AF361496

MUSSOLINI'S *DECENNALE*

Mussolini's *Decennale*

Aura and Mythmaking in Fascist Italy

ANTONIO MORENA

UNIVERSITY OF TORONTO PRESS
Toronto Buffalo London

ISBN 978-1-4426-4597-4 (cloth)

Toronto Italian Studies

Library and Archives Canada Cataloguing in Publication

Morena, Antonio, author
Mussolini's decennale : aura and mythmaking in fascist Italy / Antonio Morena.

(Toronto Italian studies)
Includes bibliographical references and index.
ISBN 978-1-4426-4597-4 (bound)

1. Fascism and culture – Italy – History – 20th century.   2. Fascism – Italy – History – 20th century.   3. Italy – Intellectual life – 20th century. 4. Italy – Politics and government – 1922–1945.   I. Title. II. Title: Decennale. III. Series: Toronto Italian studies

DG571.M67 2015   945.091   C2015-904404-9

University of Toronto Press acknowledges the financial assistance to its publishing program of the Canada Council for the Arts and the Ontario Arts Council, an agency of the Government of Ontario.

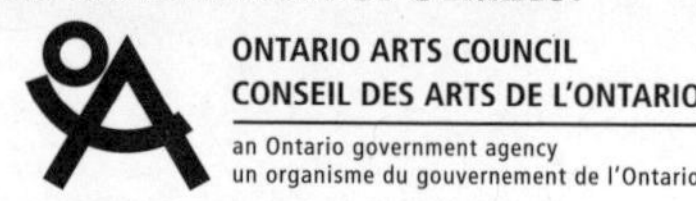

What have I in common with slaves?

Alfieri

You can't ask a nation of *dannunziani* to sacrifice themselves.

Piero Gobetti

Dictators need myths, symbols and ceremonies to regiment, enhance and scare the masses and stifle any attempt they might have to think. The fanciful and pompous ceremonies and mysterious rites in a strange language – like those of the Catholic Church – are masterpieces of their kind. It is this model that the fascists and the communists are imitating when, by means of their mass demonstrations, they appeal to the irrational impulses of the crowds.

Gaetano Salvemini

Contents

Acknowledgments

I would like to thank all those who contributed, knowingly or unknowingly, directly or indirectly, to the completion of this project. I am grateful to my readers and editors. I thank all who acknowledged the truth behind my thesis statement.

Illustrations and further notes have been uploaded to my Google+ community page. Please search for "Antonio Morena 1932."

This book is dedicated to my readers.

Antonio Morena
El Puerto de Santa María, Spain
September 2015

MUSSOLINI'S *DECENNALE*

Introduction:
Palingenetic Ultranationalism

The expiration of the first decade of the ten estimated and most certain years finds the Fascist Revolution more powerful than ever because it is certain and because it continues …

There are two immense meanings for the *Decennale* celebrations and I ask you to reflect on them intently. On one hand the Italian people, in compact and formidable masses made up of millions of men, have made a decisive leap ahead and I have interpreted, soul against soul, as never before, the anniversary.

On the other hand the doctrines, institutes and works completed by the Revolution of the Black Shirts are on the agendas of all European nations. For in this dark world, tormented and already shaky, salvation cannot but come from the truth of Rome. And from Rome it shall.

Benito Mussolini[1]

In this book I will discuss and explore a cross section of Italian culture during the *Decennale*, the year that marked and celebrated the tenth anniversary of the March on Rome. I will examine the literature, articles, public speeches, film, and even museum walks from around that time and highlight the relationship that these have with the hegemonic power. I will address the 1932 anniversary celebrations and the reaction thereto by various segments of Italian culture. My purpose is to explain how the regime, its patrons, and even its critics framed historical representation during 1932 for concrete ideological and political objectives. In conclusion I will consider the tenth anniversary as a crucial moment in Italian fascism's transition from a conservative and reactionary phase to a totalitarian, imperial, and racist phase.

I interpret the *Decennale* as a moment situated midway between the years 1929 and 1936. These were, according to Renzo De Felice, the "consensus years," a period in which fascism set out to radicalize the original movement and steer it towards an imperial and racist regime. De Felice explained that Italian fascism possessed a dual nature. Fascism as *movement* was a somewhat "red thread" that lost its vitality and importance as time progressed. This vitality was counterbalanced by fascism as *regime*. Fascism as movement was the impulse to renew fascism. This renewal occurred by means of "self-representation." Fascism as regime was Mussolini or, rather, the politics of Mussolini. Fascism as regime negated fascism as movement.[2] Studying Italian fascism and the consensus years through De Felice allows us, furthermore, to better understand post-war Italy. Emilio Gentile and Alexander De Grand have noted that it was because of fascism's overwhelming consensus that Mazzinian democratic and liberal nationalist alternatives were left weakened in the period following the war. This situation allowed alternative loyalties such as Catholicism and communism to emerge as political forces.[3] De Felice's method is also important: intertextuality, biography, and countless hours spent in the Italian Central State Archives reviewing the holdings of the Minister of the Interior, the Office of the President of the Council, and the Italian Fascist Party.[4]

De Felice's method continues to be at the forefront of research activity and has been considered most recently by Patrick Finney.[5] De Felice commented that fascism was sustained by an emerging middle class. Marxists believe that fascism stood for declining social elements. In the Po Valley a new generation of landowners was making its presence known for the first time. This emerging middle class sustained the initial movement. It was there that the fascist squads, fresh from the trenches of the Great War, confronted maximalist socialist movements. In urban centres fascism's focus on modernity and on national modernization likewise appealed to the middle class. In short, there are few historians today who can claim that neither fascism nor Mussolini had any sort of ideology. There are, furthermore, few historians who can insist that fascism was but a bourgeois reaction to the crisis that afflicted Europe following the Great War.[6]

Fascism was an authentically revolutionary movement. Fascism as movement developed into fascism as regime: a curious mix of ideology, realpolitik, compromise, and, as Zeev Sternhell writes, "an ideal prototype of a disruptive ideology."[7] In sum, Mussolini was a far-sighted thinker committed to a modernizing project that set out to mould a new fascist man, exhibit a new idea, develop a "third way" between capitalism and communism, and use every element that modernity offered to do so. Many prominent Italian intellectuals believed in this initial wave: Vilifredo Paredo, Giovanni Gentile, Giovanni Papini, Curzio Malaparte, Giuseppe Prezzolini, Benedetto Croce, Ugo Spirito, Enrico Corradini, Alfredo Rocco, and Roberto Forges Davanzati, just to name a few.

Another interpretation presents the *Duce* as an opportunist without a plan. Gaetano Salvemini was one of the first to sustain this approach.[8] Salvemini's study inaugurated historiography on Mussolini's foreign policy and stressed its inconsistence, opportunism, and violence. War was the product of aggressivity and the distance between propaganda and an imperialist project. This book accepts the idea that Mussolini's foreign policy was not, despite his opportunism, a matter reduced to improvisation. These pages maintain instead that a major motive behind the Spanish and Ethiopian wars was the main idea exhibited during the *Decennale*. Postunification Rome, we shall see in the chapters that follow, provided the regime with an exceptional laboratory. It was in Rome that "competing visions for the future clashed for spatial-visual and symbolic dominance."[9] Furthermore, Finney reminds us, referring to a study by John Coverdale on the Italian intervention in Spain,[10] that strategic considerations far outweighed ideological factors (or domestic considerations) and that Mussolini's policy continued in essence that of liberal Italy. Finney asks: Was fascism's foreign policy a mere means to an end or its raison d'être? Did the radicalization of fascism in the late 1930s signify a qualitative change, or was it merely the realization of long nurtured ambitions?[11] I will show that these ambitions were part of a long-term project. Moreover, and following De Felice, this book focuses on Mussolini as a "modernizing revolutionary ideologue" at home and a Machiavellian realist abroad. Participation in the Axis was therefore a "tactical alignment." Mussolini was a "moderate expansionist," and in the end, he set out to reinterpret, confront, and achieve the aspirations of the monarchy and the liberal elite. In this book I focus on *how* the *Decennale* attempted to complete this mission.

The *Decennale* was an exercise in self-representation that looked to the future and aspired to renew the vitality of the fascist movement. This manner of self-representation was akin to a religious celebration. This political strategy was to go hand in hand with a theological project. And the maiden voyage – at the time of the *Decennale* – had a purpose. The purpose of such a celebration was to join dogma and ritual together in the creation of a new urban space. It was to be a new city:

a regime that the world had never seen or experienced before. Ritual, writes Constantin Fasolt, is more "urgent" than dogma. Ritual is a set of "rule-governed practices designed to confirm a first-person speaker's knowledge that he or she is and does the same as everybody else." Ritual is crucial to a religious credo. It creates consensus. When dogma is "divorced from ritual," Fasolt continues, "it leaves the believer isolated or in opposition to the community of which he is a member." An effective and consensus-generating ritual has a certain rhythmic quality much as song and dance do, especially of the religious type.[12] Ritual can be abused and deny an individual's humanity. Ritual can annul an identity as totalitarian regimes do. When ritual and dogma espoused a political-theological project, it had the potential to counteract the decline of the West, as Oswald Spengler noted,[13] and cultivated a new generation of leaders. An exemplary fascist order in Italy was to provide a template for all other countries to follow.

De Felice's legacy is best represented by the scholarship of Emilio Gentile. Gentile utilizes George L. Mosse's ideas on the sacralization of politics in Nazi Germany as a template for studying the history of fascist Italy.[14] Moreover, it is especially significant that Gentile refers to the early work of a young Italian-American PhD student at Harvard University named Dante Germino. Germino leaves us with, writes Gentile, a "significant early reading of the nature of the Fascist regime."[15] Germino's argument, taking Carl Friedrich and Zbigniew Brzezinski's seven-part totalitarian model – charismatic leader, single party, all-embracing ideology, control over communications and weapons, terror, anti-capitalism, and foreign aggression – and applying it to Italy can be implausible, as has been noted. Nevertheless, this book finds it appropriate to bring to light Germino's foresight:

In an effort to emphasize the unique quality of the single mass party, numerous writers have suggested that the institution be designated by other terminology to differentiate it from the political parties of constitutional democracies. The labels "order," "church," and "army" have been proffered as substitutes for the word "party." It is undeniably true that, when it had fully developed, the single party in Italy did resemble all three of these institutions in certain respects. Like a religious order, the party demanded the unwavering allegiance of the individual – body, mind, and spirit. The party was to be revered as a sacred institution that would last beyond the death of its martyrs. The PNF [Partito Nazionale Fascista] had its own sanctuaries, saints, hymns, sacred writings, prayers, solemn ceremonies, and even marriage service. As the PNF was in part order and church, so would it also be compared to an army. Possessing its own arsenal of weapons and its own militia, it was organized from top to bottom in military fashion. Fundamentally, however, this novel totalitarian instrument, which we shall continue to call the party (although on occasion one of the other terms will be peculiarly appropriate), was neither order, church, nor army. The party was a pseudo-religious institution, but it served a *political* religion.[16]

And so, following Germino, Mosse, and Gentile, we interpret the *Decennale* as a consensus-generating "collective representation"[17] derived from a secularized religion: "a system of beliefs, myths, rituals, and symbols that interpret and define the meaning and end of human existence by subordinating the destiny of individuals and the collective to a supreme entity."[18]

The literature on totalitarian regimes during the interwar period is plentiful. This book focuses on the participatory and ritual aspects of coercion rather than on the regime's repressive apparatus. I build on research completed on the intellectual roots of fascism and the political education imposed by Gabriele D'Annunzio, the artistic avant-garde, and the nationalists. I consider the role that literary and political journals played in this process. In the period following Italian unification and the Great War, the *Duce*, rather than Vittorio Emmanuel, triumphed as a religious and mythical symbol. In a sense the "declaration of infallibility" proclaimed by the papacy at the Council of 1869–70 would be re-elaborated by the fascist propaganda machine: *Il Duce ha sempre ragione* (The *Duce* is always right). The nation's march to the Pantheon celebrating the cult of the dead and marking the anniversary of Victor Emmanuel's death would be re-enacted by a spectacular pilgrimage to the *Mostra del Decennale*. The aggressive foreign policy pursued by Francesco Crispi would be completed by the *Duce*: victory in Africa and war against France in alliance with Germany.[19]

For these reasons I argue that a storyline, complete with its own characters, was created by the regime, which reconstructed the first ten years of the fascist revolution and presented a chronology of events to be completed in the future. These elements were held together, intentionally, by the will of the *Duce*, a charismatic Author, a "supreme entity," who reaffirmed the importance of the rituals and liturgies that celebrated in 1932 the regeneration of the initial 1922 revolution. The protagonists of the tale, the new generations of fascists (those born into the regime, those too young to have participated in the March on Rome), exhibited themselves as bodies capable of revitalizing the fascist revolution. In this book I'll propose that these circumstances – "fascist Italy on stage" – allowed antagonists to critically assess the validity of the fascist way of life. I'll conclude that the anniversary provided a unique opportunity to exhibit this tale of renewal and, by the very nature of this exhibition, to criticize it.[20]

I argue that the protagonists of these historically determinant episodes in Italian history, indeed the moment in history itself, possessed a religious aura that guaranteed authenticity, historical validity, and cult value, just as, according to Walter Benjamin, an original work of art does.[21] The generation that participated in the fascist revolution relied especially on the aura of the March on Rome for its claim to power. Since the original spirit, excitement, psychological state, or *aura*, of the March on Rome could never be replicated, the *Decennale* provided a unique opportunity to recreate the aura of 1922 by mechanical or artificial means.[22] As the initial movement transformed itself into a regime, those same protagonists, now in power, needed to sustain that unique, authentic, and cult or ritual-based revolutionary spirit by reproducing it in the life of the nation. This book focuses on the cultural politics of re-enaction. What evolved therefore was a change in perception due to history. Official newsreels such as those prepared by LUCE (*L'Unione Cinematografica Educativa*) were part of this process of modernization. For the first time the masses saw themselves as protagonists; anyone had the potential to be granted a moment of fame. High levels of unemployment aided the regime's intentions. Lacking an identity, the masses could be moulded as obedient fascists by the *Duce-Prince* according to the desires of the state. Leo Strauss has considered the nature of the "ruthless councils" given by Machiavelli throughout *The Prince*, addressed not so much to princes but rather to the young. Strauss explains that Machiavelli's youth had been brought up "much too confident of human goodness" and "too gentle or effeminate." He writes:

> [J]ust as a man who is timorous by training or nature cannot acquire courage, which is the mean between cowardice and foolhardiness, unless he drags himself in the direction of foolhardiness, so Machiavelli's pupils must go through a process of brutalization in order to be freed from effeminacy ... [H]e displays a bias in favor of the impetuous, the quick, the partisan, the spectacular, and the bloody over and against the deliberate, the slow, the neutral, the silent, and the gentle.[23]

The previous passage is appropriate when considering ambition, political realism, and Italian fascism. Machiavelli dedicated his book to youth, and fascism, as is known, was based on the cult of *giovinezza* (youth). The period of brutalization to which Strauss refers – fascism was *"contro la vita comoda"* ("against the comfortable life") – would correspond to the devastation inflicted by the fascist ideological and war machine during the second half of the *Ventennio*. The protagonists of this process were the new generation of fascists. The focus on virility as a defining marker was meant to educate the masses in this process. Propaganda would have to replace rhetoric. In chapter twenty-one of *The Prince*, *"Quod principem deceat ut egregius habeatur,"* it ought to be noted, as pointed out by Leo Strauss (and others), that Machiavelli, driven by anti-theological passion, was the only non-Jew to denounce the religiously influenced (*"servendosi sempre della religione"*) actions of Ferdinand of Aragon: an enemy of both peace and faith. Machiavelli denounced the *"pietosa crudeltà"* ("pious cruelty") of Ferdinand of Aragon towards the Marranos of Spain, *"né può essere questo esempio più miserabile né più raro"* ("indeed the most miserable and rare example of cruelty"). Fascism, likewise an enemy of peace, made use of a fascist secular religion in its politics of exclusion. The masses were thus able to exhibit themselves and were a vital part of the fascist ideological and war machine. As Walter Benjamin concluded in 1936 during Italy's invasion of Ethiopia: the natural outcome of these processes was mobilization for a future war.

Returning to Benjamin's essay "The Work of Art in the Age of Mechanical Reproduction" can help clarify the approach to be taken in these pages.[24] Benjamin speaks to us about modernity, mass movements, and the visual arts. What techniques are needed to bring the masses and aesthetics together? What techniques were used to bring the masses closer to the aura of the fascist revolution at the time of the *Decennale*? Benjamin writes that in principle works of art had always been reproducible in the past. But reproducing a work of art in the modern age represents something completely different. What is lacking in a replicated work of art is the *hic et nunc*, its authenticity and essence, the aura of its origins (spatial and temporal), its historical testimony, and its authority. Reproducing a work of art, a historical event, removes it from this tradition that is alive yet ever-changing. And so, its functionality is different. When a single event is replicated, re-enacted, or reproduced into a series of events, each replication violently revolutionizes tradition. A renewal occurs.

Cinema, cinematic instruments, and the use of film techniques are the most potent agents for this renewal. The cinematic tradition, Benjamin writes, liquidates the traditional value of cultural heredity: that which is transmitted. This phenomenon is especially seen in historical films. And so, Benjamin concludes, all legends, myths, mythologies, and founders of religions will find their resurrection in film. Medium is likewise relevant. Replicating the event liberates it from its being as a parasite in ritual, and at this exact moment (the moment of replication) the event's authenticity ceases to be relevant. Its functionality changes, and the role of the replicated object or event is not in ritual but rather in politics. Exhibition value emancipates the work of art: it blasts out of the temple and sacred spaces and onto the streets. In photography, exhibition value substitutes cultural or ritual value. And yet ritual value does indeed put up one last fight: the portrait. In fact, hundreds of portraits of fascist martyrs were exhibited in the 1932 Exhibition of the Fascist Revolution.[25] In photography "exhibition value" displaces "cult value," but "cult value" does not give way without resistance: the human countenance, the portrait of a loved one.

Performance value is appreciated. In theatre an actor is on stage, so the contact with the audience and the stage is direct. In cinema the actor's essence is filtered or mediated through a camera. This performance is exhibited and transportable to another public. Meanwhile, the film industry realizes that it needs to package and sell the performance. Thus, the industry responds to this need by creating "star power": a cult image for the masses to idolize. Not all succumb to the needs of the market. Dadaism, for example, sacrificed market share to achieve other outcomes – scandal and outrage – to shock the spectator like a bullet. Fascism responds to the masses' desire for an idol to worship by creating monumental structures, events, and exhibitions. These creations are meant to hypnotize and paralyse the masses. The cult of the charismatic leader, the *Duce*, brings the masses to their knees. Lacking an identity, the masses participate in a performance – in our specific case the anniversary celebration – through illusions, representations, and spectacle. A separation between reality and illusion presents itself to the masses. They are incapable of critically assessing (because they are distracted) this separation and its ultimate goal: the horrors of imperialistic warfare that, Benjamin concluded in 1936, is an aesthetically pleasurable event for fascists. Communism responds by politicizing art.

In 1978 Rainer Stollmann published an article titled "Fascist Politics as a Total Work of Art: Tendencies of the Aesthetization of Political

Life in National Socialism." The author approached the topic "from the standpoint of aesthetics, the theory of perceptible beauty, of 'beautiful illusion' in the broadest sense." Although Stollmann focuses on the aesthetization of political life in the Third Reich, the conclusions drawn can be a useful template for this book. Stollmann concludes that the "petite bourgeoisie" organized itself as the aesthetic copy of a workers' party and that the fascist public sphere ought to be understood as a "beautiful illusion" or rather as a "private psychic flight" from reality. And, as is known, the petite bourgeoisie is the group most predisposed, both "socio-economically and socio-psychologically," to this flight. The masses step on to the stage, but they do not control the direction, nor do they act in a self-responsible manner. In short, they yearn for their self-destruction.[26] The illusion was sustained by the masses' desire to flee from reality in a time of crisis: hence the years of consensus. The *Decennale* exhibited this lie. The politics of ritual and image were thus a necessary evil, a noble lie, a beautiful illusion. This noble lie was to be exhibited and defended by a new class of citizen-soldiers. A new Italy needed to spring forth from this celebration. A renewed revolutionary spirit would have to re-educate the new generation of fascists towards self-sacrifice. At the same time the fascist regime would need to intervene in the labour market and create a new relationship between citizen and labour so as to eliminate conflict: the corporative state. A new curriculum educated the new generation. This curriculum would need to excel in the most virtuous of arts: the art of war. A war of aggression would satisfy the need for additional territory and present a new generation of soldiers with an empire. In order to achieve its goals, fascism employed myth: an illusion based on religion. The *Duce* presented himself as shepherd. The new generation of citizen-soldiers led the masses. Not all were welcome, and so the regime moved forward towards the politics of exclusion: fascism's racist and totalitarian phase.[27]

The *Decennale* was an aesthetic operation meant to anaesthetize the masses, as Guy Debord would later write in *The Society of the Spectacle*. This operation imposed a spiritualized aura onto the people and arranged that the dialogue between the state and the individual took place through a series of controlled exchanges and spectacles. Ritual triumphed over dogma. After all, the masses are naturally enslaved. And, according to the fascist dictate, enslaving the weak, those who are by their very nature slaves, is just. Justice cannot exist in an ideal city: better to have these men as slaves than free to think, act, and pursue their dreams. This enslavement too was part of the fascist project. The inclusion of certain episodes along with the exclusion of others was also meant to provide vigour to the permanent revolution that the *Duce* was advocating. Not all were enslaved to the idea. Those dissenting often did so by collaborating within the confines of the regime: an implicit rather than explicit form of dissent. And some dedicated themselves to the best life, the contemplative life, as opposed to the political life. Their presence will be examined esoterically. Their message will be read between the lines. This book considers the gentlemen of *Solaria*, the ideal city, indeed a literary aristocracy, nestled between Rome and Milan in the city of Florence. The *Decennale* attempted to regenerate the aura of 1922 and yet, as Benjamin explains, original works of art (such as the 1922 march) lose their aura when replicated. The rituals of the original revolution, which the new generation of fascists was meant to artificially relive, contributed to a critical assessment of the reality of the *Decennale*. At the time of the *Decennale*, individuals representing the varied political spectrum of Italian society set out to reconsider previously held positions. It was an epiphany within the context of the nation's narrative.

The Culturalist Approach

This book makes use of the notions of "aura," "historical representation," "memory," and "identity," not as concepts to think *about* but as instruments to think *with*.[28] The spectacle celebrated the fascist revolution as a defining moment in the nation-building process. The *Decennale* also symbolized the final stage of *risorgimento* (unification). The year 1932 was both the fiftieth anniversary of Giuseppe Garibaldi's death and the sixtieth anniversary of Giuseppe Mazzini's death. It was also the one-hundred-and-first anniversary of the founding of Mazzini's *Giovine Italia* (Young Italy) political movement. The year 1932 also defined the identity of the revolution meant to be exhibited and was aesthetically linked to the "bloody" events of 1922. The *Decennale* completed the nation-building process and set the stage for expanding the nation's borders. The traditions of the nation-building heritage of the *Risorgimento*, the Great War, and the original March on Rome of 1922 were re-elaborated and reread. As a conveyer of a collective identity, these traditions served the interests of a permanent revolution. The *Duce* was the charismatic leader who best interpreted this identity.

From a historical point of view, the matter is a delicate one. Richard Bosworth underscores the importance that the debate between intentionalists and functionalists has played in scholarship on Nazi Germany and, to a certain extent, on Stalinism. He considers himself a "structuralist" or "functionalist" historian, "anxious to explore the 'social roots' of policy rather than an 'intentionalist' historian convinced that Great Men are indeed great, the dynamos of their times."[29] In the third chapter of his biography on Mussolini, Bosworth considers the intentionalist/functionalist debate and Italian fascism, and notes that Renzo De Felice and Denis Mack Smith both "explicitly or implicitly endorse the view that Mussolini defined the regime ... a Great Man line." He then points out, "But generally speaking, the big questions have scarcely been asked – did Fascist policies originate from above? Or from below?"[30] A compromise between the intentionalist and functionalist approach can prove useful.[31] The cultural studies approach has proven particularly effective when considering the ideological intentions of and resistance to the regime at specific periods in that it deconstructs the distinction between various forms of "high" and "low" culture.[32] The culturalist approach has been at the centre of discussion for the past twenty years or so. And, as Jan Nelis explains, the key word in these recent studies is "self-representation."[33] How did fascism present itself? How did it re-enact itself? This book focuses on these main points.

Jeffrey Schnapp tells us that fascism often looked for an answer to its identity crisis in the domain of cultural politics. His approach allows us to understand how fascism aestheticized politics at the 1932 exhibition, but doesn't really tell us much about what was accomplished in the long term. Nonetheless, Schnapp's analysis of the fascist play *18BL* is especially useful from a methodological point of view.[34] In *Fascist Modernities: Italy, 1922–1945*, Ruth Ben-Ghiat claims that intellectuals did participate in the creation of a new Italy. Italian intellectuals employed a curious mix of modernity and tradition, and adopted realism, or rather a realist aesthetic, as a guiding model.[35]

As Ben-Ghiat explains, Mussolini had initially presented himself as a radical of sorts. As soon as he became prime minister in October 1922, Mussolini adopted a realpolitik approach that allowed for compromises with industrialists, the church, and interest groups. Political realism likewise dominated foreign policy. Not all agreed. On the eve of the *Decennale*, Dino Grandi remarked that ideology could not and should not interfere with foreign policy. Foreign policy itself ought to maximize all opportunity and all possibilities, including those offered by the adversary. Relations with Soviet Russia at the time were cordial, and this cordiality would be beneficial, but sooner or later ideology would have to confront itself with political realism. On 21 July 1930 Mussolini sent Grandi off to London as ambassador. In his diary Grandi reflected on the moment (2 October 1930):

> Woe in every way to those regimes that build their international program on a program of ideological expansion. Or rather on the contrast between their ideology and that of other nations. That's how you arrive at religious wars, as evidenced by the sad experience of the sixteenth century and also in part by the Napoleonic period. These have bloodied Europe without reaching another purpose other than to bring to a climax the cruelty and ferocity of men and to sow pain and misery in all nations ... Africa remains the secret anxiety and the faith of the Italian nation. Our nation has a mission of civilization to be completed on the African continent, just as our generation has a problem to be solved: the colonial problem.[36]

As the movement developed into a totalitarian regime, "the regime's aesthetic-political operation of giving style to the Italians ... ran parallel to fascism's *Realpolitik* attempt to organize a totalitarian state."[37] Both ideology and realism were implicitly part of the fascist plan in the 1930s. The research conducted by Simonetta Falasca-Zamponi centres on self-representation, texts, aesthetics, and public events or manifestations, and is thematically similar to the scholarship produced by other researchers of modern mass society such as Emilio Gentile and George L. Mosse.[38] This book is also focused along the same lines as Falasca-Zamponi's study. She explains in her volume that a month before the March on Rome Mussolini had envisioned fascism as a movement that would bring back a "fascist style" to people's lives: a line of conduct, colour, strength, the picturesque, the unexpected, the mystical. Finally, the scholarship of Claudio Fogu on the modernist mode of historical representation (*historical aura*), the role that authentic documents had in such representations and historical consciousness, is likewise an appropriate guideline.[39] This book focuses on aesthetic-ideologic discourse and considers other relevant theories regarding political realism in its conclusion.

1932

How did fascism set out to legitimize itself though the language of aesthetics and through texts? How did the Italian people present themselves as players on a fascist stage? What did this approach mean for fascism? What did this all mean for the opposition? In this book I focus on the main idea at the centre of the *Decennale*: the exhibition of a future march *from* Rome, which selectively re-contextualized the rhetoric, rituals, and aura of the original March on Rome through varied media. How did the regime fashion new identities? How were new ideas exhibited? What did this mean for the totalitarian, imperial, and racist phase that followed? How did the anti-fascist movement critically assess the moment? This present book is structured along these lines. It focuses on the development of a distinct cultural complex: ideology and cultural politics within the context of the *Decennale*.

I analyse the relationship between power and forms of knowledge "from a distance," as Franco Moretti explains:

> [D]istant reading: where distance, let me repeat it, *is a condition of knowledge*: it allows you to focus on units that are much smaller or much larger than the text: devices, themes, tropes – or genres and systems. And if, between the very small and the very large, the text itself disappears, well, it is one of those cases when one can justifiably say, Less is more. If we want to understand the system in its entirety, we must accept losing something. We always pay a price for theoretical knowledge: reality is infinitely rich; concepts are abstract, are poor. But it's precisely this "poverty" that makes it possible to handle them, and therefore to know. This is why less is actually more.[40]

In chapter one I survey the debate concerning the new generation of fascists and the manner in which the regime transposed the rhetoric of youth from the literary page to an exhibition intended to shock this new generation of 1932 into a renewed narrative. A renewed regime needed new protagonists who knew they were born to lead. The *Decennale* also marked the tenth anniversary of Giovanni Gentile's reform of the Italian educational system. Here it will prove fruitful to present a reading of official fascist textbooks used in classrooms during the *Decennale*. In chapter two I consider the creation of identities from the ground up within official school textbooks, and investigate the relationship between text and historical occurrence in this initiation process. As identities were moulded and bodies exhibited, the regime defined fascism for the first time. In chapter three I focus on ideas: the debate regarding the creation of a fascist culture in tune with the anniversary's ambitions, and the definition of fascism as seen in the *Enciclopedia Italiana* and in the docudrama film *Camicia nera* (*Black Shirt*).

The opposition responded by writing esoterically and by politicizing art. At a time when fascism was imposing itself on the rest of Europe, the philosopher Benedetto Croce reconsidered previously held positions in his *Storia Europa* (*History of Europe*). I likewise document the reception of the *Decennale* by the opposition: the most intransigent anti-fascists living abroad, anti-fascists such as Benedetto Croce, and even marginalized intellectuals best represented by the journal *Solaria*, founded in 1926 in Florence by Alberto Carocci. This book considers history as a part of literature and focuses on the common ground between history and literature. *Solaria* belonged to a long tradition of revues published in the Tuscan city (*Marzocco*, 1896–1932; *Il Leonardo*, 1903–7; *La Voce*, 1916–18). Writers would collaborate with various journals at the same time. For example, the left-wing fascist Elio Vittorini published in *Solaria* and collaborated with *Il Bargello* (1929–43). *Solaria* hosted an eclectic assortment of writers: Elio Vittorini, Giuseppe Ungaretti, Leo Ferrero, Carlo Emilio Gadda, Eugenio Montale, Giani Stuparich, Nicloa Chiaromonte, and even Alessandro Pavolini, who was executed by partisans and strung up in Piazzale Loreto along with Mussolini on 29 April 1945.

The culturalist approach remains controversial. Bosworth notes that it reports what Italian fascism "said rather than critically exploring what it meant."[41] In my conclusion I draw connections between the narrative constructed for the *Decennale* and realpolitik. I expand on the regime's historical representation at the time of the *Decennale* and the actual direction that Mussolini's regime took in the middle to late 1930s in its domestic and foreign policy. This book posits that the storyline imposed on the nation by the nation's Author (the regeneration of people and ideas) provoked a call to action across the intellectual spectrum. As such, the final chapter of this book focuses on elements of implicit and explicit dissent in literature (especially literature with psychological, social, or political overtones) produced by individuals who would eventually become the protagonists of Italian cultural resurgence, the resistance, and the post-war years. The final chapter also considers literature in *Solaria* that aspired to present a united Europe as a solution – but not an exclusive one – to the problem of the age: fascist imperialism. These circumstances invested the *Solaria* group with a need to challenge the fascist reality celebrated and exhibited, and give meaning to their lives as writers. The literature presented in *Solaria* and specific to the historical reality of 1932 was marked by the following: rationalism, humanism, and a new relationship to be formed between the individual and the state. In short: political commitment. It also called for cosmopolitanism as a response to fascism's transition to its reactionary, imperialist, and racist stage. Renzo De Felice has pointed out that the period from 1936 to 1940 led to a certain "psychological detachment" between the regime and the masses, most especially among the younger generation, the generation of the *Decennale*.[42]

Carlo Rosselli best summarized the moment in an article on Mussolini and youth published in *Giustizia e libertà* on 30 August 1935.[43] Rosselli explained that 1932 to 1935 marked the culmination of fascist force and of anti-fascist depression. But it also marked the beginning of the decomposition of fascism. Rosselli explained to his readers that fascism in 1932 found itself facing its own weaknesses for the very first time. According to Rosselli, Mussolini was acting in "bad faith," whereas the youth who followed him were acting in "good faith." Therefore, the war in Africa was also a conflict against the generation who had taken fascism as movement seriously. Carlo Rosselli concluded that the moment was ideal and that by reaching out towards that new generation, fascism could be defeated from within.

Amarcord

In a memorable scene from Federico Fellini's *Amarcord* (1973), all of Rimini empties into the Adriatic on boats and rafts. A sense of expectation fills the air. As the night edges on, the men, women, and children struggle to keep awake, and many, if not all, are lulled to sleep by the waves. Gradisca, the leading female character, entertains the others with her small-town dreams and aspirations: at the age of thirty she is still waiting for love. Then, a monstrous foghorn thunders through the night: that of the SS *Rex* returning from its inaugural transatlantic crossing. Everyone is overcome with excitement. The boats explode with joy. The blind cry out, "How is it? How is it?" A man representing the *podestà* shouts, "Long live Italy! Have a good trip!" Young and old huddle together, exchange pleasantries with the massive ship, and embrace the aura of the oncoming waves. The spectacle has a hypnotic effect. Even Titta's hot-tempered socialist father slowly raises his hat to salute the fascist regime's greatest technological achievement. Teary-eyed Gradisca, overwhelmed by ecstasy, love, hope, and a dream, sends off kisses to the massive ship, so great, so potent, so large that it overcomes the boats in its wake.

The inaugural voyage of the *Rex* occurred in September 1932. The time was ripe for the *piccioletta barca* (little boat) to cross the seas and go forth towards other lands. Fellini intentionally built his *Rex* out of cardboard and cheap lightbulbs in the movie studios of *Cinecittà*. Women, men, children, lifeguards, shopkeepers, teenagers, school-teachers, street vendors, aspiring poets, and opera singers: everyone was swept up in an idea of greatness. The scene, Fellini explained, represents a case of "total stupidity" typical of the fascist era, in which the illusions of spectacle, circus-like acts, buffoonery, group ignorance, and ritual dominated reality.[44] Finally, the episode is also an example of how fascism made use of spectacle and technology to unify the nation in all aspects of life. Illusion became reality.[45]

Defining fascism is a rather messy affair.[46] Roger Griffin speaks of "a genus of political ideology whose mythic core in its various permutations is a palingenetic form of populist ultranationalism."[47] The term "palingenesis" implies a regeneration of people and ideas: individuals are conferred membership, and sacred texts are institutionalized. A "mythic core" is evoked by a series of rituals, myths, and liturgies created by the state. The "populist ultranationalist" aspect of fascism hinges on the charismatic prowess of a single leader. An element of Emilio Gentile's definition of fascism can likewise help us in our investigation. Gentile adds that fascism possesses a "culture founded on mystical thought and the tragic and activist sense of life conceived of as the manifestation of the will to power, on the myth of youth as artificer of history, and on the exaltation of the militarization of politics as the model of life and collective activity."[48] Stanley Payne reminds us, moreover, that in matters of style and organization, fascism focuses on the aesthetic structure of meetings, symbols, and political liturgy, stressing emotional and mystical aspects.[49] Guy Debord famously wrote in thesis 109 of *The Society of the Spectacle* that fascism presents itself as a "violent resurrection of *myth* calling for participation in a community defined by archaic pseudo-values: race, blood, leader." For Debord, "Fascism is a cult of the archaic completely fitted out by modern technology. Its degenerate ersatz of myth has been revived in the spectacular context of the most modern means of conditioning and illusion."[50]

Robert Paxton goes a step further and proposes a fascist life cycle.[51] In the first, a movement is created. In the case of Italian fascism, a date and place stands out: 23 March 1919, Piazza San Sepolcro, Milan. Here the fascist movement was officially formed and a manifesto was issued. In September 1919 Gabriele D'Annunzio set out to conquer the city of Fiume. This exploit was a significant event that would resonate within the newly formed *Fasci di Combattimento*. From 1920 to 1922 (the second stage of the process), fascism proceeded to "root" itself in the political system (the fascist party was created in 1921) through the violence of the fascist squads. In the third stage, the fascist movement seized power: the March on Rome of 28 October 1922.

From the very beginning Mussolini paid keen attention to the role that technology was to have in this revolution. On 7 November 1922 a documentary film titled *A Noi!* (*To the Revolution!*) was released to the general public. *A Noi!* was an achievement in that it had been quickly edited by playwright-turned-director Umberto Paradisi. The first part of the film is dedicated exclusively to the fascist congress at Naples in the days preceding the March on Rome. The second part focuses on the march itself. This event was a bluff. It was neither a revolution, in the strictest sense of the word, nor an example of mass choreography. Instead, it was a form of "psychological warfare."[52] Mussolini was asked to form a government on 29 October 1922, and as the fascists marched on Rome, photographers were waiting to immortalize the moment. He then created his own reality: the myth of a civil war and 3,000 martyrs.[53] Authentic, original, spontaneous celebrations occurred in Rome.

Following the March on Rome, social relationships did not change, and no drastic redistribution of economic or political power took place. Liberal institutions were already weak *before* the fascist March on Rome.[54] Marxists conceptualize the March on Rome as capitalism's attempt to impose itself, violently, on the growing threat of international socialism. Others saw it as a natural consequence of the failure of the liberal state with its market economy and parliamentary politics. The period that followed (1922–32) represented the fourth stage of the fascist life cycle. Here power was exercised, and fascism began the transition from the initial movement towards a regime by proceeding to organize the state. In 1923 nationalists joined the newly formed fascist party and created a fascist militia. That same year Giovanni Gentile, minister of education in Mussolini's first cabinet, reformed the Italian educational system. In 1924 fascism confronted its first official crisis after the socialist deputy Giacomo Matteotti was assassinated. The tragic turn of events caused many initial supporters of the regime, such as the nation's leading intellectual, Benedetto Croce, to reconsider the state of affairs; in 1925 he wrote and signed a *Manifesto of Anti-fascist Intellectuals*. Croce's manifesto was written in response to a fascist manifesto published in *Il Popolo d'Italia* on 21 April 1925. The anti-fascist manifesto was published in *Il Mondo* on 1 May 1925. After pointing out the mediocrity of the fascist manifesto – it was a mishmash of ideas taken from here and there – Croce concluded:

> [L]et's leave aside the well-known and arbitrary interpretations and ma-
> nipulations of history … [T]he ill-treatment of the doctrines and of history
> is a minor thing … in comparison to the abuse that is made of the word
> religion … [T]he Fascist intellectuals would have us participate in a reli-
> gious war and in the exploits of a new gospel and a new apostolate against
> an old superstition.[55]

To summarize the manifesto: Fascism fueled hatred and resentment among Italians. Party politics in Italy had become akin to a religious war. Fascism had introduced struggle and tension, and suspicion and animosity into the life of the country. Croce cried out: What is this new gospel? This new religion? New faith? These ultra-modern ideas and mouldy old attitudes? What are these absolutest tendencies typical of the Bolsheviks? And what about this courting of the Catholic church? The anti-fascists concluded: there is nothing new in fascism.

The general state of fear created by the murder of Matteotti facilitated the transition towards a dictatorship. The *Duce* was well aware of the strategy he needed to employ in the creation of a totalitarian state, and in his Ascension Day speech on 26 May 1927 he proceeded to set some guidelines. An important aspect of this speech, a decisive one in fascism's transition from movement to regime, is that here the nation's *condottiero* (leader) stated that non-believers ("infidels" sentenced to jail or internal exile) would be pardoned in the future. The main temporal reference for this pardon is 1932:

> Now these confined prisoners (*confinati*) don't find themselves in a brilliant
> position but let's not exaggerate. They receive 10 lire a day (revaluated).
> They are separated from the common inmates. They are concentrated in
> two islands. Someone talked about an amnesty. We won't talk about an
> amnesty until 1932. And we'll talk about it in 1932 if, as I hope will happen,
> it will not be necessary to promulgate special laws … Gentlemen, you
> speak of terror? No. It is not terror just rigour. And maybe not even this. It's
> social hygiene; it's a preventative measure on a national level.[56]

The strategy to celebrate the anniversary of the March on Rome was established by the *Duce* years before 1932. He intended to radicalize the revolution once more to keep it moving towards its next stage. Once domestic policy was reinforced and consensus was established at home, an expansionist foreign policy could then be implemented. Thus a direct link existed between the *Duce*'s plan to celebrate the anniversary and, as we shall see, foreign policy. The *Decennale* was not an improvised celebration. The Ascension Day speech by the *Duce* was a turning point for a fascist regime still in its infant stage but nevertheless intent (already in 1926) on marching towards 1932. Here the *Duce* contextualized and reconsidered the original 1922 revolution – a flashback in the narrative – and anticipated a liturgy of pardon for all those who had heard of or witnessed the nation's tale of redemption but had yet to believe it.

The exceptional decrees drafted in 1926, Michael Ebner summarizes, presented a new police code, dissolved all political parties and anti-fascist organizations, empowered provincial police commissions to order political confinement, banned anti-fascist publications, created a political investigative unit within the MVSN (*Milizia Volontaria per la Sicurezza Nazionale*), and reorganized the police. This book follows the interpretation that after 1926 "violence still remained central to the ideology of Fascism, but it would be directed outward in the form of warfare and territorial expansion."[57] From a legal point of view there were some changes in the fascist system. Amnesties (1922, 1923, and 1925) had been useful in pardoning crimes committed by fascists in the earlier period. In 1932 a general amnesty (*Regio Decreto n. 1403*) was granted to celebrate the *Decennale*. This amnesty, Lutz Klinkhammer explains, extended to "minor crimes" such as "membership in dissolved parties" and "subversive propaganda" but did not cover the crime of "reconstituting a subversive association." Curiously, the amnesty "made it easier to target selected political opponents, but meant that many anti-fascists were not brought to trial, or were released from prison or had their sentence commuted or reduced."[58] The year 1932 would prove to be an ideal venue to incorporate these individuals within the state and renew the revolution's aspirations. At that specific moment, ten years *after* the March on Rome, the nation's ruler-priest-*condottiero* would administer his prayer to the nation's sinners and prepare for the next part of the narrative: empire. A march towards an imperial conquest would need to radicalize the identities of people and ideas. An official choreographer was needed to direct the performance. On the eve of the *Decennale* (7 December 1931) Achille Starace was nominated national secretary of the *Partito Nazionale Fascista* (PNF). The decision would forever change the fascist regime. The regime's bureaucratic organs went to work, and on 28 October 1932 party membership became available once again. This transformed the PNF from an employment agency into a highly structured mass party.

The *Duce*'s narrative intended to impose fascist imperial triumphalism onto a world that found itself on shaky ground. The biggest obstacles towards the creation of a modern state on the world political stage in 1932 were the economic and political crisis marked by the economic crash of 1929, the uncertainties of Stalin's five-year plan, and doubts regarding the validity of communism and democracy. These circumstances provided an ideal opportunity for fascist ideology to both contrast the menacing force of reality and impose its own. The crisis was used to generate consensus.[59] The discussion that ensued in the months leading up to 1932 focused on the opportunity for three generations of fascists to participate in the anniversary's collective liturgy: the Great War generation who had marched *on* Rome, the generation of 1932 intent on marching *from* Rome, and, finally, the children born into a regime. The *Decennale* was an opportunity for the fascists to posit an ideological template (such as defining fascism for the first time in the *Enciclopedia Italiana*) that would aid in guiding their transition towards an empire. It celebrated a collective religious experience intent on disciplining the nation (through compulsory party membership) while increasing national unity (in the school system official state-issued textbooks were implemented just before the *Decennale*; collective manifestations also increased; exhibitions were held). Historians such as Martin Blinkhorn remind us that the brutal Libyan "pacification" had come to an end, and the Weimar Republic was entering the final days of its crisis.[60] Optimism was the order of the day, and just outside Rome new cities were being built. Littoria (modern day Latina) was founded in December 1932. The storyline now had its protagonists and plot as preparations for a future march *from* Rome: the future Ethiopian campaign, which was meant to redeem the 1896 *disfatta* (defeat) of Adwa, was born.

1932–1933

The years 1932 and 1933 marked the triumph of an authoritarian hand across Europe. In July 1932 Portugal fell to Antonio de Oliveria Salazar, and on 31 January 1933 Adolf Hitler was named chancellor in Germany. The following month Engelbert Dollfuss suspended the Austrian parliament for an indefinite period, and in 1933 the Spanish right won the most seats in parliament (but not enough for a majority). Realpolitik kept the peace in Europe, especially in Great Britain. A pact was signed by France, Germany, Great Britain, and Italy on 15 July 1933.

The political circumstances surrounding the *Decennale*, much like the March on Rome, provided an ideal opportunity to discredit liberal democracy and communist ideology. They also gave the regime a favourable climate within which to plan for the long term by creating the conditions for a permanent state of revolution and redefining the primordial myth. The collective, represented by the community of the elect, were to identify with the state and, naturally, to understand their own destiny within its ideological confines. The weak succumbed to material reality, and the elect were shocked towards a spiritualized higher moral ground.[61] For the *Duce* these circumstances presented the perfect chance to plan a new moment in the history of civilization.[62]

In January 1932 British East Indies Viceroy Willingdon arrested Mahatma Gandhi and Jawaharlal Nehru, thus marking the beginning of a new civil disobedience campaign against the British Empire. For nations such as Italy, however, the situation remained relatively stable and calm. Also in January General Pietro Badoglio declared the end of Libyan resistance. In the meantime the economic crisis raged on. In Italy the regime set its sights on the new generation of fascists. The *Opera nazionale maternità e infanzia* (ONMI, the National Institute for the Protection of Motherhood and Infancy) was completely restructured in the months following the anniversary, and a day entirely dedicated to mother and child (*Giornata della Madre e del Bambino*) would be celebrated starting every 24 December. In 1933 ninety-two mothers (one from each province) were invited to Rome. LUCE documentaries projected the regime's activities to the rest of the nation. One documentary titled *Per la protezione della stirpe* (*Protecting the Italian Lineage*, 1933) focused on the work completed by the ONMI governmental office.[63] In the film, mothers proudly bring their children to the childcare centre where they are happy and clean. The children enjoy their meals together and socialize. A weekly menu is provided, and after work mothers stop by and pick up their young. Older children learn a trade. The film shows that the ONMI is also present abroad, and in one image a train arrives at Ventimiglia. Here mothers step off the train, are greeted by representatives, and brought to the residence (by private car!). The final image is emblematic. The children are now wearing the uniforms of the *Balilla* (Opera Nazionale Balilla, the fascist school-aged youth organization) and marching to the rhythm of the militarized state towards a certain future.

Labour institutions were also created at that time. INFAIL, the Fascist Institute for Insurance against Industrial Accidents, was formed in

1933. The INFPS, the Fascist Social Security Institute (later renamed INPS), was modernized the same year. In 1933 IRI, the Institute for Industrial Reconstruction, was created to rescue Italian companies in debt. Meanwhile, the spectre of the Great War continued to haunt Europe, and on 2 February 1933 a disarmament conference was held in Geneva. The crisis also encouraged further radicalization and action. On 12 February the Communist Party of Holland formed a series of unemployed combat committees. Germany in the meantime granted citizenship to one of its immigrants: Adolf Hitler. A firm totalitarian hand was sought.

Technology, design, sports, and cinema were also celebrated in 1932 and 1933. On 12 April 1932, Fiat introduced the first Italian family car named the *Balilla*. Italian engineers were also at the forefront of highway engineering. At the time of the *Decennale* the Milan-Turin highway was inaugurated, as was the Milan-Lakes and the Florence-Sea. Tourism was especially encouraged. In Rome an entire working-class neighbourhood was destroyed, and the *Via dell'Impero* (now *Via dei Fori Imperiali*) was built just in time for the *Decennale* celebrations. As urban history scholars[64] have pointed out, demolition was an effective means to promote hygienic living conditions and eliminate congestion, disease, and "social degeneracy." Demolition also improved traffic conditions and was an ideal way to exhibit landmark projects that celebrated a renewed national identity: "creative destruction."[65] In southern Italy a highway spanning 181 kilometres was constructed, which linked the Abruzzi region with Puglia and ran from San Salvo (Chieti) to Serracapriola (Foggia). At the 1932 Summer Olympics in Los Angeles (the X Olympiad coinciding with the X year), Italian athletes did quite well. In July 1933 Primo Carnera became the best boxer in the world: he knocked out American Jack Sharkey in six rounds for the heavyweight title. That same summer the first Venice Film Festival was held. And Italo Balbo, minister of the Italian Air Force, led a squadron of twenty-four airplanes (flying boats) on a transatlantic crossing towards Chicago. Their ultimate destination was the Century of Progress World's Fair dedicated to the theme of technological progress. The final stop: Lake Michigan. Seventh Street in Chicago would be renamed Balbo Drive, and Mussolini even donated a column from Ostia to the city of Chicago. The futurist's hero of 1932 was the aviator. Italo Balbo's crossing of the Atlantic further contributed to the celebration of this mythological figure. A "*Manifesto dell'aeropittura futurista*" ensued. This movement, *Stracielo*, would bond together the technological and the spiritual through aviation. In December 1932 the futurists concentrated their efforts on *aeropittura* (aeropainting) by organizing an exhibition on the topic.

On 31 January 1933 Adolf Hitler was named chancellor. He dissolved the German parliament on 2 February. That same day Hermann Goering banned communist meetings and demonstrations in Germany. On 27 February the *Reichstag* was destroyed in a fire set by the Nazis who, in turn, blamed the communists. On 4 March Dollfuss suspended the Austrian parliament for an indefinite period. On the same day Franklin D. Roosevelt was inaugurated as the thirty-second president of the United States. Meanwhile the Nazi party held a majority in the German parliament and started increasing their propaganda efforts. On 13 March Josef Goebbels became the German minister of information and propaganda. The Nazi regime's future intentions were becoming clearer and more ominous: a week later the first concentration camp, Dachau, was completed, and before the month ended Hitler became dictator of Germany. Meanwhile on 18 March Mussolini announced to the Italian Senate his plans to modify the capital. Plans for "Imperial Rome" were drawn up and executed. In April Germany moved closer to a police state. Heinrich Himmler was named police commander of Germany, and Nazi Germany intensified its anti-Semitic stance by boycotting Jewish businesses and banning Jews from much of public life. In May, trade unions were banned, and on 10 May a public book burning was held. In October 1933 Germany announced that it would leave the League of Nations. By November the Nazis held over ninety per cent of the vote.

As Ruth Ben-Ghiat has explained in *Fascist Modernities*, fascism's intention was to present itself as an alternative form of modernity against the decadence of liberal capitalism and the utopian dreams of state socialism. The economic crisis was the ideal moment to exhibit corporatism as the solution to the economic woes of the age. From a philosophical point of view, corporatism was meant to present a way of in*corporating* the individual within the state. As such, the regime needed to abandon the trade unionism of the past. An important convention on the study of corporativism and unionism, the second *Convegno di Studi Sindacali e Corporativi*, was held in Ferrara from 5 to 8 May 1932 and addressed these concerns. It was there that philosopher Ugo Spirito radically reinterpreted corporativism. Spirito had met with Mussolini on 25 March 1932. Spirito was convinced that the corporative state needed to eliminate private property completely. According to Spirito, corporativism was not to be interpreted as an instrument to defend private property, a remnant of the liberal system. Instead, he argued, the corporate state would become part of a publicly owned corporation that united capital and labour.

The individual was not to be eliminated. Rather, the individual was to become stronger as long as the state became stronger. Fascism, it seemed at the time, had become a hybrid of sorts: a mockery. Spirito met with Mussolini again on 17 May 1933. He recalled the encounter years later:

> This is not the place to recall the problems we discussed. My major objection was directed at liberalism. I supported the idea of economic action by the State through the corporations. For example, if the State became a truly corporative system, unemployment would disappear. Corporativism would achieve complete fulfillment only when it moved from the State to society, manifesting itself in a corporative way of life. Many people delude themselves into thinking that corporativism is effective and complete when it consists solely of schemes and legislated institutions. When corporativism is achieved, even the problem of abolishing the trade unions – leftovers from the class struggle – will emerge. Indeed, trade unions will be abolished. The trade unions are beginning to realize this while they are being entrusted with cultural and social functions.[66]

Corporativism would represent the third way, *the* economic system of the second decade to be exported abroad.

The *Duce* in the Triumphant Days of the *Decennale*

The time was right for the next phase in fascism. The *Duce*'s speeches (akin to modern-day "State of the Union" addresses) given for the *Decennale* focused on the dialectic between past and present. A glance at a LUCE documentary *Il Duce nelle trionfali giornate del Decennale* (*The Duce in the Triumphant Days of the Decennale*), comprised of the actual texts of the *Duce*'s speeches and excerpts from an extended conversation with Emil Ludwig, can shed further light onto the climate of *Anno X.*

In the documentary, an airplane thunders above Rome as it nears the *Altare della Patria*. There, 25,000 fascist officials are present in Piazza Venezia. The regime's hymm, *Giovinezza*, is heard in the background. A quick cut: men are marching and their chests glitter with medals and ribbons. The procession is continuous. Suddenly fascist youths burst onto the scene at a quick pace. Running, they carry their flags, banners, and the standards of Imperial Rome. A thunderous *Duce! Duce!* is now heard throughout the piazza. The camera looks up from the crowd to a balcony amid the thousands of flags. The audience participates. The tone is revolutionary.

On 16 October 1932 thousands of high-ranking fascist officials marched into Rome once more. The occasion marked the tenth anniversary of the reunion held in via San Marco 46, Milan, the place where the insurrection was decided. The *Duce* begins his speech by recalling that all but one (Michele Bianchi) of the four *quadrumvirs* (leaders) of the March on Rome are present. The crowd instinctively responds and replaces Bianchi by shouting: *Presente!* On this occasion the memory of Michele Bianchi lives on and gains meaning when revisited in 1932. In his speech the *Duce* is particularly eager to make reference to the martyrs of 1922 and to situate the fascist revolution within the context of contemporary modern history (just as he had in the Ascension Day speech). The fascist insurrection has been, he tells the crowd, the bloodiest of the modern age. The revolution is intransigent, both politically and morally. Following a brief comparison with other revolutions that changed the course of history, the *Duce* declares himself to be the charismatic leader capable of guiding this transition with the help of fascist doctrine and faith in the oath of allegiance to the party. His intentions are the intentions of the nation. A recurring metaphor is introduced and contextualized: youth and the new generation of fascists coming of age during the *Decennale*. Here the *Duce* associates the youth or generational theme with the "permanent revolution" and within the liturgical setting of the *Decennale* manifestations: one generation is meant to pass the revolutionary flame to the next. The revolution's intent is to inject a renewed sense of energy into the dead corners of the nation's life:

> We've considered the youth problem. The youth issue is one that exists on its own. Life itself presents the youth issue for life has its seasons, just like Nature. Now, in the second decade we must make way for youth. No one is older than he who is jealous of youthfullness. We want our young to pick up our torch and inflame themselves with our faith. May they be ready and decisive to continue our work.[67]

On 23 October the *Duce* spoke in Turin. The event was highly choreographed by Starace, and a certain comraderie is evident between the

Duce and the masses. In Turin he again mentioned the "fascist option."
The reception from the city is "ardent" and "enthusiastic": the working
class is moving towards the *Duce*, towards the regime, and towards the
corporative state. "I too know what it means to have an empty home
and a barren roof!" the *Duce* tells the people of Turin. In one brief scene,
a typical example of one of Starace's effectively choreographed scenarios, a group of war veterans are shown being drawn in their carriages
by young *balilla*. Two generations of Italians in uniform are now participating in the nation's regenerative spectacle. The *Duce* ends the speech
on a decisive note, a rallying cry for the new decade, towards which the
regime is moving with the spirit of a twenty-year-old youth.

On 25 October the *Duce* spoke in Milan. The LUCE documents the
sense of expectation as the crowd waits. Enormous lettering, DVX, emanates from one side of the piazza. Flags are omnipresent. The main
themes in this speech are universal fascism, empire, the martyrs of the
fascist revolution, and Rome as *the* option between Moscow and New
York. Here the *Duce* selectively reads historically determinant episodes
of the past so as to set the stage for the future. He speaks in terms of decades. The year 1932 is meant to mark the beginning of a new century:

> I say to you today, immense multitude, with my conscience completely at
> peace, that the Twentieth Century shall be the century of Fascism. It shall
> be the century of Italian might, the century during which Italy will return
> for the third time to be the leader of human civilization, because there can-
> not be any salvation, neither for individuals nor for nations, outside of our
> principles. In ten years – we can say this without being prophets – Europe
> will be modified. There have been injustices committed. Even against us,
> especially against us! And nothing is sadder than the task that awaits us
> every once in a while: defending that which has been the magnificent sac-
> rifice of blood shed by the entire Italian nation! … In a decade Europe will
> be fascist or becoming fascist! The antithesis in which contemporary civi-
> lization wrestles can't be surpassed but in one way, with the doctrine and
> the wisdom of Rome![68]

The *Duce* concludes his speech with liturgically influenced language,
and after having completed vows (*vota soluta*), he administers the
Eucharist of the state to the new generation, the generation of 1932:

> A day not too close to us – at least thirty years are needed to toughen as I
> want the soul of a nation – one day we will be truly proud to deliver our

glorious pennants to the youth who grow vigorously and splendidly under our eyes. Then we will say: These are the pennants of the Revolution, consecrated by the purest blood of the *squadristi*! Carry the pennants high, defend them – and if necessary – with your lives. And do so as if these will be kissed by the sun of new and more luminous victories![69]

The final words of the *Duce*'s speech are thematically close to the most important part of the liturgy: the consecration and distribution of the blood and body of Christ, the Gospel passion. In this case the *Duce* is the priest, and the pennants of the revolution are a signifier, a symbol, the "host" consecrated through the liturgy of violence and the blood of the *squadristi*.[70] In those days the *Duce* was active in inaugurating new projects that were meant to further perpetuate the illusion of grandeur. On 27 October quaint applause replaced the revolutionary chants of the previous days. That same day the *Duce* inaugurated the section of the *Via del Mare* that connected to *Piazza Venezia*: the road connecting the city of Rome with the waterway. In the LUCE film clip, all applaud, even a worker sitting on scaffolding from above. The *Via dell'Impero* was also inaugurated on 27 October and symbolically united the sacrifice of the Great War (*Altare della Patria*) with the splendors of Imperial Rome (*Colosseo*). On 30 October the *Duce* unveiled a monument to the war dead in Forlì. In the newsreel the music takes us back to the days of trench warfare when the nation was united against a common enemy. *"Non passa lo straniero"* ("The Foreigner Shall Not Pass"), a song from the war days, can be heard in the background. A multitude of flags fly high, and a trumpet calls the entire community to order. In his brief speech the *Duce* incites the masses: "With whom are the martyrs of the War? With us! With the revolution, with the regime!"[71] Between 30 October and 3 November the *Duce* visited Pavia, Monza, Brescia, and Ancona. In Monza he inaugurated a monument to the war dead and reminded the audience that the first fascist squad to defend his newspaper, *Il Popolo d'Italia*, was sent from Monza.

The *Decennale* celebrations were an opportunity to exhibit the doctrines, institutes, and completed works of the fascist revolution. The *Duce* was keen on being the charismatic interpreter of the nation's needs, wants, and desires. Two generations were mentioned: those who had fought in the Great War and participated in the fascist revolution, and the new generation. Both would be united in a new march towards the future and faithfully obedient to the commandments of the state. The commemorative celebrations were formalized, as we see in the LUCE documentary, with a new march by the war's amputees on the newly inaugurated *Via dell'Impero*. This action was meant to "energetically" and "decisively" inspire a new march *from* Rome, symbol of Roman imperial might and of the *risorgimento* struggle.

Mussolini also gave a series of interviews to Emil Ludwig at *Palazzo Venezia* between 23 March and 4 April 1932.[72] The interviews are interesting and appropriate to this book in that they offer a more intimate insight into the techniques employed by the regime at the time of the *Decennale*. Here the *Duce* explained that every revolution creates new forms, myths, and rites particular to a specific historical occurrence. Revolutions also inaugurate a new aesthetic. As such, it is the obligation of the "would-be revolutionist" to make use of this original aesthetic, refashion it, and create new festivals and new forms, gestures, and rites capable of keeping the aesthetic alive. In other words, the future revolutionist needs to conjure up ways to replicate an aesthetic now become tradition. Life would be determined by action: an aesthetic operation sustained with symbolisms. Keeping alive the aura of the March on Rome, Mussolini explained, meant creating the conditions for a permanent revolution, which would transcend class structures and rely on the use of myth within a collective and sacred setting. The fabrication of consensus would rely on organizing and educating the masses according to the myth of the state. Collectivism meant focusing on the annulment of the individual identity within the collective reality celebrated as a new life style, a renewed aesthetic. Each individual, the *Duce* explained, would be "replicated," "multiplied" – just as original works of art are – and would follow the precepts of the fascist secular religion unconditionally. The people's faith in the ethical state would be their reason to exist. The educational system would guarantee this faith by imposing a new aesthetic onto the new generations of fascists. Celebrating previous victories would provide the conditions for actuating this ideological program. The *Decennale* satisfied these needs.

1

Exhibition Value: The New Generation

Mussolini's Italian

In 1930 Mario Carli published *L'Italiano di Mussolini: romanzo dell'era fascista*, a novel written for a reader in tune with the fascist movement's accomplishments. Carli was the co-founder of the *Arditi*, the assault troops of the Great War, along with Filippo Tommaso Marinetti and Ferruccio Vecchi. *L'Italiano* was an intentionally populist novel. Clichés and fascist ideology dominated the novel, as did a certain tendency to focus on storytelling, propaganda, and fascist spirituality. Carli's Italian was Falco d'Aquilonia, an ex-combatant now in his early thirties and a spokesman for fascism. At the beginning of the novel we encounter Falco's uncle Riccardo returning home after twenty-five years of voluntary exile in the United States. While travelling on Italy's modernized railways, *zio* Riccardo reflects on the nation's transformation:

> Italy was unrecognizable. He felt a vague moral malaise. Perhaps it was remorse for not having contributed energetically to the transformation of the face of the nation as the war and the fascist revolution had done … But his sense of marvel was fed even more by the encounter with the new generation. Falco appeared as its best representative. This thirty-year-old had already lived an entire life and had undergone profound experiences. His adventures had been both spiritual and corporal. He had gambled with death without ever losing and had enriched his blood with steel schrapnel and the powder of fuses. This young man, all of a sudden just as he was becoming a man, was finding in himself the virtues of command or obedience … [T]his blue-eyed young man appeared to him as a completely new human figure, an unedited model of Italian virility. To find

something similar, his imagination had to go back in history. His eyes saw that Falco incarnated a type of "civilized barbarian": in other words a modern man striding towards the future in a spiritual manner but completely free from conventionalisms and that sort of cowardice that weakens the character. What couldn't a nation that was now reborn historically do with similar men? What couldn't a nation do that was guided by a charming and bright Leader? The most legitimate hopes could be conceived for the future of Italy, and now he understood the chants and slogans that had been in the press for a couple of years now. These slogans made the *Duce* seem magnificent. They spoke of an Empire and of a new civilization. These insights immediately penetrated the spirit of the man coming home once again, and in an instant he saw and understood what the words "fascist revolution" were all about.[1]

The passage presents a judgment of both Italy and Falco. Both had undergone a complete transformation due to the war and the fascist revolution. Riccardo feels a sense of remorse for not having freely given himself and his energy to this collective effort. The Italian people, he now understands, have been redeemed from their past. Falco, *exemplum* and hero of this progression, Carli explains, had heeded the call of both leadership and obedience. His adventures, furthermore, had been both spiritual and physical. These adventures had transformed Falco into a new kind of Italian man. In sum, he was an example of fascist modernity: spiritually purified through violence and free from bourgeois convention and decadence. His values exemplified the movement's values.

The encounter with the young man immediately transforms Riccardo's spirit, for he is now able to see, touch, feel, and perhaps contribute to this born-again nation. Riccardo, we infer, identifies with this aesthetic transformation – both Italy and Falco are now "beautiful." In addition, a religious metaphor is implied: the saviors of the Italian nation had suffered the cross (the Great War, the fascist revolution) to grant deliverance to the nation. Through their sacrificial offering, Italy had been resurrected, aesthetically and morally, as the birthplace of a new civilization and a new empire.

The cult of virility was well established in nineteenth century Europe. Piero Meldini reminds us that language focusing on virility can be traced to the first colonial wars (Abissinia, 1895–6; Pacification of Libya, 1922–32).[2] Both nationalists and futurists appropriated this language. *Lacerba*, a leading literary journal edited by Giovanni Papini, celebrated this tone in a 1914 article titled *"Amiamo la Guerra,"* ("We Love War"). The article contained phrases such as "we love war and we love to taste it as long as it lasts" and "[w]ar is fearful and in fact just because it is fearful and tremendous and destructive we must love it with our masculine hearts." The Great War had provided an excellent opportunity to renew the political playing field. And when the fascists met for the first time in Piazza San Sepolcro, Milan, on 23 March 1919, the *Duce* called upon Ferruccio Vecchi, who had once famously stated in his book *Arditismo civile* that "man's mask is peace, his soul is war."[3] Around that same time, Papini published another book on this subject, *Maschilità* (Manliness).[4]

Mario Carli went a step further and put together a series of notes to describe the ideal fascist male. According to the futurist Carli, the ideal fascist male (1) was a genius, lively, and had thick, dishevelled hair, (2) was fiery and proud, with naive eyes that did not ignore irony, (3) possessed a sensual and energetic mouth ready to kiss furiously, sing sweetly, and command imperiously, (4) had lean muscles irradiated by beams of ultra-sensitive nerves, (5) had a dynamo heart, lungs like tires, and the kidney of a leopard, (6) had the legs of a squirrel to climb all the peaks and conquer the abyss, and (7) was extremely elegant but also manly and sportive, which allowed him to run, to fight, to struggle, to break free, and to harangue a crowd.[5]

These ideas were still relevant at the time of the *Decennale*. In 1932 Manlio Pompei wrote in the pages of *Critica fascista* about the need to encourage "virile education." Fascism was to be, Pompei explained, a school exemplifying courage that championed virility and combat. The new generation needed to understand that war is the greatest event the future can hold. One must be ready for war, because war is a constant. It is an event that always was and always will be. The rest of the article focuses on the lack of male teachers and the steps needed to close this gap.[6] More recently, a solid study on other aspects of this concept can be found in the pages written by George Mosse in *Nationalism and Sexuality: Respectability and Abnormal Sexuality in Modern Europe.*[7]

Now, if we consider the connection between aesthetics and fascism, then both Italy and its youth can be read as original "works of art" possessing a certain uniqueness or, if we prefer Walter Benjamin's term, "aura." Carli explains to us that the combatant had been *presente* (present) at specific times and places: the Great War and the March on Rome. His presence in these historic events guaranteed his status as a cult figure participant in the ritual of revolution. Falco belongs to a distinct class: the generation of 1922. We discover that he is well mannered but a brute, solitary but still sociable, an MP and a personal friend of the *Duce*. He is at home both in the city and in the country. He is a "civilized barbarian," virile, altruistic, and selfless, and a fearless aviator and patron of land-reclamation projects in the Puglia region. The ex-combatant is a fascist man of action and experience.

Falco d'Aquilonia personifies the fascist revolution's first decade. Towards the end of the novel, his younger brother Lucio (the fascist "light" of the future) decides to sign up for the Libyan front. Lucio, at eighteen, is ambitious like his older brother. He represents the new generation's coming of age. Dionisia, their mother, stoically accepts her son's decision to enlist voluntarily. A chorus of voices ("the Italian people"), similar to a chorus employed in ancient Greek tragedy, acknowledges the young man's decision:

> You don't know my torment; you don't know it, Falco. I never told you anything not to sound ridiculous … [Y]ou've been my idol, an example to follow, my teacher, but also my constant anguish. You acted, and I admired you in awe.
>
> Let those like us – those not fortunate to have been an infantryman or *squadrista* – live our adventure. Let us fight. I've had enough of envy and of living in the reflection of others. I want my part of the glory. I want my own risks, my own wounds, my own hardships, my own war. Are we not a race of warriors, yes or no? And when do you want me to leave? When cowardice and the shoe blisters of the world have decided to abolish war forever? Come on, Mother! Smile. You can't die when your heart is so light. Let me go forth and participate in my own orgy of youthfullness. And when I return to you I'll have more steel in my blood and more love in my heart!
>
> May the Lord be with you, my son!
>
> The elderly Mother blessed him with kisses, and tears fell on her son's tanned face.[8]

Lucio wishes to continue the march initiated by his older brother and aspires to redeem his own generation, members of which did not participate in the Great War or the 1922 March on Rome. War, violence, virility, youthfulness, and the rhetoric of maternal sacrifice were all important parts of a fascist belief system. These characteristics defined the individual by allowing him to participate in something greater: the ethical state. The success of this movement, furthermore, depended on its ability to regenerate, redeem, and instil a revolutionary consciousness (or aura) in youth, an aura that insisted on the potentiality of character reform. If we look again at Carli's novel we notice that Lucio identifies with his older brother's unique experiences, but with one substantial difference. Whereas Falco had been called upon by fate to change the course of Italian history, Lucio has been educated and created in the image of the true Italian fascist after the revolution. Lucio appears to the reader as a mere reproduction of the "original," since he lacks Falco's authority, historical testimony, and, generally speaking, life experience or aura. He is an "authorized copy" of an original work of art: a mere product of the movement's efforts to mass produce "new men" within the fascist state. In short, Lucio possesses "exhibition" or "political" value (as opposed to "ritual" value) ten years after the March on Rome.

Youthfulness was an adventurous performance rhetorically construed by the collective state, a myth staged on the ideas of martyrdom as ascension, war, destiny, and the aura of ritual sacrifice.[9] The aesthetic rebirth was to be accompanied by a moral one. In 1932 the journal *Ottobre* republished a well-known text by Mussolini titled "*Quant'è bella giovinezza*" ("How Beautiful Youth Is"), initially printed in the first issue (1920) of the student newsletter *Giovinezza*. By implication, these writings, directed towards the nation's youth, would be immediately transformed into sacred scripture that defined and created a new national order consisting of one voice: His. Mussolini's textual references were verses written during the Renaissance by Lorenzo de' Medici (*Quant'è bella giovinezza*). The *Duce* counterposes the age of the Medici with the present. It is an age devoid of happiness, where joy is but a brief pause in the battle, a seemingly endless war that will heal the world through its violence. In 1932 the implied message of this article would have been obvious: the sacrifice of the new generation, an imitation of the martyrs who preceded them, would bring the light of Rome to all the peoples of the earth through universal fascism. Events, however, would turn out differently. Ten years after the March on Rome, measures had to be set in motion to collectively assemble the nation's youth into a modern mechanized entity capable of redeeming both the world and fascism in a time of crisis. A very important report written by Carlo Scorza to Mussolini on 11 July 1931 (and also represented to us by Michael Ledeen in *Universal Fascism*) is especially useful in clarifying the issue. Scorza was the head of the fascist university student association:

The *Duce* needs to have at his beck and call an army composed in close-order formations: immense, masculine, steadfast in its faith, and irresistable in its advances. In other words, an armed religious formation: an army capable of predicting the Leader's will even before he expresses it; an army capable of finding in itself the spiritual and human elements to make it work even before the Leader can give them the material elements. An army rooted to the land through love. The passion links it to the nation, and it is always ready to quit camp and move on anywhere else … Are we to let the youth generation act on its own for the government's sake? … The Fascist Revolution, having only ten years of life, can't afford such luxury. For twenty centuries every Sunday the Church has explained the Gospel and considers blasphemous any other interpretation. The university masses are not as the *Duce* wants. The reasons for this are diverse and not easy to explain. Those farthest from us are Law students, students of literature, and philosophy students: those in abstract disciplines. Those closest to us are instead Medical and Engineering students: the exact sciences. I found among the university students a lively sense of autonomy with respect to the Party and a lively intolerance with disciplinary and hierarchical regulations.[10]

Scorza advised the *Duce* on the current state of fascist indoctrination among university youth. He noted, for example, that anti-fascist professors were often the most esteemed and influential scholars, that discipline was lacking, and that a relatively high percentage of anti-fascist teaching assistants were present in the universities. Since the removal of these faculty members would not have been an effective measure, Scorza advocated the use of myth and youth-centred fascist spirituality. These new warriors had to be educated through myth and theology, perhaps even by listening to untrue stories, indeed to noble lies:

We need to give youth a myth, because youth needs to believe blindly in something and consider itself at the centre of something. At the present time students are spiritually uncertain because they have to deal with two great events: the War and the Revolution, in which they have not participated and to which they have not contributed. Youth seeks something that its instinct feels as urgent but that it still can't explain precisely in its mind. Youth is fascist, yes, but not the way the *Duce* wants it to be. I'd say that it is fascist as a mass, whereas it ought to be fascist just like an aristocracy at the Command. In every age young Italian students … have had a flag, a belief, a myth.[11]

The members of this new generation lacked the aura ("myth" according to Scorza) that their older *camerati* possessed. Creating an aura for them within the cultural politics of the regime would therefore allow this generation to identify strongly with the revolution and, in turn, eliminate dissent. It appeared that defending and guaranteeing the future of the revolution had become a technical problem after the March on Rome. The production of an artificially construed aura that bordered on the irrational – a "noble lie" of sorts – was contingent on transforming history into spectacle. After all, Machiavelli too was not always concerned with historical truth and, as Leo Strauss remarks, frequently "changed at will the data supplied by the histories ... [T]here may be examples which are beautiful without being true. In the language of our time, Machiavelli is an artist as much as he is an historian. He is certainly very artful."[12]

A new institution that championed these ideals, *La Scuola di mistica fascista Sandro Italico Mussolini* (The Sandro Italico Mussolini School of Fascist Mysticism), was inaugurated in Milan. The school was founded in April 1930 by Niccolò Giani under the patronage of Mussolini's brother, Arnaldo Mussolini, and renamed active until 1943. It was named after Sandro Italico Mussolini, Arnaldo's late son. The term *"mistica"* ("mysticism") was used at the school to represent a series of ideas to be relied upon and adhered to by means of a tradition or feeling, even if these ideas could not be justified in a rational manner. Giani's idea of *"mistica"* was applied to the idea of the *Duce*. It underscored that fascist mysticism was anchored in Benito Mussolini, the *Duce* and infallible spiritual father of fascist culture. Arnaldo Mussolini's contribution focused on the new age, the new generation, and the passing of the torch. The school invoked faith in life, fascist spirituality, and *giovinezza* (youth) as a "state of grace" to which all fascists ought to aspire. The school aimed to create future fascist leaders and cadres for the fascist party with specific characteristics. There were to be no privileges, only duties, and students had to accept all responsibility. Fascists were meant to be intransigent, just like the Dominicans of the Inquisition. Fascists had to be capable of commanding and obeying. They had to have faith and believe in faith strongly. They were to do good and do it in silence. The true fascist was meant to have a different relationship with wealth. For the true fascist, wealth should only be a means to an end, and in the long run wealth alone would not be sufficient to create a great civilization. Fascists were not to indulge in inappropriate greedy transactions. They were not to be vain or careerists. Fascists were to provide true examples of probity: they had to act on their own before preaching to others. Fascist works and deeds would always be more eloquent than words in speeches. The fascist would disdain mediocre events and never be vulgar. The fascist would believe in all that is good. The fascist was to have truth and goodness as his personal confidant.

The *Scuola di mistica fascista* focused on this sort of mysticism as an absolute truth presented by the *Duce*. Fascist mysticism was best exemplified as fascist action set within absolute faith in the truth of fascist doctrine. Albert Sorel and Friedrich Nietzsche influenced the main ideas sustaining the school, as did Niccolò Giani, Berto Ricci, Telesio Interlandi, Arnaldo Mussolini, and the *Duce*. And Julius Evola. The protagonists of the school were many, represented the Italian elite, and merit further study. The school is an important element in the creation of the cult of the *Duce*, which sustained the fascist movement in the second part of the *Ventennio*. It was responsible for the regime's politics of exclusion. This influence is especially seen in the role played by the school in the development of an anti-Semitic program in the second half of the 1930s.[13]

The generation coming of age in 1932 set out to distinguish itself from those who had witnessed the first hours of the fascist party. This new group was a threat to the previous system and also to the movement's future or destiny. At the same time the new generation was insecure about their newly acquired status since they had not participated in the Great War and the March on Rome. One example of this existential conflict is the character Lucio in Carli's novel, discussed earlier.

Indro Montanelli, generally considered the greatest Italian journalist of the twentieth century, clearly defined the issue.[14] Montanelli compared the *squadrista* past of the first generation of fascists with the ritualistically staged exercises (and schooling) of the later fascist avantgarde: less intense, disassociated from the urban warfare of 1919, and wrongfully mocked. Montanelli explained that the regime's efforts to re-create the original 1922 fascist spirit in his generation were not appreciated by the youth masses and therefore ineffective. This lack of experience undoubtedly affected the issue of authenticity. The matter was one of conscience and autonomy. The true revolutionary movement allowed its protagonists to dissent, renounce, and even disown its past. This approach produced several results. Some of Montanelli's *camerati* inebriated themselves in myth and religiously identified with the *Duce*. Others, however, sought to overcome the regime's intentions (forced social control and passive acquiescence) and to regain their own individuality and dissent, especially on moral grounds. This new mentality, created from the aura of the past (the rituals of the Great War and the revolution of 1922), developed into a regenerated aesthetic centred on *giovinezza*. Fascism had aestheticized the politics of youth to such an extent that only another war, or rather, if we read between the lines, a march *from* Rome, could redeem and indeed define this new generation. Montanelli concluded that they, the new generation, did not seek positions but only reclaimed their battles and wounds.[15]

The generation coming of age in 1932 was expected to do much more than simply be introduced into society. Its mission was to change history and redeem the world through universal fascism. These young men of 1932 set out, much like the fictional character Lucio, to claim their own battles and wounds. Blinded by the precepts of *giovinezza*, they would strive to earn their own "certificate of authenticity" by presenting Mussolini with an empire in 1936. The aesthetics of youth, or rather the "beauty" of this generation, linked each young man coming of age in 1932 with a specific mission. The concept of beauty carried both exclusive and inclusive meanings. In the exclusive sense it described the exterior manifestation of this beauty: the exhibition value of the new generation. In the inclusive sense it pertained to the morals and character of the new generation.[16] Both elements combined, thanks also to the regime's efforts to grant this generation an aura, to create the fascist "new man" and initiate him into society via a collective representation, much like the *Decennale*. However, simply living within the regime's walls could not suffice. Berto Ricci, Montanelli's teacher and editor of an important fascist revue, *L'Universale*, was convinced that a rather large contingency of the regime's youth would not accept the regime's truth passively.[17] Instead, he argued, the so-called process of normalization had only contributed to the new generation's critical assessment of fascist orthodoxy in 1932.

Giuseppe Bottai attempted to reconcile the diverse aspects of the youth question in 1932. The regeneration of youth was to focus on eliminating those materialistic elements that alienate the individual and are typical of capitalist societies. He summed up the main points of the youth question, after three years of debate, in an article published during the *Decennale*.[18] In his article, Bottai responded to an article by Giulio Santangelo, which had just been published in *Bibliografia fascista* and only touched the surface aspects of the youth question by reducing the entire issue to job placement. Bottai responded by considering the spiritual regeneration of youth. Finding a solution to the youth question would guarantee a renovated political elite and the future of fascism. Bottai reflected on the previous decade and on what he believed to be a successful process of legislative and ideological normalization that would encourage a reformist spirit. A critical analysis of fascism and the new generation's function within the regime would certainly bring to light issues of autonomy, freedom, and dissent. Bottai was also responding to Camillo Pellizzi, who wrote that the new generation of intellectuals ought to collaborate with the regime by dissenting, thereby providing an example for the rest of society. Not everyone was so optimistic. In the same issue a young Romano Bilenchi added a bit of realism to the discussion by concluding that the new generation (between twenty and twenty-four years old) coming of age in 1932 was indifferent to the entire issue. These young men preferred to live "comfortably" rather than as revolutionaries. Bottai responded to both these views by focusing on a practical solution to the youth question. He concluded by proposing ways to instil a revolutionary consciousness in the new generation through fascist syndicalism, schools, and cultural institutions, and thus incorporate the generation within the regime. An editorial published in *Occidente* contained the most relevant conclusions regarding the youth question. The youth of 1932 were apparently sceptical about the validity of a fascist secular religion: aura, fascist aesthetics, the tradition of the past, and all. For them, history was something to think *with* and not just about.[19]

This process of normalization (reflected in Bilenchi's words, as well) urged fascist intellectuals such as Bottai to increase the regime's efforts to create a revolutionary conscious "new generation." Youth journals such as *Saggiatore*, *Orpheus*, and *L'Universale* responded to this attempt to modernize the original revolution by establishing a dialectic with reality rather than putting their trust in a secular religion. The discussion that ensued divided the party into a "revisionist" faction and an "intransigent" faction, as Ben-Ghiat points out. Intellectuals such as Luigi Chiarini reminded young intellectuals that the regime "already had a perfectly defined history and doctrine," while Gherardo Casini "stated the regime's intention to 'exert control over emerging tendencies' and warned youth away from 'negating' existing values and institutions."[20] This last group promoted an inauthentic and choreographed revolution, and eventually transformed the regime into a technically advanced "instrument" of sorts, which was determined to artificially fabricate a new generation of revolutionaries, aura and all, by keeping dissent at a minimum and "bringing [its] leisure-time activities under State authority."[21]

The *Decennale* celebration, therefore, presented an ideal opportunity for the regime to exhibit the semantic web of youthfulness through new forms of media such as parades and even museum walks. These pages, therefore, focus on demonstrating the manner in which the regime transferred the myth-based rhetoric of youth from the literary page to a visual space re-enacting the aura of history. This last strategy was particularly appreciated at the *Mostra della Rivoluzione Fascista* (Exhibition of the Fascist Revolution) – the first political exhibition of its kind – which inaugurated the *Decennale* celebrations. It was at the *Mostra* that the rhetoric associated with *giovinezza* redefined the nation's narrative by building upon the literature of the past (Mazzini, D'Annunzio, Mussolini) and transposing the semantics of *giovinezza* onto the narrative space of an exhibition walk.

1832: 1932

The rhetoric of youth defined the fascist movement from the very beginning. It was not, however, an exclusively fascist concept but a recurring theme influenced by specific events belonging to the nation-building experience. Scholars such as Emilio Gentile have reiterated that nationalism, the ideology of sacrifice, and the rhetoric of youth were common themes in Mazzini's writings and especially in those associated with the *Giovine Italia* (Young Italy) effort. Gentile explains that a civil religion has been present in Italian political culture since the *Risorgimento*. This civil religion created its own symbolic world. The nation was attributed a sacred aura. Mazzini and his religious concept of politics as mission and duty further contributed to the creation of a civil religion, a lay form of religiousness that would be considered an essential component in cultural modernization.[22]

Fascism believed that it could unite the nation and complete the unification process. Each important Italian march of the past (Mazzini's, Garibaldi's, D'Annunzio's) was part of a continuing process of redemption. As such, fascism was seen as a completion of the nation-building process begun in the *Risorgimento*. Mazzini idealized the young men fighting as a morally righteous revolutionary force. In a text titled "*Une nuit à Rimini*" ("A Night in Rimini"), Mazzini's heroes are a hundred young men. They are the pride of their families and the hope of their land. The oldest is but twenty-five years of age. At that age years represented centuries. This collective group was not interested in love, pleasures, and petit bourgeois concerns, simply because they did not care about these things: "*Eux, n'avaient pas regardé!*" (recall the fascist slogan:

"*Me ne frego!*" – "I don't care!").[23] And so, Mussolini wrote, the signal had been given, the cry had been understood, and the young men had rushed into combat.

War initiates the young man into a new religion. Consequently, the combatant dismisses those activities traditionally linked to a bourgeois upbringing. War allows him to identify with a cohesive group and with a system created by historical circumstances. The battle regenerates identity. The battle initiates the young man into history. The aforementioned texts underscore the rhetoric of sacrifice, maternal sacrifice, fate, and destiny. They speak to us of a generation united by ritual and blood in a secular religion. These men fight for their land. They fight against traitors and against those who have neglected or sold the honour of the nation.

In the *Manifesto della "Giovine Italia"* (1831), written ten years after a group of refugees had fled to Genoa following a failed insurrection against Austria, Mazzini explained the mission of the *Giovine Italia*: today, a religion of martyrdom; tomorrow, the religion of victory.[24] Thus, history and time bestowed an aura of authenticity upon these combatants. Mazzini's apostles appear to us as protagonists of a new age: purveyors of a reformist spirit, instruments of redemption, and participants in the ritual of revolution. The manifesto of 1832, *Della Giovine Italia*, underscored the young generation's role. This youth collective, "new souls … rising like Prometheus against Fate" would be capable of liberating Italy and the rest of Europe from its past.[25] They were the ideal protagonists of a universal movement at a time of incertitude, just as universal fascism aspired to be in 1932. In another document that focused on those forces impeding the development of freedom in Italy (*D'alcune cause che impedirono finora lo sviluppo della libertà in Italia*), Mazzini expanded on the theme and explained that the true revolutionary takes advantage of youth's potential and transforms each combatant into a zealous apostle of a new religion. The essay stated that only war and martyrdom can prepare these revolutionaries for other more sweeping conquests that transcend life on earth. He described the young generation as authentic, experienced, and in possession of an aura, proclaiming that they must perform as instruments of deliverance. He wrote that these young men must have a mission.They must believe in something, in a myth-based faith. And they must identify with the mission and with the rhetoric of glory, homeland, and might, and be ready for mobilization.[26]

Mazzini's lesson was not lost on the young Mussolini. After being expelled from the socialist party in 1914, he wrote an inflammatory article promoting the interventionist cause in his newly founded newspaper, *Il Popolo d'Italia*.[27] Mussolini's rallying call, "War!," was directed towards those young in age and youthful in spirit: a collective defined as history's destiny, those willing to march into combat and redeem the nation from its past. Many of the nation's youth, especially those associated with the futurist movement and Prezzolini's *La Voce*, gladly supported Mussolini's interventionist stance.[28] War was an effective way to realize the complete potential of the revolution. The nationalist Filippo Corridoni explained that war was a necessary long-term strategic consideration. Corridoni believed that the "proletarian brain" was not capable of fully understanding the problem of war. The proletarian only sees the massacres, misery, and hunger. But war can also be a revolutionary event. It can pave the way for a social revolution and eliminate the last remnants of feudal dominance by eradicating standing armies. Corridoni cried out: "Give the proletarian bread, yes! But give them also ideas and an education. And tend to their spiritual and cultural needs."[29]

Ideological and political continuity between the *Risorgimento*, the Great War, and fascism was claimed. For example, in a book review published in the literary journal *Occidente*, Giulio Santangelo considered both the *Risorgimento*, which was an urban revolution, and the Great War in relation to fascism, which was a rural revolution. Santangelo's article reviewed Mario Missiroli's latest publication, *L'Italia d'oggi*, as a "well-meant yet unsatisfactory attempt" to position fascism within the general context of Italian history. Missiroli's study concluded that the war effort had cost Italy "something" when it came to national unity. Santangelo disagreed, and in 1932 quoted a paragraph previously written by Emilio Bodrero for the journal *900*.[30] The experience of the trenches had unified rather than divided the Italian nation, wrote Bodrero. This "wondrous consequence," the result of blood and pain, had united the classes socially and the nation's youth.

Rhetoric of this sort was also present in Gabriele D'Annunzio's speeches and writings, especially those delivered following the 12 September 1919 taking of Fiume (modern day Rijeka, Croatia). Mussolini had been cautious, whereas D'Annunzio had not and was quick to make this clear to the *Duce*. As Renzo De Felice and other scholars have pointed out, we have two versions of a letter that D'Annunzio sent to Mussolini reprimanding his lack of fundraising for the *impresa* (campaign). The letter was sent on 16 September 1919. A censored version appeared in the *Il Popolo d'Italia* on 20 September. De Felice indicates, furthermore, that fundraising efforts in New England had been effective. For example, *L'eco della Nuova England* of Springfield, Massachusetts, sent $1,775.40. The Argentinian newspaper *Italia del popolo* sent 25,000 lire from Buenos Aires.[31]

D'Annunzio proclaimed the *Reggenza Italiana del Carnaro* (Italian Regency of Carnaro) on 8 September 1920. The self-proclaimed state would later be replaced in December 1920 by the Free State of Fiume under pressure from the Italian navy. The constitution, *La Carta del Carnaro* (The Carnaro Charter), written by D'Annunzio and the anarcho-syndicalist Alceste De Ambris, was a combination of socialist, anarchist, pre-fascist, Nietzschean, and utopian ideals intended to establish a corporatist state with ten guilds, nine of which were reserved for "workers" (unskilled labourers, merchants, and so on). The tenth (X) guild, led by D'Annunzio, was to include the "creative" people, geniuses, "new men," and, we can assume, supermen or warriors. The charter is notorious for triumphantly proclaiming that the fundamental principle of the state be "music." Music redeems the individual. Music allows the individual to be born again and free. The religious beliefs proclaimed at Fiume centred on the regeneration of virtue, the beauty of life, and the centrality of work: a theme adapted from revolutionary unionism.[32] These elements would liberate the individual (potentially granting him freedom) and allow him to identify with a larger group, the collective.[33] After seizing the city in 1919, D'Annunzio's legionnaires were now called the redeemers of victory.[34] The youthfulness embodied by his soldiers had already become a raison d'être for D'Annunzio in the months preceding Fiume.[35] Years later, in a speech dated 21 September 1922 (following the loss of Fiume and one month before the March on Rome), D'Annunzio redefined *giovinezza* as "destiny" and "fate," even when it errs.[36]

Youth possessed "cult value" in the ritual of war for Mazzini, D'Annunzio, and the young Mussolini. Furthermore, as the literature of the time suggests, the experience of war had created a fellowship in a public setting for the previous generations. In 1932, ten years after the March on Rome, the fascist movement had evolved into a regime, and the aura of activism had been replaced by consensus-creating technicalities. Discourse on youth would have to adapt to the historical events commemorated by the *Decennale* celebrations so that it could incorporate the role that the generation of 1932 would have in Italy's future imperial conquests. The very notion of empire, therefore, associated fascism with *dinamismo* (dynamism) and *vitalità* (vitality): spiritual and moral expressions typical of youth rhetoric. This fascist way of life, characterized by discipline and sacrifice, would permit the Italian people to redeem themselves and the world from its economic and moral crisis. The journal *Gerarchia* published a series of articles dedicated to the topic in 1932. The journal's editor, Margherita Sarfatti, was convinced that Mussolini's universalistic aspirations were also meant to defend, intentionally, the racial integrity of the West.[37] Indeed, wrote Sarfatti, Mussolini had taken control of the world political scene.

The *Decennale* was an ideal platform for presenting the fascist solution as an alternative to both liberal democracy and communism.[38] Western civilization itself was menaced by an economic and moral crisis that only *lo stile del Fascismo* (fascist style) and Mussolini's "new Italian" could defuse. The most important event of *Anno X* to consider universal fascism was the *Convegno Volta* (Volta Convention), dedicated to the theme of "Europe." The mission of *Ottobre*, a publication inaugurated on 28 October 1932, exactly ten years after the March on Rome, was to reconcile Italian *giovinezza*, universal fascism, and the theme of redemption.[39] *Ottobre* insisted on a complete spiritual renewal of the present times and new ideals, all in the name of a generation-based rebirth.[40] In a front-page article published in the 5 January 1933 issue of *Ottobre*, Asvero Gravelli noted that the convention participants belonged to another generation that was "no longer relevant for the future of Europe." The nation's youth were now called upon to sustain the fascist movement's universalistic aspirations. The article promoted a future *Conferenza della Giovane Europa* (Conference of Young Europe), which would be the definitive expression of Europe's new Renaissance and rebirth in the name of *giovinezza* and fascist *azione* (action).[41] The European Renaissance of 1932 would focus on a campaign to spread both the Italian race and the "Fascist International." It would be a catalyst for a new civilization, a new Renaissance, and a new world order, which would do away with the false idols and rituals of the past. *Ottobre* had dedicated its inaugural issue to both the universal aspirations of fascism and the dynamic state of this continually evolving revolutionary spirit. In November 1932 it began publishing a series of articles on the history of the fascist youth movement. Gravelli explained to his readers that these pages were not to be read as a melancholic review of youth's role in the previous decade. Instead, the literature presented was to commemorate the specific function that youth had within fascism. Gravelli then urged his readers to study the documents made available on the subject at the *Mostra della Rivoluzione Fascista* in Rome. Gravelli's editorial was probably influenced by his own personal experience at the 1932 *Mostra*, where the modernist aesthetic and the representation of the past in the present was intended to redeem the new generation and give it a new mission: empire.

The previous pages not only consider the semantics of youth from Mazzini to 1932, they also show that the rhetoric of youth could not rely exclusively on words. The rhetoric associated with youth involved a performance of sorts, a ritualistic passing of the aura from one generation to the next. This aspect differentiated the generations of Mazzini and of the Great War from the generation of 1932. In the case of fascism, one generation owed its very existence to the actions of the previous one within the same historical narrative. The new generation, however, was asked to march *from* Rome and to become the future protagonist of a now radicalized fascist revolution. In the absence of a war to fight (at least for the moment), the new generation would have to limit itself to "study documents" and participate in debate. Among the thousands of documents present in the National Archives in Rome, we find one from the Youth Avant-garde of the PNF in Fano that contains all the elements present in the aforementioned texts:

Young workers and students!
   The youth avant-garde of the National Fascist Party warmly calls upon you to embrace its flag, which knows the thrill of victories won for the good of the Nation.
   Youth – this healthy volatile entity which, with the impetus of its vigour, of its enthusiasm, has written sublime pages in the history of the Homeland – must not remain absent from the great forge of history.
   The National Fascist Party is the sole political group that claims for itself, as a dominant part of its doctrine, the national sentiment understood in its ethical and material sense. Faced with the lowly speculation of other political parties that negate the Nation to get hold of the youth, it calls on you.
   Listen to it: it is the voice of those who saved the Homeland from imminent ruin. It is the voice that emanates from thousands and thousands of red, white, and green pennants soaked with the sublime blood of martyrdom. It is the voice of the bloodied mother speaking to her youngest children.
   Do not remain deaf. Run to the Party. The Nation expects from you its future. A long labour of full and beneficial national reconstruction awaits you.
   Italian youth!
   Dedicate yourselves to the Homeland right now, your soul and your life. Strengthen yourself in it, run to it quickly, and work hard.
   This is your hour: **A NOI! [To the revolution!]**[42]

The original passion sequences of the *Risorgimento*, the Great War, and 1922 (rituals in their own right) would be transferred from the literary page to the experiential at the *Mostra della Rivoluzione Fascista*. The exhibition was meant to inform and artificially confer a revolutionary aura onto the new generation. It intended to shock this generation into a new role as the future protagonists of a renewed and awe-inspiring narrative now to be exported from Rome.

Public Intimacy: The Exhibition of the Fascist Revolution[43]

Anno X also represented the fiftieth anniversary of Garibaldi's death. Garibaldi was considered a historical figure who had been a protagonist of the nation's regeneration. The study of Garibaldi's presence in the sacralization of politics – the cult of the leader (Garibaldi was also called *Duce*) – is an important template for the study of fascism. Garibaldi, the *Duce*, was also revered as a sacred leader for Italian youth:

> Q. Make the sign of the cross.
> A. In the name of the Father of my country, the Son of the people, and
>   the Spirit of liberty. Amen.
> Q. Who has created you a soldier?
> A. Garibaldi has created me a soldier.
> Q. Who is Garibaldi?
> A. Garibaldi is a spirit most generous, blessed of Heaven and Earth.
> Q. How many Garibaldis are there?
> A. There is only one Garibaldi.
> Q. How many persons in Garibaldi?
> A. In Garibaldi there are three persons really distinct: the Father of his
>   country, the Son of the people, and the Spirit of liberty.
> Q. Which of the persons became man?
> A. The second, that is, the Son of the people.
> Q. How was he made man?
> A. He took a body and soul as we did in the most blessed womb of a
>   woman of the people.[44]

The myth of Greater Italy has taken on a distinctly religious tinge. Mussolini referred to it as "the new religion" and had furnished fascism lavishly with the rites, ceremonies, and visible symbols of a cult. The following creed, taught to the *balilla*, or boy recruits, speaks for itself:

"I believe in Rome Eternal, the Mother of my Homeland,
And in Italy, her first born,
Who was born of her virgin womb by the Grace of God,
Who suffered under the barbarian invader, was crucified, slain, and buried,
Who descended into the sepulcher and rose again from the dead in the
    Nineteenth Century,
Who ascended to Heaven in her glory in 1918 and 1922,
Who is seated at the right hand of Mother Rome,
Whence she will come to judge the quick and the dead.
I believe in the genius of Mussolini,
In our Holy Father Fascism and in the communion of martyrs,
In the conversion of the Italians,
And in the resurrection of the Empire.
Amen![45]

Claudio Fogu has studied the link between fascism and the *Risorgimento* with specific reference to the 1932 Garibaldi celebrations. Fogu's study on historical representations and modernist rhetorics has served well for these chapters. The *Decennale*, Fogu explains, allowed the regime to "reverse the traditional concept of historical legitimation and consciousness: it was not fascism that gained historical legitimacy from the affirmation of its historical continuity with the past; it was the past that gained real presence and meaning ... Thus the Garibaldian celebrations ended by providing the Italian masses with a prototypical representation of the relationship between fascism and all other events in the Italian past."[46] The *Decennale* presented an ideal opportunity for the regime to legitimize the new generation of fascists coming of age. The most spectacular response to the generational question ever conjured can be found at the 1932 *Mostra della Rivoluzione Fascista*, the regime's first political exhibition of the fascist revolution.

Above all, the exhibition was to spectacularize the *Duce*. In 1932 one of the main organizers of the exhibition, Luigi Freddi, affirmed that the "leitmotif" of this gigantic symphony was to be the thought, action, and dominating personality (*personalità dominante*) of Mussolini. Historical events would have to ride on the "wave" created by the *Duce*. Similar ideas were put forth by Dino Alfieri in 1933 at the Third Congress on Fascist Culture.[47]

The exhibit was a "manifestation of will and might" (*una manifestazione ... di volontà e di forza*) created to educate, stimulate the visitor's imagination, and regenerate the spirit (*si rivolge alla fantasia, eccita l'immaginazione, ricrea lo spirito. Il visitatore ne resterà conquistato e preso fin dentro l'anima. Sicchè noi abbiamo fede che lo scopo educativo della Mostra della Rivoluzione Fascista sia felicemente raggiunto).*[48] It was there that the *Decennale* was institutionalized, as people and ideas were conferred new value. Its purpose was to instantiate a narrative, starting from Rome and authored by the generation of 1932. It was also a modernist celebration (where politics joined forces with aesthetics and architecture) and, furthermore, a point of arrival for the exhibition of fascist culture.[49]

In December 1933 a competition was announced for the creation of the new headquarters for the fascist party in Rome, the *Palazzo del Littorio.* The exhibition was to be held in Milan at the *Castello Sforzesco* in order to pay homage to the fascist movement's San Sepolcro origins but was moved to the *Palazzo delle Esposizioni* in Rome. In Rome, just months before its inauguration, the *Palazzo del Littorio* hosted an exhibition honouring another anniversary: the fiftieth anniversary of Garibaldi's death. The *Palazzo* also permanently hosted the 1932 exhibition as well as Mussolini's new office, libraries, and other bureaus.

The *Mostra* was divided into five sections and told the nation's story from an omniscient perspective. The first four sections centred on history: interventionist policy versus neutrality in the Great War (1914–15), the Great War (1915–18), the birth of fascism (1918–21), and the March on Rome (1922). The remaining areas focused on the rebirth of fascist Italy . (1922–32). Experienced by nearly four million visitors (Italians and foreigners), the *Palazzo delle Esposizioni* was transformed for the occasion, writes Jeffrey Schnapp, into a sort of "fascist Saint Peter's Square," where the regime's faithful renewed their creed ten years after the March on Rome.[50] The nation's capital was an ideal venue for fascism to bring a sense of closure to the nation-building process (begun one hundred years earlier by Mazzini), which was symbolized by Rome, and moreover, simultaneously to self-generate and reaffirm the city's identity as the starting point for a future march *from* Rome.

Numerous LUCE newsreels were dedicated to the exhibition.[51] Outside the exhibit an establishing shot set the scene. Four giant *fasci* were raised and connected together by the phrase: MOSTRA DELLA RIVOLUZIONE FASCISTA. Inside, twenty-four halls recounted the history of the movement. The first section of the exhibition was meant to captivate the subconscious and subvert traditional schemes by juxtaposing varied phenomena in a sequential pattern: large photographic montages, enlarged texts, and even sculptures within a modernist architectural setting.The *Mostra* furthermore is an exceptional case study for the history of typography and modern-day branding techniques "with an iron fist," as Steven Heller has most recently illustrated.[52] Its main purpose was to relive the aura of Italian fascist history. Moving along, the five halls located on the first floor celebrated fascism's conquests at home and abroad.

Visitors were able to participate, as protagonists, in a narrative that began with the events leading up to the March on Rome (analepsis: a flashback) and ended with a performative ritual focusing on fascism's future empire (prolepsis: a flashforward). Technically speaking, participants experienced a series of collages in a scripted sequence. The whole event had a somewhat pleasurable cinematic flair to it, as Sergei Eisenstein, the pioneering Soviet Russian film-maker of the period, would have it.[53] When situated within a fascist secular religion, the itinerary resembled the Stations of the Cross, the procession completed by Christ, redeemer of all humanity according to the Christian tradition. Similarly, the participant's ultimate destination at the exhibition (just as in Christ's procession) was a Golgotha-like stage complete with a cross. In both instances observing meant participating and identifying emotionally and psychologically with a redemptive narrative that pushed the neophyte out of a liminal state in order to fully engage with the community. Ada Negri noted: "This is not an Exhibition. It is an act of faith ... just like exiting the catacombs towards the open air and the sun."[54] It was at the 1932 exhibition that the rhetoric of regeneration and sacrifice (as expressed in the literary sequences presented at the beginning of this chapter) was transported into the realm of spectacle and exhibited for all to assess. The techniques involved were exquisitely modern. A sense of fellowship was artificially created in a public space.

In *Public Intimacy* Giuliana Bruno introduces the reader to Eisenstein's essay (mentioned above) and explains that the modern "architectural itinerary" (the museum walk) collects "various fragments of cultural phenomena from diverse geohistorical moments open for spectatorial recollection in space."[55] The cinematic event involves passing through different "light spaces" and is the very spectacle of the cinema screen and the architectural wall. In our specific case it provided an ideal opportunity for the new generation of fascists to experience and participate in a modernist spectacle that involved a series of chronological movements seen through the dimensions of time and space, and was held together by an ongoing narrative. The dialectic relationship developed by the images was marked by a synthesis that in turn created a narrative of redemption (for the new generation of fascists) and universality (empire). The narrative strategy was not new. In the Christian tradition Christ's passion was also a performance subsequently re-enacted by the faithful. In the case of the exhibition, the faithful re-enacted fascism's initial rituals of sacrifice by using a sophisticated assembly of images, halls, and stations that mechanically reproduced the original passion sequences, the semantics of which were intimately connected to the texts presented at the beginning of this chapter.

Halls A and B centred on the beginning of the Great War and the birth of *Il Popolo d'Italia*, the *Duce*'s newspaper. Particular attention was given to the protagonists of the war generation. They were at the centre of montage sequences that united text and image. In Hall A, designed by Esodo Pratelli and Luigi Freddi, the first issue of *Il Popolo d'Italia* was conferred special status. Its front-page enlargement was the largest ever created and occupied an entire section. The *Duce*'s article *"Audacia!"* was endowed with a new status. Its cry, "War!" (*"Guerra!"*), was elaborated into the narrative scheme of the exhibition hall as an inscription on the wall, complete with a dagger in the letter "G." LUCE newsreels documented and publicized the event. LUCE newsreel B0177 is a brief walkthrough of the rooms dedicated to fascism's origins and the events leading to 1914. LUCE newsreel B0181 is dedicated to 1915. LUCE newsreel B0191 is entirely dedicated to the war effort: images, portraits, and pictures. Dino Alfieri, the exhibition's main organizer, spent the months preceding the inauguration of the exhibition writing and collecting these documents. The fundamental success they had in exhibiting the thoughts of the *Duce* were indeed the pictures and documents relating to *Il Popolo d'Italia*. One notable autograph, Mussolini's article for the interventionist cause (*"Audacia!"*), was especially appreciated.[56] A mosaic of pictures, images, and words were exhibited. The aura of *Il Popolo d'Italia* was recreated through a larger-than-life pastiche of letters, documents, and figures. These artefacts regenerated, from within, the aura of an initial myth that a new generation of fascists could believe in.[57] The original "work of art" (*"Guerra!"*) had now been mechanically replicated. The aura of the original had been replaced by a traumatic effect attributable to a series of enlarged letters bursting forth from the hall's walls. The original and ritualistic call for audacity – *"Audacia!"* – was now regenerated as part of a narrative that recollected the past while, at the same time, was meant to inspire the future generation of fascists.

Halls C and D celebrated the interventionist cause. One wall of Hall C was decorated with a series of enlarged photographs featuring the desolate wasteland created by trench warfare, the cannons of battleships, and a machine gun at rest. As Bruno would have it,[58] a narrative space was created for the visitors as a field of visual space in which they could participate. After being initially encouraged to gather their strength, visitors were now asked to consider the rituals of the battlefield, the aura of the war generation, and to replicate the call for mobilization. The following hall, E, was dedicated to the period leading up to the creation of the fascist movement and the struggle against the Bolshevik "folly." The aura of that period was recreated by an architectural design that relied on avant-garde montage techniques: mechanical replication of the *Duce's* name. The design of this hall united both architectural and cinematic techniques: a "passage through light spaces," which created a narrative "engaging psychic change in relation to movement" for the body in transition. The resulting piece employed the "architecture of memory," a manner of "mapping space" and a type of "inner writing," the result of which was "an emotional affair providing access to knowledge." The story being told to the new generation of fascists coming to this exhibit acquired meaning as the visitor passed through and assimilated these historical sequences.

Bodies were also needed to project or exhibit these ideas. Hall G featured statues replicating larger-than-life soldiers of all sorts (both healthy and mutilated), covered with newspaper clippings, photographs, and headlines. In this instance the exhibition suggested that the events leading up to the Great War had redefined the borders between the public and private sphere. The documents that formed the skin of these statues were part of a *battaglia cartacea* (paper war) symbolizing the battle between fascists and subversives in 1919. The exhibition also defined the modern political struggle as one that relied on the hegemonic power's total control of the press.

Follow the Flag[59]

Fascist flags were predominantly exhibited in the "Gallery of the Fasces" and in the "Martyr's Shrine." These flags were sacred, and two LUCE newsreels dedicate scenes to them. LUCE newsreels A1019 and B0150 focus on the work of mounting the exhibition. Here we see the organizers opening boxes and unwrapping carefully packaged flags, in this case fascist pennants later to be exhibited in the Martyr's Shrine.

The cult of martyrdom was especially relevant after 1930. The *mito squadrista* (myth of the fascist squad) was inserted into the PNF constitution in 1932. At the time of the *Decennale* the myth was at the centre of celebrations. On 22 and 23 October 1932 a solemn ceremony for fifty-three *squadristi* was held in Bologna. Months later, on 24 March 1933, the young nationalist Ines Donati, a martyr of the post-war struggles, was memorialized. On 27 October a special ceremony was held in Florence for thirty-seven martyrs of the fascist revolution (pre–March on Rome) on the eve of the closing of the exhibition in Rome on 28 October. A leading journal, *Il Bargello*, dedicated thirty-six pages "written entirely" by *squadristi* to the affair. Following the ceremony the leading Florentine newspaper, *La Nazione*, published a biography titled *L'olocausto di Firenze* (*The Holocaust of Florence*). Ritual and civil liturgy dominated the scene.

Flags are important elements in collective representations and consensus building. They are mythic symbols, often viewed as an extension of the body, and are considered on religious terms. War enhances the flag's value. Blood consecrates it. The logic underpinning flag symbolism was cunningly manipulated by Nazi intelligentsia. Robert Shanafelt reminds us that the Nazi "Bloodflag" was a relic of the "Beer Hall Putsch."[60] This flag was exhibited and venerated during collective celebrations. It represented death and apparently held the blood of sixteen Nazi martyrs. Likwise, this book supports the idea that institutionalized violence served a ritual function through which participants renewed their faith. Furthermore, as Michael Ebner has demonstrated, the "appearance of one red flag could lead dozens of suspects to be arrested and held for days, weeks, or months." Ebner recounts the story of one communist named Natale Camarra who spent the periods from 1927–9, 1936–9, and 1939–42 in island *confine* (confinement) colonies. He also spent time in jail after he was released. In 1934 Camarra was considered "suspect" in exhibiting a red flag and spent two months in jail.[61]

An excellent example of the spectacularization of flag imagery can be seen in Sergei Eisenstein's *October* (1927), a film commissioned by the Soviets to commemorate and relive the revolution of 1917 *in* 1927. In one scene, a Bolshevik runs with his flag and crosses into the wealthy section of the city. A couple notices the intruder, and the worker is attacked. The Bolshevik attempts to defend the flag. Meanwhile, other Russians run to the scene seeking to destroy the flag by force, even with their teeth. They are convinced that by destroying the flag they can rid themselves of the Bolshevik threat. In *October* the Bolshevik banners and flags are clearly the more forceful and potent of the mass party documents for, as a symbol, the flag guides the masses. In times of crisis or even during an uprising, the (mostly illiterate) masses flock to the flag. There are those who defend the flag, those who seek to destroy the flag, and others who intend to capture and exhibit the flag as a spoil of war.

In January 1978 Carla Gobetti discovered approximately 190 flags in the National Archives in Rome that had been shown at the 1932 exhibition. These were flags captured by fascist squads in the years preceding the March on Rome. Exhibiting these flags symbolized dominance and would encourage critical dissent. Furthermore, it would bring about a sense of closure to the troubles (the "Red Years") before the March on Rome. In reliving the violence of those years, the regime was bringing the nation's narrative to a new level. Fascism had won the fight by force. These flags belonged to various groups: Catholic and "Red" associations, co-ops, anarchist groups, workers' unions, mutual-aid societies, and the socialist and communist parties. An exhibition of the flags was quickly organized at Palazzo Carignano. A book, *Un'altra Italia nelle bandiere dei lavoratori. Simboli e cultura dall'Unità d'Italia all'avvento del fascismo*, was published by the Centro Studi Gobetti in 1980 that commemorated the event. In his brief preface Sandro Pertini, president of the Italian Republic (1978–85), wrote that these flags document the "long red line," originating with Mazzini and leading to Garibaldi, libertarian groups, and the socialist party.[62]

All these flags were exhibited in Hall G of the *Mostra*. In the exhibition catalogue we read:

> [A]t the entrance we sense an impending menace: the tangle of subversive flags. But from these, the triumphant colours of the national flag emerge triumphantly.[63]

Those visiting the hall, we infer, were meant to violate the spaces covered by the amassed flags only to emerge from the chaos and see the national flag. From chaos: order. Hall H was dedicated to 1920. Again, flags were present:

> [B]etween one board and another, in cavities blocked by the pennants of the fascist squads, the red flags taken from enemies of the homeland are amassed.[64]

The flags are some of the signs left to us by the exhibition. Upon further inspection it should be noted that the subversive flags had not been scrupulously identified in 1932 for the exhibition. Instead, the flags were intentionally piled all together in one chaotic mess so as to symbolize disorder and danger. The flags documented those signs and signifiers of subversive symbolism that had once threatened the state. Finally, within the collective representation of the *Decennale*, these flags became primary source documents meant to be exhibited, critically assessed, and done away with. Each flag documented and exhibited an experience and told visitors about the groups that revolved around it. Flags also documented change, as was the case with the numerous flags belonging to those socialist groups who had moved on to become the Italian Communist Party and had updated their flag by adding a black thread to a red background.

Flags documented conflict, as was evident when anarchists and socialists united to protest against war on 1 May 1912: "Not a coin, not a soldier / neither servants nor masters." In this case the flag referred to the speech given by Andrea Costa, the socialist member of parliament, after the Dogali incident in 1887. The episode marked a decisive blow by antimilitarist anarchists *against* colonial ventures in Africa. On 3 February 1887 Costa remarked that the African adventure was not a noble project but rather a foolish one, and that the members of parliament would give neither a man nor a coin.

In another instance flags documented the women's movement against war, denounced existing societies ("Neither God nor Master"), and called for utopia. Flags also represented the workers' corporation and were often decorated with colourful mottos by Garibaldi, Marx, Mazzini, Blanqui, and Rosa Luxemburg.

Squad violence was likewise exhibited and celebrated. The campaign of violence inaugurated between 1920 and 1922 culminated in the March on Rome. Blackshirted *squadristi*, a police inspector wrote in 1921, "devoted" themselves to manhunts, chasing, confronting, and beating those who belonged to socialist organizations by breaking into homes; destroying furniture, documents, and objects; lighting fires and shooting into houses at night; and patrolling in armed groups so as to intimidate and traumatize people. More importantly, this campaign prevented the socialists from entering into public spaces and confined them to their homes.[65]

The fascist squads attacked the city of Fiesole hard in 1922. On 29 August the communist headquarters at Ponte alla Badia was pillaged, and a flag was taken as loot. On 22 October the squads hit the socialists in Fiesole as well. The defeated consigned their flags in a semi-official ceremony. The colours of this socialist flag – catalogued in the National Archives as MRF 14281 – are red and black. The symbol is that of a rising sun on a horizon overlooking the sea. It is the aura of a socialist sun inaugurating a new day or rather, when read from a fascist point of view, the aura of socialism extinguishing itself for good. Flags also incorporated subversive images belonging to the sacralization of politics: broken chains, the aura of a radiating sun, and the aura of a revolution.

The intent of the flags' visual iconography and texts is pedagogic. The manner is didactic. As Gobetti's team at the National Archives in Rome reminds us, the aura of the radiant sun goes back to the days of the French Revolution and to the Fraternal Democrats, a club born in London in 1845 under the influence of Marx and Engels. In the Emilia-Romagna region, the socialists even had their own newspaper called *Sole dell'avvenire* (*The Sun of the Future*). Filippo Turati referred to the metaphor in his workers' hymn, *Inno dei lavoratori*, written in 1886. The radiating sun is a unique symbol adopted by these organizations. In 1919, the Italian Socialist Party (PSI) adopted the Soviet hammer and sickle as a symbol. The hammer and sickle over a radiating sun could be seen on the front page of *Avanti!*, the PSI newspaper.

Other flags catalogued by Carla Gobetti's team include the following.

MRF 14541: the aura of the sun shines forth from the bottom right-hand corner of a flag representing the *Lega di Miglioramento* of Porotto, a small town in the province of Ferrara. The bibliographical note compiled by Gobetti's team tells us that this association was created on 1 September 1882. By 1885 it had twenty-three members. A curious note: in the organization's by-laws, article 49 states: "[D]iscussions on political and religious matters are excluded." Sign-up fees varied from two to four lira; monthly dues were one lira. After twelve months all members were covered in case of sickness for up to four months. In the years that followed, the association expanded and incorporated other workers, and by 1911 it had 970 members. In 1920 the members found themselves on the front lines of the agrarian strikes. In February 1921 headquarters were attacked by fascist squads led by Italo Balbo.

On 3 March 1921 a fascist league was created in Porotto. On 13 March Umberto Tognoli, a fascist who had shot and killed two members of the association, was killed with two shots. On 5 April the fascist squads, most likely led by Italo Balbo, assaulted the headquarters of this association (this time with the complicity of lawmen). The flag was taken down and later shown at the 1932 exhibition.

MRF 9675: At times a flag was more or less anonymous. In this flag farmers' tools radiate from the earth, forming a crudely designed rising sun. The flag once belonged to the Italian Communist Party branch at Cinquecerri, a town located in the province of Reggio Emilia. At a moment when universal fascism was being exhalted, this flag exhibited the universal brotherhood of workers of the Italian Communist Party. MRF 9675 was meant to be exhibited and critically assessed.

MRF 15791 documents the activities of a socialist association, the *Circolo Rosa Luxemburg* in Spineto, Aosta. Very little information on this association exists. References to Rosa Luxemburg and Karl Liebknecht by youth associations that existed during the years following the Russian revolution are frequent. These individuals would have especially been acknowledged by left-wing fascist elements active at the time of the *Decennale*.

X: Flags Nailed with Daggers Illuminated by Spotlights

The next hall documented the martyrs of the struggle. One wall was dedicated exclusively to the student avant-garde. The article *Quant'è bella giovinezza*, discussed in this chapter, was enlarged for all to experience. Its presence there is another defining element of the youth-centred narrative. The initial narrative was further developed as the visitor continued his or her journey. Halls L and M were consecrated to D'Annunzio's adventure at Fiume: after the call to audacity and mobilization, reckless abandonment to the cause followed. Hall N exhibited the most important events leading up to the March on Rome. Historially set in 1921, ample space was dedicated to Mussolini's published articles from that specific year. Also included were the bloodied remnants of clothing belonging to the martyrs for the fascist cause. A discarded garment, Bruno reminds us by referring to Kierkegaard, "enacts recollection; the material embodies a projection: the textile surface acts as a screen; the stories of histories are inscribed on it."[66] In this case the story being told was the aura of revolutionary blood leading up to the March on Rome.

A spectacularly large X, symbol of the *Decennale*, hovered above the visitor's head. The X created an ideal link, a cinematic "bridging shot," between the events leading up to the original passion, the March on Rome, and the aspirations of the *Decennale*, mobilization for a future march *from* Rome. Even here, flags were the protagonists. Exhibiting the looted flags re-enacted and projected the history of the years preceding the march. These flags were nailed with illuminated daggers to an enormous X. An aura of light surrounded the weapons and gave the illusion of a crucifixion. The X signified the murder of subversive ideology:

> This model is completely covered with socialist and anarchist flags set in semi-darkness. This display demonstrates that in the year 1922 the true effectiveness of the subversive parties ends. These flags are nailed to the framework with daggers illuminated by spotlights.[67]

Halls P, Q, R, and S were the creation of Mario Sironi and addressed the March on Rome. The march, the guide explains, was a pre-emptive show of force that actually saved more lives than it sacrificed. In this section, Hall Q was set apart and named the *Sala dell'Avvento* (Hall of Advent). The montage sequences presented here implied that the March on Rome had initiated the beginning of a new chapter in the nation's narrative. A quote by Benito Mussolini: *"Maestà, Vi porto l'Italia di Vittorio Veneto"* ("Your highness, I bring you the Italy of Vittorio Veneto") burst forth from the wall towards those visitors participating in this rite. Nearby, Hall S, the *Galleria dei fasci*, hosted ten fasces: the primitive totem and symbol of might, beauty, and redemption.[68] The design of each *fascio* was identical, and yet each was distinguishable from the next by a year. As a spectator walked through this station, he or she recollected the previous ten years of the fascist revolution. Time also created an allegoric narrative that in turn could be transported to the visual field.

Hall T, designed entirely by Leo Longanesi, was devoted to the nation's leader. The hagiographic setting emphasized the humble origins of the nation's high priest. In this sacred space the visitor observed not only personal documents but also the *Duce*'s relics tainted with blood from various assassination attempts. The phenomena belonged to another important aspect of the narrative exhibited: the cult of the *Duce*.

The final hall, Hall U, designed by Adalberto Libera and Antonio Valente, was meant to bestow the long awaited aura onto the new generation. Alessandra Capanna tells us (by referring to a study completed by Gigliola Fioravanti) that Valente, a personal friend of Dino Alfieri, had been the set designer for the futurist photographer Anton Giulio Bragaglia as well as a projectionist at the *Centro Sperimentale di*

Cinematografia. In Hall U the avant-garde aesthetic united cinematic technique and modernist design to shock the new generation into a new chapter of the fascist revolution's narrative. The Martyr's Shrine (*Il Sacrario dei martiri*) was chosen as the last station to be experienced by those visiting the *Mostra*. The circular hall's most striking feature was a black metallic cross, just as in Christ's passion, rising out of a blood-red pedestal in the centre of the room. On the cross, replacing the biblical INRI (*Iesus Nazarenus Rex Iudaeorum*) were the words: *Per la Patria immortale* (For the Immortal Homeland).The allegory would have been immediately clear: the fascist revolution's martyrs had redeemed Italy just as Christ redeemed Adam's disgraceful fall. The veneration of this black fascist cross, moreover, was also meant to remind visitors of the "Exaltation of the Cross" or "Feast of the Cross," during which Christians celebrate Christ's passion, crucifixion, and resurrection. Celebrating the fascist cross in this hall would have been akin to witnessing fascism's triumph over "past sins," "disorder," and "chaos." Hall U would have elicited an emotional response from the individual. It was embraced by the word *"Presente!"* ("Present!"), which was illuminated one thousand times along the wall and grouped together in six rows of "Trinities" – perhaps a reference to the Holy Trinity and to Garibaldi's *Mille*.

<pre>
    ...!Presente!Presente!Presente!...
        !Presente!Presente!Presente!...
            ...!Presente!Presente!Presente!
...!Presente!Presente!Presente!...
        !Presente!Presente!Presente!...
            ...!Presente!Presente!Presente!
    ...!Presente!Presente!Presente!...
            !Presente!Presente!Presente!...
    ...!Presente!Presente!Presente!
</pre>

Or perhaps the reference was meant to be the one thousand victims of the *Giovine Italia* movement celebrated one hundred years before by Mazzini:

This is what Young Italy knows. It understands the importance of its mission, and it will complete its mission. We swear this on the one thousand victims who succeed tirelessly from ten years to prove that even under persecution opinions are not extinguished but reinforced. We swear by the spirit (that teaches us what progress is) of the young fighters of Rimini. We swear by the blood of the martyrs of Modena. There is a religion in that blood. No force can suffocate the seed of liberty that has grown from the blood of the strongest. Today our religion is the religion of martyrdom. Tomorrow it will be the religion of victory.[69]

The martyrs' response ("Present!") to the scene created an ineffable and surreal (*irreale*) atmosphere to be grasped by the visitor as an absolute or higher notion of rationality. Along the walls the pennants of the fascist squadrons were illustrated. Each was inscribed with the name of a fallen martyr, and even here the succession appeared continuous and constant. The regime's official hymn, *Giovinezza!*, played softly in the background and brought the spectator back to the culture of the *Arditi*. A lone *Milite* (a volunteer soldier of the *Milizia Volontaria per la Sicurezza Nazionale* [Blackshirts] that operated in Italy from 1923 to 1943) stood guard.

The allegorical interpretation of these symbols was meant to be immediate: the sacrifice of the first generation (the martyrs of the revolution/war) was meant to incite the young generation of 1932. The *Sacrario dei martiri* was meant to confer upon this new generation, by means of a surreal ritual, an aura. It would grant *these* young combatants, the ones who had participated neither in the Great War nor in the March on Rome, "authenticity" as revolutionary conscious protagonists of the second decade. The acknowledgment of the names of those same martyrs who had died in the years preceding the March on Rome, which were now inscribed on the pennants, was intended to give the visitor a sense of closure. Born-again, redeemed, and, most importantly, incorporated into the nation during the *Decennale*'s collective representation, the young men of the 1932 generation were then asked to accept their new responsibilities and give themselves freely to the revolution. The *Mostra*, and in particular the final station, provided an ideal opportunity for the regime to take on a definite "autonomous religious dimension"[70] within the universalistic aspirations of the movement.

The religious overtones would have been particularly appreciated after Pope Pius XI's encyclical (*Non abbiamo bisogno*) of 29 June 1931 that condemned statolatry in fascist Italy. On 28 October of the same year, the regime obligated Italian university professors to swear an oath of loyalty. Only thirteen refused. Following this purification visitors could visit the first floor of the *Mostra* dedicated to universal fascism, which contained literature created by and for the regime, as well as an informational hall complete with charts and numbers associated with fascism's accomplishments. The technical (rather than purely political) aspects of the *Sacrario* (the fascist cross, *Presente!*, the lone solder, *Giovinezza!*) guaranteed the validity of the regime's most spectacular solution to the youth question on a macro-political level. It intended to shock the masses into identifying with and seeing themselves as a modernist spectacle in 1932. More importantly, it transferred the basic elements of discourse considered in the previous pages from the strictly literary page and political speech to an exhibition walk by selectively choosing elements from the past and incorporating these elements into the exhibition. The rhetoric of youth had now confronted itself with the modernist experiment, thanks to the coming together of traditional literary rhetoric and elaborate representational rites. At the same time the *Sacrario* was meant to be the final ritual that formally ended the tradition of the March on Rome. The result was a pseudo-mythic experience that many accepted as truth.

Others, rationally prone, did not sanction this product of politically realist doctrine. In 1932, intellectuals such as Camillo Pellizzi and Massimo Bontempelli were keen to point out that this semiotic explosion, distanced from actual reality, was counterproductive.[71] The hall acted as a double-edged sword: by exhibiting the aura of the revolution, the regime was making itself more vulnerable to critical assessment and dissent by the new generation. The shock effect, meant to instantiate a new narrative (the March *from* Rome), was effectively produced by visuals of the avant-garde type – in this case the seemingly endless repetition of the word *Presente!*, now transformed into a mantra of sorts for the new generations to repeat. The playing of *Giovinezza!* in the background as a "voice-over" of sorts held a similar function. The result was an awakening, an abrupt shocking out of a liminal state for the new generation of fascists. They were now redeemed and entrusted with the universalistic aspirations of the second *Decennale*.

Sound and visual imagery are important spaces of critical exploration. If we continue incorporating *Public Intimacy* in our reading, the *Sacrario* was an intimate encounter experienced in the public sphere. The *Mostra* was the first of its kind and could not be compared to any other political exhibition. As such it intended to reveal the truth and produce meaning, and assumed that those visiting would accept this truth as unquestionable. The regime's solution to the youth or generational issue was ingenious – the creation of an intimate spiritually based experience capable of shocking the audience into a different psychic state while, at the same time, archiving or mapping out a narrative into the memory of those same participants. Whereas the legions of youth who fought with Mazzini, Garibaldi, in the trenches of the Great War, with D'Annunzio, and even with the fascists of the first hour marching on Rome were conferred an aura of sanctity and considered themselves, thanks to the intimacy of collective violence and other rituals of fellowship, as part of a clan, these young men of 1932 were participants in a modernist experiment that intended to mechanically replicate and exhibit the aura of the revolution, inspire cohesion, and continue the original narrative. Just as cinema allows viewers to reinvent themselves and experience an intimate encounter in a public sphere, so too did the museum walk, especially the *Sacrario*. The experience was meant to serve as a catalyst for a new narrative, the March from Rome. The architectural strategy set into motion by the creators of the exhibition made use of design as an art of space and time. The protagonists of this renewed narrative were the bodies of young fascists. The exhibition reaffirmed the new generations' duty on a macro-political level and manipulated reality so as to impose a new chronology of events onto a now-radicalized fascist revolution.

2
Textbooks for *Il balilla Vittorio*

The economic crisis of 1929 increased school enrollments and facilitated the regime's consensus-making schemes, at least on paper.[1] That same year all schoolteachers were forced to swear their allegiance to fascism. An oath was also imposed on secondary school teachers. On the eve of the *Decennale*, university professors were asked to oblige as well. In 1931 the state issued its first batch of *libri-unici* for elementary school students, and for the first time all students were to read from the same textbooks.[2] The stage was set for 1932. At the time of the *Decennale* the legislative period was officially over. In short, no other touch-ups were needed.

IL CAPO DEL GOVERNO (THE HEAD OF STATE)
JULY 27 1933-XI

Dear Ercole,
[With] these last provisions – the transferal of elementary schools
to the State, single textbooks for classes, the creation of new institutes, program touch-ups ... I maintain that Italian schools have now reached in all of their grades an asset that is, if not definitive, to be considered stable for a long time. The program of reform, reorganization, and fine tuning has been completed. Now there's nothing new to invent ... Now we have to administer the schools ... I don't want to hear about any more "touch-ups" and new provisions, ecc. Now we need a period of stability and calm. The legislative period in the field of education has finished. Now we begin the executive and administrative period.
   I believe that your Excellency will agree with my conclusions.
                                                          Mussolini[3]

Children were the product of an experiment that aspired to unite classroom instruction with the militarized nation at large, ten years after Giovanni Gentile's reform.[4] As Monica Galfré has demonstrated, the regime did not have the means to satisfy the demand for these textbooks.[5] The responsibility was given instead to publishers. These publishers were allowed considerable freedom in their editorial decisions. In short, the *libro-unico* genre was not exactly a success for the regime.

This chapter does not investigate the circumstances surrounding Gentile's 1923 reform or even the history of pedagogy in Italy. Rather, I examine the textbooks with the following questions in mind: What would an elementary school child (first to fifth grade) read in 1932? What can these short stories tell us about the *Decennale*? Were these textbooks written with the *Decennale* in mind, perhaps even on a subconscious level? What was really fascist about a fascist education?

What emerges from these pages is a representational rite to be imitated. In a sense the *Decennale* allowed the regime to package and sell a performance. The scenes examined in these textbooks are realistic. The short stories included encourage children to elaborate their own view of life but always within the confines of the state. The older figures represented, moreover, are not the protagonists of sentimental scenarios. They act as guides with a clearly defined political agenda. The language is concrete and realistic. Optimism prevails.

EIA!

The first textbook examined in this chapter is titled *Sillabario e piccole letture* (The ABC's and Brief Readings). The first lessons present isolated words and simple phrases. They introduce the student to the basic structures of the Italian language and lead to more complex thoughts and brief dialogues. The first lesson focuses on vowel pronunciation, and the first word is created by joining three vowels: "e," "i," and "a." *EIA!*, a sort of ululation of Greco-Roman descent, was a battle cry first suggested by D'Annunzio during war operations in 1917.[6] *EIA!* was intended to substitute for the otherwise barbaric "Hip, hip, hurray." This exercise is accompanied by an illustration of a healthy child in uniform writing *EIA!* on the blackboard: an example to follow. Learning the alphabet, a seemingly rational operation under normal circumstances, was now transformed into a rhetorical performance that sought inspiration from selective moments in the past and looked to the future: empire. As Walter Benjamin would have it, the social function of the performance would not be founded on ritual but, rather, on politics. The technique brought the masses of schoolchildren together with the *hic et nunc* of the Great War. *EIA!* burst into the classroom like a scene from a historical film that could be easily transported from classroom to classroom. The child acquired "star power" by performing for the state, and the performance was an aesthetically pleasurable event whose ultimate end would be war. A seemingly non-rational act, pronouncing this battle cry in unison, initiated each child into the militarized state. The *Decennale* necessitated a new language capable of reliving the aura of the Great War. This language also presented a new reality structured along hierarchical lines. Learning the ABC's provided the first opportunity for the child to embrace the collective and militarized state. This daily performance sustained the cultural politics of the *Decennale*.

The next lesson is a bit more complex. The words "I" ("*io*") and "we" ("*noi*") are introduced: the individual and the collective. The subject pronoun *io* is accompanied by a drawing of a child. The subject pronoun *noi* introduces a girl holding her older brother's hand. They both play with a model train (a reference to the regime's renewed railway system and fascist modernity). The number "one" ("*uno*") is presented, and a child is introduced. Her name is Nannina. She is healthy and, furthermore, is never bored and never boring. Nannina is a product of her age. She is a well-nourished, efficient, and active daughter of a redeemed nation. The students complete their lesson by finishing the phrase "I am an ... (Italian)": ("*Io sono una ... / Io sono un ...*").

The exercise creates a visual identification with the paramilitary uniform through didactic imagery: a constant in these textbooks. We infer that the actual learning process is meant to be instinctual. The final page of the exercise unites each individual child with the collective sphere. It features a young boy in uniform saluting the Italian flag. The drawing (in colour) is accompanied by the phrase, "*Una ... e un ... A noi!*" ("Girls... and boys ... for the revolution!"). The next time we encounter the pair, they are saluting each other. All the necessary elements are present: national identity (*italiana / italiano*), individuality (*Io*), the collective state (*l'Italia nostra*), duty (*Per l'Italia nostra*), and the paramilitary structure within which the abecedarian espouses instinctual behaviour and activism. On the next page, a squadron of *Alpini*, the "Italian sentinels," is depicted. The children, now in uniform, are told to salute them, their *camerati*.

A cult image for the masses is presented: the *Duce*. In these pages he personifies the ideals of a redeemed nation. The text is hagiographic and reminiscent of saint veneration. After saluting each other and a squadron of *Alpini*, the children salute their hero: Mussolini, a father figure who loves his children. Other important elements are present: a young student saluting a portrait of the *Duce* and a group of students saluting the flag. The ritual that unites them is the salute to the *Duce* and to the flag. These two pages are neatly juxtaposed on the same visual plane. Both symbolize Italy and merit acknowledgment as higher or spiritualized entities from the individual and from the collective. The charismatic *Duce*, man and leader, his humble rural origins, his heroic past, his presence are all elements of a divine and universal will. The *Duce* is omnipresent in both the private and public sphere. He influences the very idea of self that the children possess. He normalizes their existence as young fascists and eliminates distinctions between those activities conducted in the public and private sphere. In short, the *Duce* functions as a surrogate father whom the masses are content to appease.

These pages underscore the responsibilities facing the new generation of Italians and also focus on themes such as brotherhood and unity. In a short story titled *"La forza del numero"* ("Strength in Numbers"), the author draws from Rousseauian ideals and presents the story of a farmer and his children. In the tale, a farmer instructs his children on the benefits of unity by referring to a bundle of sticks that, bound together in a *fascio*, does not break. The *fascio*, he tells his children, represents the will of the Italian people. It is a will that is strong, invincible, justifies violence for a greater cause, and eliminates all forms of individualistic dissent.

Particular attention is given to the soldier: a symbol of might that appeals to the imagination and psyche of adolescents. The paramilitary uniform of the *Balilla* is much more than an obsession for these young boys. The uniform represents the aspirations and destiny of an entire generation. The cover page of *Il libro della II classe* (Second Grade Book) neatly projects these ambitions. It is, of course, a privilege that must be earned.

Unity also implies absolute obedience. In another one-page scenario, we come upon an older gentleman – *un sapiente* (a wise man) – hovering over a young child. The child asks his elder: What should the first virtue of a child be? The second? The third? "Obedience" is the *only* response in the state's catechism. In another page taken from the *Sillabario*, a group of children (the new generation of fascists) are playing. An elderly man sits on a bench and enjoys the spring sun. A group of soldiers marches past, and the old man takes the time to recall his own past.

Meanwhile, the children familiarize themselves with the uniforms and try to outdo each other as to which military group is more appealing: the *bersaglieri, soldato di marina, alpino, aviatore*. The children accompany the soldiers with their eyes, and, the text reads, with their hopes. The page concludes with a moral. Students are encouraged to express their preferences (in preparation for a future march) as long as they accept that they are, above all, Italian soldiers.

In an episode from *Il libro della II classe*[7] Bruno is allowed to wear the *balilla* uniform on 24 May, the day in which Italy entered the Great War alongside Great Britain, France, and Russia. Bruno's dad recounts Italy's participation in the war and emphasizes the victory secured by the Italian soldiers at the final battle on the Italian front, the battle of Vittorio Veneto (1918). In typical childlike fashion, Bruno asks his dad if he made it to the front line and if he had been the most valiant soldier. The veteran responds that he fought alongside the others and that the war effort was a collective effort. Now, years later, both father and son participate in a celebration and relive the aura of those days. Evoking the past legitimizes the present and sets the stage for the future.

In the same textbook, another *balilla* named Renzo meets his uncle Marco, "a soldier of the air," and aspires to be just like him. The image would have been especially effective at the time of the *Decennale*. In 1930 Italo Balbo had crossed the Atlantic and arrived in Rio de Janiero. It was not a solitary feat but rather a collective one, accomplished by twelve Savoia-Marchetti S.55 flying boats. Balbo outdid himself during the *Decennale* celebrations. During the summer of 1933, he led a group of twenty-four flying boats (twice as large as the Brazilian expedition) straight to Lake Michigan in Chicago, Illinois. The city of Chicago later received a Roman column from the city of Ostia (still visible near Soldier Field along the Lakefront Trail) and renamed the street after Italo Balbo. The name still stands today. New York City, not to be outdone, greeted Balbo and his squadron with a ticker tape parade and an invitation to lunch from President Roosevelt. Balbo's spectacular feat, sponsored by the (corporative) fascist state, certainly distinguished itself from (the capitalist) Charles Lindbergh's solitary (or perhaps even egocentric) crossing of the Atlantic.

On Towards the People

On 25 October 1931 Benito Mussolini presented one of the *Decennale*'s main objectives: *andare verso il popolo* (go towards the people). By doing so he deliberately associated "the people" with "the nation": a form of populism already espoused by the *Narodnicestvo* (Narodniks), a Russian political and cultural movement of the previous century that considered the people as the best representative of those values exemplifying justice and the nation.[8] Peasants, factory workers and the proletariat, artisans, and government employees: all were able to fit into the schemes of the regime's ideological apparatus. These themes were also present in the textbooks considered in this chapter. The following examples underscore the potential, ambition, aspirations, and intentions of those ordinary people. Read during the *Decennale*, these short stories were certain to coincide with both the populist message and the universalistic aspirations of the regime now exhibited on a much larger scale.

The state-issued textbooks considered here reflected the *Duce*'s populist directives for this new age. These directives were meant to satisfy the intellectual requirements of a refined middle class as well as those of the lower classes: a dynamic and upwardly mobile group not constrained to their condition as the communists would have them believe. In *Il libro della IV classe elementare* (Fourth Grade Book), a short story titled *"Pionieri"* ("Pioneers") focuses on four Italians keeping company on a ship bound for South America. The main theme is evident: the Italian nation is no longer exporting manpower but ideas and know-how. These pioneers are asserting their own unique form of Italian hegemony through colonization.[9]

Four examples are introduced. The first pioneer is a venture capitalist who has expanded his textile business by opening it up to the South American market. His monologue informs the reader about (false) urban legends of dishonest Americans, unsafe trade routes, and limited capital gains. He has modernized his machinery and contributed to Italy's future.[10] The second pioneer is a young lawyer, a former anarchist on the road to redemption. He symbolizes the nation's son who once strayed into the vice of subversive ideas. The young lawyer, now redeemed thanks to a missionary (the hand of God that legitimizes his choice to move from anarchism towards fascism), decides to become a colonist. He is, much like those pardoned by the *Duce* during the *Decennale*'s collective pardon, incorporated into the fellowship of the state:

"I have a Law degree," continued the second traveler, "but I've never practiced. At university I damaged myself a bit with subversive ideas; I imagined that poverty was caused by governments and by rich people, and that one could solve the problem of poverty not by hard work and discipline but with an unlimited amount of freedom. I became an anarchist … The love for my country has taken me back. I asked a concession in Libya; I brought Italian colonialists there. That colony will be a region not less rich than others in great Italy."[11]

The third pioneer is a teacher sent by the Dante Alighieri Society to open up a new school for the sons and daughters of Italian immigrants. Here the text focuses on the redeeming qualities of emigration.[12] The fourth pioneer is an aviator who pronounces standard fascist rhetoric. The entire episode ends on a positive note:

It would be very fortunate if every Italian would consider himself as a missionary. Be the first to arrive in every place, be always the first. This is, after all, my uniform.

"I think," said the old man, "that Italy in my time was very different. The long period of slavery had lowered its status in the eyes of the world and in its eyes. There wasn't any faith in anything, and men like me were laughed at. Now Italy has arisen and walks; and to the men who have faith you tip your hat at them. I would like to still have fifty years of life to see Italy, with my eyes, the great and potent Italy of tomorrow."[13]

These themes are traceable in another textbook titled *Il balilla Vittorio* (Vittorio, the Boy Soldier). In the opening pages we are introduced to Vittorio's classmates. The last child introduced, named Murrisi, is the son of a postal worker originally from the province of Caltanissetta. When the school teacher asks Murrisi how many people live in his hometown, the child responds in Sicilian dialect, *"Chi 'u sapi?"* ("Who knows?"). Murrisi feels ridiculed and looks down, grim. The setting provides an opportunity for the teacher to present a brief history lesson on the earliest example of Italian poetry, the *Scuola Siciliana*. She encourages Murrisi (the "people's son") to continue working, for he too is potentially capable, through hard work, of moving up in society, just as the *Duce* had. Murrisi is asked to speak in Italian. In this instance he is able to retain his own individuality (dialect, memory of hometown) and yet is asked to participate in the collective state (official language, Rome).

Murrisi is not isolated because of his background. He performs better than Gherardo, the son of an engineer. One day Gherardo invites Murrisi to spend an afternoon with his parents. Meanwhile, Vittorio convinces himself that Gherardo's excellence in the classroom is due to his economic status. Vittorio stops to say hello to Lucchesi, another classmate. They are not alone in their efforts. Rather, just like the soldiers fighting in the trenches of the Great War, they participate in a collective effort:

> One comes to school to learn how to act later on in life and to learn even from the things that are needed unless you want to be a labourer in life, someone who works with his hands following the orders of others. But tell your brother this – actually tell yourself this if you can – think about this: At this very moment, in all of Italy, four million students are, in elementary schools just like yours, learning.[14]

In these textbooks the dead, mutilated, and wounded of the Great War are now re-elaborated into four million schoolchildren learning and participating in a collective liturgy at school:

> Today, fascist Italy, the Italy of Mussolini, is the Italy of order, of discipline, of a will worthy of a common effort. The labour that unites us is the greatness of the homeland, the prosperity of our families, of our land, and of our cities, which needs a unifying rule observed by all, which is, of course, the fascist law. And so, just as the universe has its geometric laws, society has its laws, language has its syntax.[15]

In *Il libro della IV classe*[16] we are introduced to Lucio, the son of a lowly bricklayer working in the *officina* (factory) of Santino Avondo. Lucio is an exemplary worker and virtuous citizen, and just like Alessandro Manzoni's Renzo, avoids the tavern. Santino on the other hand is getting older, has not created a family, and is not doing too well. He recognizes Lucio's potential and makes him an offer. We infer from the text that Lucio takes over the *officina* in 1922. It is a deliberate coincidence, marking the beginning of a new age for the working class. Celebrating the anniversary of the 1922 march was meant to reaffirm these aspirations.

An episode taken from the pages of *Il balilla Vittorio* is similar. Here we are introduced to the Balestrieri brothers, Francesco and Giacomo.[17] Both have inherited substantial property from their parents but are spendthrifts and forced to work. Giacomo focuses on his studies and becomes a bureaucrat at the local town hall. Francesco is less fortunate in his decisions and seeks his fortune in Argentina. The brothers are united in 1915 when Italy joins the war effort. After the war Francesco is thinking about leaving Italy again, but the initial stages of the March on Rome make him change his mind. And so, the brothers put on their black shirts (they were members of the *Arditi* assault squad), organize the first *fasci* in their hometown, and March on Rome. The moral is obvious: peasants once forced to leave Italy are now able to march towards a better life.

These textbooks also focus on historically determinant dates: 28 October (March on Rome), 4 November (Armistice Day, WWI), 11 November (the king's birthday), 21 April (founding date of Rome), and 24 May (Declaration of War day). The holidays presented an opportunity for children to relive the past in the present, display their affection for the uniform, and project an image of order and obedience. In the *Sillabario* the student's learning experience runs parallel to the main protagonist's obsession to wear a *balilla* uniform. Thanks to the fascist revolution, Rome had been redeemed as *caput mundi* (capital of the world), and on 21 April all children were asked to participate in these festivities. More importantly, 21 April celebrated the fascist Labour Day (*Festa del Lavoro*). The fascist decision to nationalize Labour Day by associating it with the founding of Rome distanced the Italian workers' movement from the Socialist International. It was a deliberate and effective move that sowed the seeds for the corporativist revolution. Bruno understands the importance of the holiday after he sees his dad return home dressed in his black shirt and wearing his war ribbons. Another festivity, the anniversary of Italy's entrance in the war effort (1915) on 24 May, allows Bruno to participate alongside his father in a parade. Bruno wears the uniform and promises his schoolteacher that he will surpass her expectations and finish the year at the top of his class. The intentions are clear: the simple desire to wear the uniform facilitates entry into a redeemed society. Parades were also effective in instilling a sense of aura in these children. Bruno, on his part, assumed that these parades were meant for him, for he and the fascist state had now become one:

> And how proud he was when his black shirt–wearing dad would bring him around in the streets covered with flags and crowded with people! It seemed to him that the party was for him, this young and happy *balilla* who raised his hand in a Roman salute at every pace.[18]

Anno X was also the fiftieth anniversary of Garibaldi's death. According to Fogu, the Garibaldian celebrations ended by providing the Italian masses with a "prototypical representation of the relationship between fascism and all other events in the Italian past."[19] Nowhere was this more evident than in the state's renewed treatment of the *Risorgimento*. The defining moment occurred with the taking of Rome on 20 September 1870, when the *bersaglieri* entered the papal city through a breech in the Aurelian walls just a few metres from *Porta Pia*. Resistance was largely symbolic, and casualties were low. The episode led to a series of consequences. The papacy lost control over much of Rome, and Catholics refused to participate in future elections. Right-wing nationalists rebelled, and in 1910 the Italian Nationalist Association was formed. These people looked to Mazzini and authoritarianism for inspiration. Teachers were noticeably present in the association, and among them we find Giovanni Gentile and Roberto Forges Davanzati, author of *Il balilla Vittorio*.[20] Several pages of *Il libro della terza classe elementare* (Third Grade Book) are dedicated to the history of this period and its protagonists. The heroes of the *Risorgimento* are "good Italians" and the virtuous disciples of the state. The ideals of patriotism and *cameratismo* (camaraderie) unite the various classes: peasants, workers, and gentleman. All participate in the state's theatrics. It is also important to note that the oath of the *Giovine Italia* can be found in *Il libro della terza classe elementare*. Reciting the oath in 1932 united the three marches: the *Risorgimento*, the march of 1922 *on* Rome, and the march of 1932 *from* Rome. The pages of these textbooks also clarified the relationship between the taking of *Porta Pia* (1870) and the March on Rome (1922). Emphasis is also given to symbols – the red shirts of the *Risorgimento* and the black shirts of 1922.

In an episode taken from *Il libro della IV classe*, a grandfather speaks to his nephew about his past experience as a *Garibaldino*. In *Il libro della terza classe elementare*, a gentleman named Goffredo meets a group of students visiting Rome. The setting is *Porta Pia*. Goffredo remembers the battle for *Porta Pia* in 1870. He spends a considerable amount of time recounting the sacrifice of a young man named Pino and the remorse felt by his company's sergeant for Pino's death. Recalling the event inspires Goffredo to explain that something similar happened in 1922. The connection is obvious: the blackshirts of 1922 had completed a process begun in the 1870s. More importantly, Goffredo's tale is a perfect opportunity for the children to learn about the threat of communism:

> "Communists," Mr Goffredo explained sweetly, "are people who do not respect order. Order is good not only for the individual but also for human society. And above all they do not understand those rights conquered by sacrifice."[21]

Goffredo then tells the children another story. It is the tale of a land-owner named Guccio and his neighbours, communist farmers:

> Near Guccio's castle was the house of very evil communist peasants. They had little desire to work, saying that the bosses took advantage of them. But instead, and remember this, my children, the true gentleman works even harder than others and doesn't show off.[22]

A group of fascists, a sad bunch injured from fighting and without any firewood, is in hiding. Guccio is instinctively drawn to them and selflessly offers to fetch some dry wood from the communist peasant's barn. Guccio is discovered and tied up for a beating, even after present-ing himself as a "good Italian." Meanwhile, the fascist squad arrives and is worried about Guccio's fate. A violent fight broods in the air, but it is Guccio who pardons his captors. Eventually the *contadini* (peas-ants) come to their senses for, the text reads, their daily contact with nature makes them unable to commit violence. Guccio's actions (the pardon of the *Decennale*) convert the communist peasants into believ-ers! The fascist squad is comforted with food and hospitality. A name, a cross, the *fascio*: the pedagogy of examples presented in these *libri-unici* encouraged the new generation of 1932 in their march *from* Rome. The education process clarified a distinct political agenda in tune with the exhibition value attributed to the new generation.

The cultural politics of the regime did not limit itself to these school-books. Among the many documents preserved at the National Archives in Rome are materials sent to Dino Alfieri and exhibited at the exhibi-tion by an overzealous Beniamino Carrozza.[23] In an accompanying let-ter, Carrozza describes the documents. One document is a deliberation by a group of communists. The meeting determines their passage from communism to nationalism. A list of names is included. According to Carrozza's account, the communists not only become nationalists but also publicly repent for their evil and criminal acts of the past and, fur-thermore, create a nationalistic section of their own: exhibition, critical assessment, and dissent.

Il Libro della V classe elementare: *Il balilla Vittorio*

Il balilla Vittorio was much more than a textbook. It was a textbook writ-ten for a child who had already accepted fascist reality as undisput-ed. Students reading *Il balilla Vittorio*, a diary that accompanies the schooling of a typical fifth-grader named Vittorio,[24] no longer needed to be convinced of the state's accomplishments.[25] In these pages, author Roberto Forges Davanzati expands on themes such as the *Risorgimento*–fascism link, the cult of the *Duce*, and universal fascism. These aspirations are especially reinforced in one particular section, *"L'Italia sul mare"* ("Italy on the Seas"). Here students acquaint themselves with Italy's latest war ships: the *Ugolino Vivaldi* (named for an explorer of the Middle Ages) and the *Giovanni da Verazzano* (named for a pioneer who reached the shores of New York). Students are urged to study their past and relive it within a mythic framework. A final reference to Dante's Ulysses (*Inferno* XXVI) urges them to defy fate beyond recognized borders. Read during the *Decennale*, this book set the stage for imperial expansion.[26] In this episode Vivaldi and Verazzano's exploits are legitimized by the renewed meaning that they acquire in the fascist era, one in which Dante's verses were now associated with universal fascist hegemony:

> I don't need to explain these words to you. They are clear, even for you, because whatever a Leader needs to persuade his followers on land, sea, or sky to confront a danger, be it nearby or far away, he cannot say anything to himself but this:

> You were not made to live as brutes
> but to follow virtue and knowledge.

> *Fatti non foste a viver come bruti,*
> *Ma per seguir virtute e conoscenza.*[27]

Il balilla Vittorio is divided into twelve chapters. If we consider the textbook as an entire year in the life of Vittorio, then chapter ten represents October (the month of the revolution) and is particularly relevant when considered in relation to 1932. The first chapter, *"Una vita nuova"* ("A New life"), centres on Vittorio's new life after his dad is promoted to a new job in Rome. *Capitolo X* opens by advertising the regime's most important success: the Pontina land-reclamation project. What follows is a brief piece on malaria, a centuries-old menace now eliminated thanks to the reclamation projects, which have, furthermore, through the mixing of Italians from different regions, also bettered the Italian race. The reader infers that these reclamation projects have set the stage for a prosperous future.

The protagonists of *Il balilla Vittorio* do not visit Rome on a school trip. They march on Rome and transform the city into a stage. In a final episode Vittorio reflects on all of this. It inebriates his mind, and just before he falls asleep, an image grants sanctity to the event: the apotheosis of the *Duce*. When Vittorio awakens he understands that a new day has begun. During the night a child has been born in the city of Rome. Vittorio (perhaps alluding to the battle of Vittorio Veneto) now must make room for his brother Romano (as in Rome 1932, universal fascism, *Romanità, gens italica*). The *Duce*, their father (Vittorio and Romano were the names of the *Duce*'s sons), mediates through a dream as a modernized Caesar. As a side note, a similar image is likewise present in the concluding scene of *Camicia nera*, the film of the *Decennale*.

As a conclusion, we can now ask ourselves the following question: what was really "fascist" about these textbooks? Fascist textbooks celebrated the beginning of a new age by educating new men capable of striving towards an empire. Under the watchful eye of the *Capo* (and according to the precepts of the cult of the *Duce*), children would naturally identify their will with the collective and impose themselves on reality, at least in theory. Young women were educated differently. The secretary of the National Fascist Party (PNF), Augusto Turati, codified a series of precepts that were designed to educate the future mother of the new generation. She was (1) to be a dutiful daughter, sister, student, and friend, and fulfil such a duty happily, (2) to serve the homeland as if she were the greatest and best mother of all good Italians, (3) to love the *Duce*, he who has made the country stronger and greater, (4) to happily obey her superiors, (5) to have the courage to go against those who give bad advice and belittle honesty, (6) to educate her own body to conquer physical battles and her soul not to fear pain, and (7) to flee from vanity, but also to love beautiful things.[28]

The decade that preceded the *Decennale* has been recognized as the decade of progressive education. This approach was child-centred, presented a curriculum based on student interests, and aspired to identify and solve social problems. The Depression of 1929 seriously affected this approach towards education, and a "worldwide reaction against what was increasingly seen as indulgent permissiveness in an era racked by poverty, disease, inequality and incipient world war"[29] modified the goals of and subsequently weakened the progressive movement.

In Russia the Soviet educational system confronted itself with the dilemma between "individualism" and "collectivism." Lenin died in

1924, and Stalin overcame Trotsky in 1928. This last event marked the beginning of a new era in which curricula became set and standard textbooks were used. Schools now needed to confront themselves with the goals set by the first five-year plan (1928–32), and on 25 August 1932 the Central Committee of the Communist Party of the Soviet Union decided to formalize the "lesson" system (*urok*) and centralize education by focusing on discipline and authority, along with collaboration and critique.[30] A brief sample of pages taken from Soviet textbooks can be useful in illustrating certain similarities and differences between the Soviet and the Italian educational systems.[31] The aura associated with the revolution politicized artistic expression and lent itself to the creation of an easily assimilated narrative.

Socialist textbooks celebrated the spectacular achievements of the first five-year plan (1928–32). Thousands of socialist workers had contributed to the effort, and *War with the Dnieper River* (*Voina s Dneprom*) became the best-known children's book on the subject. Stalin battled against a river and built a dam; Mussolini attacked swamplands and reclaimed land for Littoria. Both were celebrated.

Attention was also given to youth organizations. Soviet books included didactic imagery celebrating pioneers learning about the construction of the socialist state and acquiring technical skills as students in the laboratories of a polytechnic school system. These student leaders are capable orators who encourage other workers to contribute to the progress of the Soviet state. Women (and here the Soviet texts differ considerably from the fascist ones) also play a determinant role in the post-revolutionary state.

Soviet and fascist textbooks aspired to create a "book for life." Coming to school was an exercise in micro-politics and an everyday occurrence suggestive of normality. Leaving the classroom and joining the ranks of society allowed the student to make the transition onto the macro-political stage. Education was intimately connected to propaganda as the individual completed him- or herself in society. The socialist school, true to the workers' revolution, introduced manual labour in these texts and guided the child towards the creation of a socialist state. Women were expected and encouraged to do their part. The Soviets, building on the aura of the revolution, produced workers (at least for now). The fascists produced soldiers. The cult of the *Duce* preceded Stalin's cult of personality by a few years.

In abridged form, the fascist classroom was where theatre, text, performance, and language set the stage for future mobilization. What emerges from these pages is a ritual-based pedagogical dimension, patterned and formulaic, meant to organize the legions of schoolchildren within the classroom setting. A relevant aspect of the fascist regime's strategy of indoctrinating and preparing the very young for the state's theatrics at a time when all eyes would be on Italy and its new generation of fascists is that in 1932 the *Foglio d'Ordini* (a newsletter first published in 1926 that listed party events) began to publish a yearly calendar of official party activities.[32] Indicative of this agenda is the walk orchestrated by Achille Starace and taken by Mussolini on 28 October 1932 from the Colosseum to Piazza Venezia on the newly constructed *Via dell'Impero* (now *Via dei Fori Imperiali*). The 1932 walk inaugurated a new march (*from* Rome and tending towards an empire): one that had been created by destroying an entire working class neighbourhood (an ideal setting for subversives) in time for the tenth anniversary.[33]

The *Decennale* allowed this shift from theory to practice to occur.

3
"Writing" 1932

Dialogue on Culture: 1932

In the period following the Great War, the Italian Socialist Party fractured. In 1921 Antonio Gramsci created the Italian Communist Party (PCI) at the Livorno Congress. Mussolini entered parliament in 1921. The March on Rome happened a year later. Writers and intellectuals adhered to fascism. A few such as Gobetti, Gramsci, and Matteotti were particularly vocal in their opposition. *Solaria* retreated to its own Aventine Hill.

Dialogue on the cultural politics of the time occurred in the pages of literary journals and magazines. Many of these journals have been digitized and can be found online today. For example, Antonio Gramsci wrote in the pages of *Ordine Nuovo*, and Piero Gobetti published *Rivoluzione Liberale*. *Il Baretti* was founded by Gobetti as well. *La Ronda* published *prosa d'arte* (artistic prose). The journal *900* was tied to the *Stracittà* movement and focused on creating a dialogue with Europe. In *900* we find nineteen articles dedicated to French literature, eleven articles dedicated to Russian literature, and seven to Spanish literature. Fourteen articles are dedicated to English and American culture; *900* published Virginia Woolfe, James Joyce, and D.H. Lawrence. *Il Selvaggio* belonged instead to the *Strapaese* movement and was published until 1943. *Il Selvaggio* was anti-intellectual, exalted the primitive lifestyle, and engaged in polemics against *Stracittà* and other forms of cosmopolitan elitism. *Il Selvaggio* famously sent its readers out to the marketplace and declared in the first issue published in 1928: "*Strapaese* has for years proclaimed the need to defend the rural character of Italian life from the importation of foreign civilizations ... This is a political principle and not some sort of literary recipe. Go to any marketplace in our towns: there you'll see people who are robust, tanned and proud, active and full of ingenuity. This is the basis of an Empire." *Stracittà* on the other hand was interested in the futurists and all that was new: jazz and cinema. The journal *900* published (in Italian) James Joyce but also André Malraux and Rainer Maria Rilke.[1]

Prose didn't fare too well during this period. Notable works appeared, such as Alberto Moravia's *Gli indifferenti* in 1929, Ignazio Silone's *Fontamara* in 1930, and Carlo Bernari's *Tre Operai* in 1934. As a side note Silone turned out to be an informer for the fascist police – but that's another story. It is not the intent of this book to focus on poetry, especially the *Ermetismo* (Hermeticism) movement (Giuseppe Ungaretti, Eugenio Montale).

The year 1922 was a year that celebrated English modernism. Joyce published *Ulysses* and Eliot published *The Waste Land*. Giovanni Papini and Filippo Marinetti had read Walt Whitman, but most readers of American literature were scholars of English literature. We can recall Carlo Linati, Emilio Cecchi, and Mario Praz. After 1930 a new generation of writers, most notably Elio Vittorini and Cesare Pavese, went on to create a *mito dell'America* (American myth) that was not only a literary myth but also a myth glorifying America as a land of freedom and creative energy. Publishing houses jumped on the opportunity. In Milan Valentino Bompiani published James Cain and John Steinbeck. An anthology of American literature was compiled by Vittorini by 1942. Giulio Einaudi established the publishing house Einaudi in 1933 and introduced Italians to Gertrude Stein and Ernest Hemingway. Arnoldo Mondadori presented Sinclair Lewis, John Dos Passos, William Faulkner, and William Saroyan.[2] For fascist Italy, however, the greatest literary achievement of the period was the publication of the Italian encyclopedia, the *Enciclopedia Italiana*.

Discourse at the time of the *Decennale* encouraged culture capable of writing this new age and re-contextualizing the aura of 1922 in 1932. Each re-enactment of the March on Rome continued this strategy. Dino Alfieri, organizer of the 1932 exhibition, was especially interested in exhibiting photographs of victims, tumultuous crowds, barricades, seditious manifestos, and communist banners.[3] Alfieri's intention was to exhibit not only the Great War but also the fascist revolution.[4] In a letter to Giuseppe Cocchia written on 4 July 1932, Alfieri asked Cocchia to send him an anti-Bolshevik manifesto published by Roman fascists on May Day (1 May) 1920.[5] Such a manifesto, wrote Alfieri, was especially useful (the dialectic is obvious) for the exhibition and would, he notes, also satisfy the intentions and will of the *Duce*. In another letter Alfieri asks fascists from Bologna to send him a bloodied jacket, a car fender involved in a raid on communists, and a program of political renewal published in 1919.[6] Manifestos of political renewal arrived from all over Italy, and documents commemorating those who had died for the fascist cause were also exhibited.[7] For example, leaflets sent to Alfieri indicated that the birthplaces of certain fascist martyrs continued to commemorate the anniversary of their deaths, as was seen in a leaflet published by the *Fascio* of Forlì for the third anniversary of the death of Anselmo Melandri.[8]

Documents rallying against other political parties were also displayed at the exhibition, such as one against the *Partito popolare* at the time of the 1924 elections.[9] Socialist manifestos were likewise exhibited to encourage critical dissent. In the archives we find an anti-war manifesto published by the socialist section of Mantova on 19 May 1915[10] and a leaflet ("subversive propaganda") published (and confiscated) in September 1924 from a branch of the Italian Communist Party in Rome. The leaflet denounced fascism as a revolution intent on defending capital and one that arrested "the redemptive ascent of the proletarian."[11] Another document, published by the Italian Communist Youth League (*Federazione giovanile comunisti d'Italia*), warned of the war mongering that fascist propaganda exhibited.[12] Those were the old manifestos. New manifestos and a renewed sense of realism were needed in 1932. In short, the *Decennale* needed to "write" its own reality.

My Fascist October

On the anniversary of the *Decennale* Elio Vittorini published a short piece in *Il Bargello* titled "My Fascist October," in which he recalled the days leading up to the March on Rome:

> [O]ne of those mornings I woke up with the rolling drums of the fascists leaving for Naples. Never before had I seen so many. And they were really armed. One could say that, absorbed by what I was reading … I had never noticed the marvelous reality of these boys wearing the black shirt who were turning upside down the province's slimy bottom … But that day I heard the drums roll and I saw them leave – the happy ones were from the third year in high school – in a game that had become so real, with flags, with trumpet blares, and with rifles. That day I choked with tears of anger,

and I did not know how to comfort myself but by becoming friends with the few fascists left. Anyway, that foggy morning that they left for Rome, I was there.[13]

"I was there": his presence guarantees his authenticity as a participant in a ritual meant to be re-enacted, we infer, in 1932. In the text the adolescent Elio Vittorini identifies with the shouts, flags, trumpet squalls, and rifles of the fascists. His words focus on the theatrics of the revolution, "a game that had now become so real," and the historically relevant conclusion of the punitive expeditions that preceded it. The fascists are described as a loud bunch. They grab him by the hair and want to send him home. The child-man protagonist Vittorini answers back by telling them about his own experience at Gorizia during the Great War. The men, probably ex-combatants themselves, listen (in this intimate setting) as the narrative confers upon Elio an aura that legitimizes him. Asserting a presence in the March on Rome or the Great War confers a revolutionary status on author and text. The next day the gang awakens to find itself stranded on the coast of Calabria only to discover that their wagon had been untied from the rest of the train. News arrives: Mussolini has taken matters into his own hands. The text ends there.

Vittorini's essay was written in 1932. It reflects on the experience of 1922 and projects new aspirations onto the new generation: a dialectical process that synthesized past and present and projected a new reality onto the future. However, as Giuseppe Bottai pointed out, risks did exist on the eve of the *Decennale*:

[O]ne needs to know why one marches, why one grabs a weapon, why then one can kill, in the name of what ideal one can do this … It's important not to forget that often in the past a regime's enemies were educated by the schools of that same regime. The regime was not able to look deep down into the souls of its disciples and students. It did not realize that through the falseness of its systems it had educated these students to become its future destructors.[14]

Bottai's words are pertinent to our discussion and will prove to be accurate. He notes that regimes are often responsible for their own demise. Their critical assessment and eventual destruction, from within, is often instigated by the deceptiveness and falseness of the systems created by those same regimes. Bottai concludes by speaking of the need for an awakening capable of confronting the lessons of history and the actual reality of a great historical occurrence such as the *Decennale*. In 1932 the only other option was the Soviet Union. It is not a coincidence, therefore, that articles published at a time when Italy was "on stage" focused on the affinities and differences between these two examples of political modernity.

Fascism's insistence on spirituality, as opposed to Marxist materialism, influenced discussions regarding realism and the state's role in artistic expression. This issue was the "problem of our times," Sergio Pannunzio wrote on the eve of the *Decennale*.[15] Roberto Fiorini believed that both Moscow and Rome exhibited political modernity.[16] Mario Rivoire wrote that these two political realities could not be reconciled. Notwithstanding these differences both political movements were relevant.[17] The discussions regarding this renewed political landscape coincided with the successful completion of the Soviet's first five-year plan, begun in 1928 and completed a year early in 1932 following which (in 1934) Stalin inaugurated socialist realism.

The *Decennale* was an ideal opportunity for the Italian intellectual class to reform culture according to the spirit of the year. The result was a re-evaluation of terms such as "life," "culture," "the realist aesthetic," "representative modes," and the "collective."

The realist aesthetic influenced other fields such as advertising and typography. For example, Anton Giulio Bragaglia wrote in 1932 that nationalism and a new form of realism, *neue sachlickeit*, were at the time "battles organized by artists conscious of life." Rationalism and *neue sachlickeit* were also expressed in the printed word and especially in publicity.[18] Bragaglia's articles focus on the art of the book. He explained that writing by hand is not that different from writing on a typewriter. And when we speak of typography we likewise speak of architecture that can bring us back to gardening or even to a film screenplay. For Bragaglia the two pages of a book were two *palazzi* bordering a boulevard composed by the inner margins.[19]

In the first months of 1932, *Critica fascista* called for a renewed sense of realism in all forms of fascist life, and on the eve of the anniversary Gherardo Casini published articles that set the tone in cultural discourse.[20] Writers, explained Casini, were meant to identify themselves as legislators with a clear function. Casini did not call for a politicized form of literature but, rather, one that would consider these changing times. Similarly, Pannunzio focused on the role of the intellectual in this new age and the need to bring the writer out of the ivory tower and into the life of the nation.[21]

This chapter suggests that the call for cultural renewal in fascist Italy – new culture that would best represent the spirit of the age – was a consequence of the exhibitory value attributed to the *Decennale*. It is not a coincidence therefore that *Il Saggiatore* focused on the link between realism, the present age in 1932, and the opportunity for Italy to assert itself on a universal level.[22] In January 1933 a group headed by Berto Ricci, who were "more seekers of knowledge rather than reciters of a catechism," published a "Realist Manifesto" in *L'Universale*. The manifesto was signed by Giorgio Bertolini, Romano Bilenchi, Diano Brocchi, Gioacchino Contri, Alfio Del Guercio, Alberto Luchini, Roberto Pavese, Icilio Petrone, Ottone Rosai, Edgardo Sulis, and Mario Tinti. The crisis of the present age, the age of the *Decennale*, was one that had enveloped nationalism, capitalism, and Christianity. Nationalism was in a state of crisis due to its selfishness and egoism. Capitalism was in crisis for a number of reasons: industry was suffering, mass unemployment existed, and state intervention was rampant. Finally, Christianity was experiencing a moment of decadence because it had lost sight of its original mission. The manifesto explicitly called for a universal form of fascism, best expressed by means of a fascist empire, as a civilizing force. Empire, in the fullest geographical and metaphysical extent, the manifesto stated, would be an act of love for the world. And this empire would ensure the subordination of the individual to the state.[23]

Ricci's journal, aptly titled *L'Universale* (founded in 1931), called for writers to participate in the nation's life and, at the same time, defeat the "petulant sterility" of certain elitist literary circles. Ricci called for a renewed fascist culture that would contribute to the revolution through dissent and transform the theory of fascist spirituality into action. In October 1932 another group gave birth to *Occidente*. The journal aspired to compare the Italian literary experience with that of other nations. The debate was picked up by journals such as *Il Bargello* and *Il Selvaggio*, and started to die down around the time of the May 1933 issue of *Critica fascista*, as an article by Ricci noted. A month later Casini published an article along similar lines. In sum, the spirit of the *Decennale* encouraged or at least indirectly influenced the discussion on cultural renewal and seemed to define the chronological timeline of the debate.

Defining Fascism in 1932 ·

Fascism was defined for the first time in 1932. The publication of the *Dottrina del fascismo* (co-authored by Gentile and Mussolini) is unique in that the document formalized fascism as a modern political idea to be exported.[24] Defining fascism also formalized a "code of command-ments" within the parameters of a now universalized secularized reli-gion.[25] The *Decennale* also inaugurated the publication of pamphlets belonging to the *Biblioteca della Enciclopedia Italiana* series. This series was inaugurated by the lexical item "fascism," and was followed by "Ethiopia": a clear indication of the relationship that existed between culture published in the spirit of the year (meant to instantiate a new form of culture) and the future march *from* Rome.[26]

The 1932 definition of "fascism" in the *Enciclopedia Italiana* set out to illustrate a completed past, create a dynamic present, and lay the groundwork for the future.[27] The idea of an anniversary initiating neo-phytes and consecrating ideas as a preparatory event for a future march *from* Rome could be interpreted, if we adopt the Marxist interpretation of fascism, as a strategy celebrating capitalism's imperialist aspirations. At the same time it could be read as a political doctrine originating from the manipulation of a general state of crisis. The *Decennale* was a relevant episode in the history of fascism in that the idea was formal-ized and adopted for consumption by the masses. Just as the *Encyclopédie* of Diderot set out to collect, present, and formalize the knowledge available in his time (and according to the precepts of the Enlightenment), so too did the *Enciclopedia Italiana*, with obvious differences. The new generation of fascists (and the anti-fascist movement as well) were now presented with the Word. Defining fascism was an absolute necessity "if fascism [did] not wish to die or, worse still, commit suicide." Thus read the doctrine's first footnote.

The encyclopedia entry is divided into two sections. The first, com-posed of thirteen paragraphs, considers fascism's fundamental ideas. The second, thirteen paragraphs as well, is a personalized account of fascism's political and social doctrines compiled by Benito Mussolini. Naturally predisposed to violence, fascism relies on peace at home and war abroad as a means of maintaining power. Fascism unites the inter-ests of the individual with those of the state and elevates the individual as the protagonist of the nation's future narrative. The fascist concep-tion of life refutes liberalism. The individual is annulled within the state. Life itself is conceptualized as a struggle. In this drama the individual is an instrument capable of moulding reality through individual acts of heroism. The *fascio* replaces the Christian cross, symbol of compassion. Might (and violence) are its crucial components. The doctrine exalts self-sacrifice, the renunciation of self-interest, and a spiritual view of the world. The true fascist disdains the "easy life" (*la vita comoda*).

In the second section an Author emerges. Here, in the eleventh paragraph, the *Duce* considers the state of affairs at the time of the *Decennale*. Fascism denies the validity of socialism, liberalism, democracy, and even monarchical absolutism, and opts instead for the totalitarian state as the product of post-1929 modern mass society. Only a strong, centralized corporative state can resolve the crisis of the age. The document concludes by presenting fascism's future aspirations: empire. In a sense, just as Christ's disciples were encouraged to set forth and colonize the world according to the redemptive message and precepts of Christ, so too were the protagonists of the *Decennale*, with the obvious differences that need not be explained. And so, the *Decennale* provided the new generation of fascists with the necessary manifesto capable of sustaining a now radicalized revolution. The philosophy of action behind the newly exhibited fascist doctrine intended to satisfy the masses' need for "authority, direction, order" and was meant to instantiate a new chapter in the nation's narrative. In the spirit of the *Decennale* and as a celebration of modernity, the official doctrine was translated into images and complemented by a political liturgy: the film *Camicia nera*.

Il Cinematografo

Cinema was especially appreciated during the *Decennale*. In August 1932 the *Esposizione Internazionale d'Arte Cinematografica* (now known as the Venice Film Festival) was inaugurated. In 1933 the journal *L'Italiano* dedicated an entire issue (January–February 1933) to the study of cinema, and the LUCE sponsored an open competition for a screenplay that would best celebrate the anniversary of the March on Rome.[28] The quality of the screenplays submitted was so mediocre that the LUCE decided on a documentary (*Il Decennale*) as the film to be shown in elementary schools.[29] A letter (dated Rome, 19 December 1932) to Minister Ercole written by Francesco Bascone, director of the *Istituto Nazionale di Assistenza Magistrale Rosa Maltoni Mussolini*, states:

[T]here is no municipality that does not thrive thanks to the atmosphere of Fascism and that has not benefited and developed from the constructive politics of the Regime. However, there are many that, on the occasion of the *Decennale*, have not had the opportunity to experience an immediate and concrete, albeit synthetic, vision of the grandiose work that has, in ten years, transformed the country. The LUCE film titled *Il Decennale* is the most suitable instrument to permanently impress upon the minds of youth the living and real images of Men and the Projects of the Revolution. Above all, the film can engrave the gaze, the voice, and the gestuality of the *Duce* onto the hearts and spirits of the students. These intentions are of unquestionable value.[30]

Bascone then presented his proposal: the institute (named in honour of Mussolini's mother Rosa) would promote the film in all elementary schools. Costs would be sustained by well-to-do families, and any financial obligation from poorer families would be exonerated.

The *Duce* had also become a star abroad at the time of the *Decennale*. In 1933 Columbia Pictures produced *Mussolini Speaks*, a documentary narrated by Lowell Thomas (of Lawrence of Arabia fame). The film grossed one million dollars, an enormous sum at the time. Around the same time Giovacchino Forzano was directing *Camicia nera*, a propaganda film shown during the *Decennale* and discussed in this chapter.[31]

Camicia nera

Camicia nera: the film incorporates fascist action, dialogues set in a determined historical situation, and objective and subjective realities. As *the* film of 1932 *Camicia nera* was to relive in 1932 the aura and rituals of the war and the fascist revolution through the liturgy of cinema. It aspired to project truth onto the spectator on a subconscious level with a clearly defined end result: to make the spectator recognize as reality something which he or she had not experienced or seen. The film also possessed archival value. It retrieved selective moments from history to legitimize them in the present. It consecrated ideas and created fascist reality as a documentary film. "Film," Leo Longanesi wrote, "was to replace the novel and presented itself as a new model for the new generation to emulate," for this new generation "live their lives as if they were part of a film."[32]

The film tells the story of a blacksmith (Mussolini's father was a blacksmith) from the Pontine Marshes who spends the day fashioning iron until he heeds the call to war. The young man leaves his family and is himself fashioned by his experience at the front. Then, in the final days of the war, the blacksmith is wounded and loses his memory, only to regain it just in time for the March on Rome. The connection is clear: the trenches (an intimate experience in a public space) had awakened the combatant.

The opening scene is telling. A soldier from the Great War is in the foreground running towards the spectator. A fez-wearing and dagger-holding fascist is in the background. Both are situated in a battle scene. An aura, in the shape of a *fascio*, surrounds them. The meaning is immediate: the aura of war *is* the movement, its origins, present, and future. The title, *Camicia nera* (Black Shirt), is a signifier that unites both groups – those who had fought in the Great War and the new generation of fascists, the generation of 1932. The time coordinates (1914–32) are equally important. Here the events of the past are legitimized when considered in the present. The protagonists of this cinematographic synthesis are realistic or exact interpreters of the events that took place from 1914 to 1932. This technique was later used by the neorealist director Luchino Visconti in the opening scenes of *La terra trema*. In both films the director makes use of a collective identity as a carrier of meaning. Both groups are potentially capable of experiencing an awakening of consciousness. They represent the future of the nation.

Adverse forces represented by the socialist party hinder the interventionist cause. A turning point presents itself: Mussolini's 15 November 1914 article, the same one that eventually led to his expulsion from the socialist party and the founding of *Il Popolo d'Italia*. Here the *Duce's* article "writes" history. After reading it the blacksmith and his family members consider the political situation. A moment of doubt is resolved by the arrival of a new Word. Ideas are consecrated. The blacksmith replies:

– This is the truth.

He then reads Mussolini's article out loud. His father responds:

– Who writes this way?
– Mussolini.

The episode is particularly effective. The setting is the blacksmith's home, poor and rustic. The home fire burns. As the blacksmith speaks "the truth" (Mussolini's article), the director zooms out and to the left. There, next to his mother, a young child (representative of the generation that was too young to have fought in the war, the generation of 1932) is lighting an oil lamp. As the blacksmith reads the final words of the article an aura of light shines on the child, who is admiring the lively flame. The moment is defined clearly and represents a spiritual experience in the presence of the numinous: *mysterium tremendum et fascinans*.[33] The audience would have immediately recognized that a transformation has occurred in the film. The initiation process has begun.

Clear oppositions are created: believers and non-believers, socialists and non-socialists, pacifists and interventionists, the interests of the parliament and the interests of the people. Forzano applies the same logic to another scene. The reasoning is clear and without any hesitation. In a scene that follows, a well-known article by Mussolini ("*Audacia!*," also present in the *Decennale* exhibition) is shown. The call to arms and audacity – once recognized as part of a ritual event in the lead-up to the Great War – is now replicated through modern or mechanized propaganda. It is a refrain that is reproduced a seemingly infinite number of times on screen only to lose its original value or aura. As Walter Benjamin would have it, the modern technique of reproduction "detaches" the "reproduced object" (the word *Audacia!*) from the "domain of tradition," and "by making many reproductions it substitutes a plurality of copies for a unique existence."[34] In short, the aura surrounding the letters is but an attempt to "adjust" this reality for the distracted masses.[35] The Italian front now becomes relevant. The blacksmith leaves his family and joins other soldiers in the liturgy of battle. Here Forzano utilizes the words of D'Annunzio in order to justify the sacrifice that awaits the nation: "Blessed are those who have the most, for they are those who can give the most." At the centre of the screen, the aura of the Great War projects out towards the spectator.

As the child thinks about his father, an aura of light surrounds him. The next scene shows the father performing an act of valour in the trenches. The use of film techniques that combine methods from both silent and sound films is particularly effective. Realism leads the way to a spiritualized, hyper-realistic mode: the extraordinary ritual of war cannot be defined through logic. The blacksmith is awarded a medal. The experience touches his family as well, because individuals and generations are bound together by a moral law. The son learns to write and writes to his father, who is injured in a final offensive. Unconscious, the blacksmith suffers memory loss and winds up in a hospital. His awakening (which is also an awakening of conscience due to the war experience) coincides with the first reunion of the *Fasci di combattimento* (an awakening of the nation) on 23 March 1919. The blacksmith recovers from the ordeal, yet is unable to participate in the life of the nation. His son (representative of the new generation) completes his father's duty and happens to be present in Piazza San Sepolcro that same day. Two close-ups are superimposed via an effective montage: the child hearing "the truth" for the first time and an adolescent wearing a hat and witnessing the San Sepolcro reunion. The technique employed by Forzano can be associated with Eisenstein's montage theory as well as with Marxist dialectics. Two images are edited together, and both are in conflict with each other. The new idea that emerges presents a new concept.

Forzano dedicates a considerable amount of time to the electoral strife and violence that led to the March on Rome. Those who "vote black" are promised the "kingdom of Heaven," whereas those who "vote red" are promised factories and industrial complexes. Oppositions are clearly present: the materialism of the communist credo versus fascist spirituality, chaos versus order. Chaos ensues. In the film we see the communists tattooing the palms of peasants and forcing them to respect the demands of their strikes. Fascists are thrown into ovens by the communists, and a young *squadrista* named Giovanni Berta is thrown into the Arno River. His name is not mentioned in *Camicia nera*, but it is clear that the episode would have been known to all. Images of martyrs are continuously portrayed. As the doctrine states, in the years preceding the March on Rome fascists knew how to die. The sacrifice of these martyrs is then vindicated by the violence of the *squadristi*. The blacksmith joins a group marching towards Rome in a Fiat 18BL. The collage of images is particularly effective. Images of fascists marching are superimposed over images of Dante and sculptures. The correlation is clear: the fascists marching on Rome are redeeming the people of Italy from their past.

A new voice is now heard, that of Mussolini in his first speech in parliament on 16 November 1922.[36] The scenes that follow narrate the reconstruction of Italy following the March on Rome and are equally important. The state concentrates and creates harmony between the interests of the social classes. The church understands and accepts this new relationship. Mussolini and Gentile explain that the state is not "indifferent" to Roman Catholicism and that the state does not possess a theology of its own but rather a "moral code." The state furthermore expresses the "will to command." Empire is but an expression of the vitality of the state. Never before, we read in the final paragraphs of the doctrine, have the masses thirsted for authority, for direction, and for order as they do now. Every age has its doctrine, and *this* age, the age of the *Decennale*, has the doctrine of fascism: a decisive moment in the history of human thought.

Camicia nera concludes with the images of a nation celebrating a new reality in 1932: the land-reclamation projects in the Pontina area and the founding of Littoria. The film ends with the blacksmith's son, now a young boy, raising the flag in Littoria (modern day Latina) on the day the *Duce* inaugurates the city. The final image is particularly eloquent and best represents the dialectical nature of the montage sequences present in Forzano's film. The *Duce* is now attributed Caesar-like qualities and leads his nation's young as they march *from* Rome towards new conquests: empire.

Camicia nera leaves the spectator with a sense of absoluteness. For one, the image presents, via a "tight" structure, an entire narrative sequence as a singular pictorial representation. The *Duce* is projected onto the viewer as an idol, an emblematic figure, and, as Luigi Sturzo wrote around the time of the *Decennale*, a "symbol of the collective force," for "idolatry is collective rather than individual."[37] All of the necessary elements are present: the *fascio*, the *Duce*, and the youth squads, now exhibited on stage for the *Decennale* and the concluding act of a political liturgy. The masses were now shocked into accepting the state's official narrative. Even here viewers experienced a sense of intimacy in a public space, just as they had at the 1932 Exhibition of the Fascist Revolution. And so, in 1932 the encyclopedic tradition likewise confronted itself with modernity: *Camicia nera* translated the doctrine of fascism into a political liturgy.

4

Critical Dissent:
An Alternative *Decennale* and Beyond

Croce and Gobetti

Dissent through culture selectively considered literature capable of inspiring change. What was needed at the time was a humanist re-evaluation of the individual as an expression of communal life in opposition to the barbarity, rituals, and myths of fascist civilization. Dialogue through culture was at the centre of discourse. Arnaldo Mussolini and Luigi Chiarini were convinced that "contaminating" Italian culture or "opening up" to Europe would deform artists and Italian culture. Others such as Alberto Moravia and Giuseppe Bottai believed instead that Europe had always influenced Italian culture and was perfectly adaptable to fascism. On the anti-fascist side dissent implied the reformation or revoking of the totalitarian project to mould a new Italian and a new civilization.

The *Decennale* presented an ideal setting for change. In a speech given on 1 October 1932 the *Duce* stated that intellectuals should leave their ivory towers and study the reality of the times. Intellectuals opposing fascism viewed this strategy for cultural renewal and commitment as an opportunity to restore the dignity of a nation from the outer boundaries of society. Often, if not always, it meant presenting and interpreting literature by reading between the lines. A decade earlier, Piero Gobetti had already presented his strategy. He wrote in *Rivoluzione liberale* (15 July 1924): "With a regime that suppresses freedom of speech (*stampa imbavagliata*), the real writer of the article is the reader: he is the one who needs to read between the lines (*il vero articolista è il lettore: egli deve leggere tra le righe*). Critical dissent meant interpreting the reality of 1932. It also meant providing guidelines that would inspire an awakening focused on values such as equality, truth, and freedom. The intellectual was now called upon to redefine himself. Both parties, the hegemonic power and the opposition, were well aware of this strategy.

In December 1931 the influential philosopher and statesman Benedetto Croce published his *Storia d'Europa* (History of Europe). The most important theme arising from the pages of the *Storia* is the relationship between ethics and politics – a premise for intellectual resistance against fascism. Croce's insistence on a "religion of freedom" on the eve of the *Decennale* makes it an ideal text to examine in this final chapter. Equally important is the link with another volume, the *Storia d'Italia dal 1871 al 1915*, published in 1928 by Laterza and recognized as Croce's response to the 1927 publication of Gioacchino Volpe's *L'Italia in cammino: l'ultimo cinquantennio.*[1] These pages written by Benedetto Croce can be read as a response to the age of the *Decennale*.

In a letter to Thomas Mann (to whom the volume is dedicated) written that same year,[2] Croce explained that the *Storia d'Europa* was meant to be an examination of beliefs once held but now reconsidered in a new light. The *Storia* was an "appeal to reason" and a quest for truth. The Dantean verses placed at the beginning of the volume set forth the *Storia*'s function. They are the words pronounced by Virgil to Dante as they escape the *Malebranche* devils in the fifth *bolgia*:

> Just now your thought commingled with my own,
> alike in attitude and aspect,
> so that of both I've formed a single plan.
>
> *Inferno*, xxiii, vv. 28–30

The *Storia* was immediately recognized as an anti-fascist manifesto, for it combined thought and action. In the first chapter Croce presents freedom as a religious concept. Following Hegel, Croce writes that history naturally strives towards freedom and that only freedom can allow culture and civilization to flourish. For Croce, the religion of freedom possesses the aura of a radiant star. Freedom has also withstood the trials of time. All other religions are instead "artificial" and will eventually be destroyed by their own hand. In the following passage Croce opposes fascism as a secularized religion:

> Now the person who gathers together and considers all the characteristics of the liberal ideal does not hesitate to call it a "religion." This person calls it by that name, of course, because he looks for what is essential and intrinsic in every religion, which always lies in a concept of reality and an ethic

that conforms to that concept. This excludes the mythological element that constitutes only a secondary differentiation between religion and philosophy. The concept of reality and the conforming ethics of liberalism were generated, as has been shown, by modern thought, dialectical and historical. Nothing else was needed to give them a religious character, since personifications, myths, legends, dogmas, rites, propitiations, expiations, priestly classes, pontifical robes, and so forth do not belong to the intrinsic and are taken out from particular religions and set up as requirements for every religion with ill effect. Such a process is the origin of the numerous artificial religions of the future that were devised in the eighteenth century. These were all ridiculed and rightly so, since they were counterfeits and caricatures.[3]

In the *Storia* Croce equates the suffocation of truth, which he suggests is the moral equivalent of human life, to a form of murder. Recuperating truth implies experiencing unspeakable suffering, such as that which takes place during a civil war or a war of liberation. Consequently, any political doctrine that aspires to artificially create reality – a false aesthetic system – is destined to be extinguished. These false ideals, born from the spiritual and philosophical void of post-1870 Europe, set the stage for the Great War and its aftermath. Activism, concluded Croce, had become the moral equivalent of a satanic mass.

An awakening of conscience meant uniting contemplation and action. It meant reconsidering previously accepted positions and learning from the lessons and accomplishments of the past as a strategy for the future. Croce explained that it would not be the "history of the future" but the "history of the past" in the present and illuminated by the light of truth. On the eve of the *Decennale*, Croce called upon exiled intellectuals and victims of fascism to disseminate freedom in the name of a united Europe:

[W]hen the question is asked whether liberty will enjoy what is known as the future, the answer must be that it has something better still: it has eternity. And today too, notwithstanding the coldness and the contempt and the scorn that liberty meets, it is in so many of our institutions and customs and our spiritual attitudes, and operates beneficently within them. What is more important, it lives in many noble intellects in all parts of the world, which, no matter how they are dispersed and isolated and reduced almost to an aristocratic but tiny *respublica literaria*, yet remain faithful to it and surround it with greater reverence and pursue it with more ardent love than in the times when there was no one to offend it or to question its absolute lordship, and the crowd surged around it hailing it by name, and in the very act contaminated its name with vulgarity, of which it has now been cleansed.[4]

Croce's epilogue is a true prophecy that sums up the pedagogical intent of the *Storia d'Europa*. In the last paragraph Croce explains that the *Storia* is to be read as a strategy for the politically committed. His indications, however, were not to be considered as absolutes. In a true liberal spirit, he recognizes that other ways of thinking could also prepare the way for the resurgence of truth and freedom:

Meanwhile, in all parts of Europe we are watching the growth of a new consciousness and of a new nationality … And just as, seventy years ago, a Neapolitan of the old kingdom or a Piedmontese of the subalpine kingdom became Italian without betraying his earlier quality but raising it and resolving it into this new quality, so too the French and Germans and Italians and all the others will raise themselves as Europeans. Their thoughts will be directed towards Europe, and their hearts will beat for her as they once did for their smaller countries – not forgotten now but loved all the better. This process of a European union, which is directly opposed to nationalist competition and has already set itself up against it and one day will be able to liberate Europe from it altogether, tends at the same time to liberate Europe from the whole psychology that clings to this nationalism and supports it and generates kindred manners, habits, and actions. And if this thing happens, or when it happens, the liberal ideal will be fully restored in men's minds and will resume its rule.[5]

Croce's final words emphasize fellowship in the name of a united Europe. These words were directly opposed to fascism's imperial aspirations. Furthermore, Croce underscored the need to unite the contemplative aspects of the intellectual life with action and establish a renewed relationship between culture and the reality of the times. Benedetto Croce's *antifascismo europeo* had been at the centre of Piero Gobetti's strategy of dissent a decade earlier. Gobetti's program for a cultural revival defined anti-fascism as a "matter of style" meant to awaken the conscience of those enslaved by the rhetoric of fascism. The literary or cultural review was the preferred medium. It was in the pages of these literary reviews (*Rivoluzione liberale* and *Il Baretti*) that a strategy of opposition by those belonging to what Marco Gervasoni calls "pedagogic aristocracies" was formed.[6]

A defining moment for Gobetti occurred after Mussolini's *discorso del bivacco* (16 November 1922). This was the first speech that Mussolini gave after the March on Rome. Gobetti responded with the article "Questioni di tattica" ("A Matter of Tactics") in *Rivoluzione Liberale*, 23 November 1922. Gobetti's opposition was founded on intransigency and a "serene" disposition towards analysis of the matter: "an antithesis of style" that would "combat" that "other Italy" by means of, if necessary, a "long-term" project, which would be developed "amongst friends" and directed towards those predisposed to intellectual reasoning rather than activism. "We don't fight against Prime Minister Mussolini specifically," he said, "but against that *other* Italy." Gobetti believed that the Italian people and the institutions of the state were meant to live this experience. His intransigency was, above all, a pedagogical experiment. Fascism was a necessary evil. Fascism would educate the ignorant masses on the value of freedom and, above all, on the effects of tyranny. Gobetti hoped that Mussolini and his government would take its full course. This too was a necessary evil meant to educate Italians on the meaning of tyranny. The country needed to prove itself ("*Il paese ha bisogno di una prova*").

In an article "Elogio della ghigliottina" ("In Praise of the Guillotine") published in the same issue of *Rivoluzione Liberale*, Gobetti famously defined fascism as the "autobiography of a nation." A nation that does not believe in class struggle is a nation that is not worth much. Antifascist strategy was meant to be something a bit mad – slightly Quixotesque – indeed, something serious. So serious, wrote Gobetti, that no one laughed, because all seemed to feel a desperate religiosity ("*ci si sentiva una disperata religiosità*"). He concluded that in the end Mussolini might even turn out to be an excellent Ignatius of Loyola![7]

Ten years later the writer Renato Poggioli would also mention that same image – Don Quixote – in the pages of *Solaria*, a literary review read by a tight-knit group of friends who considered themselves the successors of Piero Gobetti's vision.[8] In short, Gobetti's and Croce's visions would have been favourably accepted by a literary aristocracy. The strong ideological connection between Gobetti's *Il Baretti* and *Solaria* reinforced this critical strategy at the time of the *Decennale*.

Solaria

Solaria spent the first years of its existence (1926–7) on uncertain ground. In the early years it struggled to present its course of action and put up little resistance to the fascist regime. The arrival of Giansiro Ferrata as co-editor renewed the journal. And so, writers such as Vittorini were able to compare Italo Svevo's style with, for example, other European writers such as Stendhal and Balzac.

In *Love and the Idea of Europe*, Luisa Passerini dedicates a chapter to a young writer who also championed the idea of Europe: Leo Ferrero. Europe was, for Ferrero, the land of science, progress, enlightenment, and modernity. Europe *was* the Enlightenment. In 1916 the Ferrero family moved from Turin to Florence and participated in a very active cultural life. Florence had, Passerini mentions, a strong "European heritage." This heritage was best exemplified by Gaetano Salvemini and the Rosselli family, who "kept alive" the tradition of Mazzini. Florence was a centre for Italian literary Judaism. Ferrero would participate in this experience through *Solaria*. In September 1932 Ferrero arrived at Yale University thanks to a Rockefeller scholarship. He died in 1933 in a car accident in New Mexico.

In 1928 Ferrero published an article in *Solaria* titled *"Perché l'Italia abbia una Letteratura Europea"* ("So That Italy Might Have European Literature"). Leo Ferrero believed that "Europe" meant, above all, "redeeming" one's own national literary tradition. Ferrero explained that European literature "writes" a country by understanding other forms of literature. The European writer compares. The European writer who writes about Italy must have knowledge of the world.[9] And literature is a form of expressing a people's own "moral character." Morality, art, and literature, especially in the form of theatre: these were the main ideas. Not everyone believed in the same idea of Europe. For example, Alberto Consiglio returned to Gide, Rilke, Proust, and Valéry. There was also an implicit openness to Judaism in *Solaria*, thanks to the literature of Saba and Svevo. It is clear that Ferrero was "familiar" with the positions expressed by other Italian Jews such as, for example, Nello Rosselli.

Ferrero encouraged this sort of discussion at a time when the regime was becoming increasingly insular in its attitude towards culture. In the years that followed (1931–2), *Solaria* began to open itself up to Russian, German, and even Spanish literature. The journal discussed English literature (Joyce and Woolf especially) and Ernest Hemingway. Umberto Morra in February 1930 reviewed *A Farewell to Arms*.

The months following the publication of Croce's volume began a new period for *Solaria*. In a letter dated 4 January 1932, Carocci considered a new program for *Solaria*. He proposed a series of issues dedicated to contemporary foreign literature that would give a slanted character to the journal. The renewed editorial strategy was to be read as implicitly anti-fascist. The next day Carocci wrote to Renato Poggioli and requested his assistance for an issue dedicated to Slavic literature. In another letter, dated 15 October 1932, Alberto Consiglio explained (to Carocci) that a reformed *Solaria* needed to consider the reality of a new world now defined by Rome and Moscow. *Solaria* needed to publish literature that described this new age. He encouraged a new form of literature that considered land reclamation, unemployment, and the political battles fought in 1922. Consiglio would later co-write the screenplay for *Rome, Open City*. In another letter, dated 20 November 1932, Giorgio Marchi explained to Carocci that *Solaria* needed to create a dialogue with other literary currents from abroad. These letters clarify the cultural debate surrounding *Solaria*'s renewed strategy at the time of the *Decennale*.[10]

The following paragraphs present a general overview of the literature published at the time in *Solaria*. Four distinct periods will be treated here. The first period (February–October 1932) considers Renato Poggioli's review of Leone Ginzburg's translation of Pushkin (as requested by the editor of *Solaria*). The second period centres on Poggioli's review of the French translation of a book by Jaroslav Hašek. In the third period (January–February 1933), a more direct critique of the spirit of the *Decennale* can be read. This period is distinguishable by the elimination of a section dedicated to literary reviews and criticism (the *Zibaldone* section). Publications of poetry also disappear (except for two unedited poems by Rilke in the August–October 1933 issue). In February–March 1933, the fourth period considered here, *Solaria* began to publish episodes of *Il garofano rosso* (*The Red Carnation*) by Elio Vittorini.

The last explicit presence of an intransigent fascist intellectual in the pages of *Solaria* can be found in February 1932. Alessandro Pavolini's "*A mare bianco*" is a simplistic poem that exalted the vibrancy of youth, sport, and a collective representation: the flag. In the same issue, Renato Poggioli thanked his friend Leone Ginzburg, professor of Slavic literatures at the University of Turin and future editor of the Einaudi publishing house (co-founded with Giulio Einaudi in November 1933, perhaps as a response to the general climate of the *Decennale*), for his gift ("*bel dono d'anno nuovo*") – a translation of a Pushkin story ("*Le donna di picche*"/"The Queen of Spades"). Poggioli praised Ginzburg's preface and Pushkin as a model for "Europe." Ginzburg was one of the first to introduce Russian authors and their literature to Italian intellectuals. This move was intended to deprovincialize the Italian literary scene. The *Zibaldone* section of the same issue presented an ideal opportunity for literary criticism. For example, Aldo Capasso's review of *Saint-Saturnin* (NRF edition) by Jean Schlumberger (co-founder of the *Nouvelle Revue française*) focused on existential issues. Capasso wrote that he appreciated literature centred on the figure of "man," the psychological subtleties of which are elaborated into art. Capasso's reading of Schlumberger implied that cultural discourse was capable of inspiring an awakening. Capasso considered a renewed identity that maintained a morally fit attitude towards life even when reality forced the individual to hide behind a mask. He presented a strategy. Writing could be an act of resistance against evil and was a way of going "towards the people."

The populist rhetoric of the *Decennale* had now been transformed into a strategy for the opposition. Furthermore, memories of the Great War, or rather the aura of the war, were also present in the pages of *Solaria*. The February 1932 issue also contained a brief review, written by Carlo Emilio Gadda, of Giani Stuparich's *Guerra del '15*. Stuparich was a writer from Trieste, a city that represented a gateway to Europe. Gadda's observations were based on his own personal reading, as an ex-combatant and member of the war generation, of a war memoir. He applauded Stuparich's realism and "extreme objectivity": "[F]or the soldier … 'fatigue and death' are the only truisms." And so, Gadda's appreciation for "truth" in Stuparich was a critical assessment of fascist reality. This aesthetic, founded on truth, was created to guide true patriots in the nation-building process:

> On what will the history of the future and the future victory and truth of the Italian people be founded? They will come from the seeds found in the book by Stuparich. Oh! It won't be the village fair and neither the wreath nor the trombone, but rather the crude examination of actual situations and a crude confession based on sacrifices, on the sins of the military, and an intelligent reconstruction and a lively and appropriate sense of reality. I insist that the portrayal of war is not something of minor importance. It's something of extreme importance and an extreme educational necessity in a theoretical sense and in a moral sense when, let's make it clear, it's eliminated from the filthy kitchen garbage of rhetorical and patriotic preoccupations. One serves the nation with valour, with intelligence, and with the true beauty of true works. One serves, above all, by stating the truth so

that through the truth a true and intelligent experience and a secure future may be created. Talking about nonsense is the most incredible swindle.[11]

Absolutist political systems were also critically assessed. Aldo Garosci's article on Cesare Beccaria ("Notes on the Eloquence of Beccaria") in the April 1932 issue focused on the dangers of absolute power. Here Garosci clarified that Beccaria's outrage was directed against a "system of abuses," the by-product of the transformed relationship between society and the individual. Furthermore, he noted that Beccaria's "lack of faith" in society had increased with the advent of imperialism. Beccaria's horror towards capital punishment ("war of a nation towards a citizen") and other offences against humanity and justice had given him the courage to meticulously examine injustices and reclaim the dignity of the individual just as, Garosci concludes, Giuseppe Parini did with his poetry. The article is a perfect example of implicit dissent at the time of the *Decennale*. The next article (same issue, April 1932) in the *Zibaldone* section of *Solaria* is a review by Morra of Croce's *Storia d'Europa*. Here Morra focused on Europe as a defining element in history. The history of Europe, Morra wrote, is indeed the history of freedom and of the European spirit. Morra also focused on the validity of the liberal system. He did not agree with Croce's absolutist view of liberalism as a religion, but looked forward to an all-inclusive moral high ground. Morra applauded Croce's confidence and, above all, his determination and strategy.

A new translation of Tolstoy's *War and Peace* presented an ideal opportunity for the reviewer, Leo Ferrero, to extract a critique of the climate surrounding the *Decennale*. Tolstoy, a writer representing the European literary tradition, teaches us that all ideas, sentiments, and sensations created by man are false. Furthermore, "truth" is obtained not through intelligence but through "courage." Tolstoy teaches us that in our quest for truth we must dig beneath the surface of an exhibited reality and that we must have the courage to examine our own conscience. Literature was supposed to inspire an existential reflection on behalf of the individual in response to the spirit of the *Decennale*.

"Consalvo e Candida": Aborting the Nation's Soldier

In June 1932 *Solaria* published a short story written by Antonio Aniante titled *"Consalvo e Candida."* It is the story of a surrealist nightmare, an abortion, and a futurist resurrection. Aniante's real name was Antonio Rapisarda. His earliest writings were published in futurist literary revues. After the war, Aniante moved to Paris and was influenced by Dadaism and Surrealism. He returned to Rome in 1925 and wrote six *commedie* for Anton Giulio Bragaglia between 1926 and 1930. Aniante's theatre was applauded by Marinetti but not entirely successful.

In "*Consalvo e Candida*," the modern age (in essence, the climate of the *Decennale*) is so terrible that a mother would prefer having an abortion to giving birth. The short story's narrative sequences are revealed in the opening scene. As we read these paragraphs, visual elements remind us of Bontempelli's magic realism (the fetus-doll reconstitutes itself and comes to life), French Surrealism (the use of a dream sequence), and Dadaism (the anti-war motif).

"*Consalvo e Candida*" is composed of six distinct scenes: a hospital, a clandestine abortion clinic, the couple's bedroom, the same hospital, the world outside, and a weapons factory. The opening paragraph juxtaposes the infernal chaos of the modern age (the reality of fascism) with the relative tranquility present beyond the hospital walls. The reality of the age is a harsh one, and Consalvo is only able to take a short break from work to visit Candida as she recovers from her clandestine abortion. The hospital is a *hortus conclusus*, an enclosed paradise secluded from the chaos of the modern city where tranquility and peace reign. The biblical reference (Song of Songs 4:12) is not casual in that the imagery can also refer to a virgin's womb as an enclosed (*conclusus*) garden as she longs for her spouse. The situation depicted by Aniante, however, is a different one, and the next scene is a flashback in the narrative: Consalvo's visit to the abortionist's tenement, a run-down building that had not yet been demolished in a working class neighbourhood inhabited by "questionable people" (*gente equivoca*). There, Consalvo searches for Candida. The decision to abort is read as an explicit protest against fascism's intrusion into the private sphere.

The text also speaks to us about modernity, fascist demographics, and urbanization. It presents the abortion issue not as a bourgeois vice (as considered in the pre-war era) but rather as an urban working class practice and, most importantly, as a political crime against the state and against fascist demographic policy. The demographic campaign, which Ebner summarizes in *Ordinary Violence*, had been launched in 1925 with the establishment of the ONMI, the institution of a bachelor tax, prizes for mothers and large families, and the outlawing of birth control devices and information about birth control. The campaign also made emigration illegal. In 1926 a public security code called for police confinement for doctors and midwives suspected of performing abortions. In Aniante's tale Candida does not work and at least here does not interfere with the *Duce*'s wishes regarding the role of women in the workplace.[12] In an infamous article published in 1934, the *Duce* would write:

> The working woman generally affects, apart from unemployment, also the demographic challenge … An exodus of women from labour would no doubt have an economic impact on many families, but a legion of men would raise their humiliated brow and a hundred times the number of new families would enter into the life of the nation. We must convince ourselves that the same job that causes the loss of the female generative attributes gives a man the strongest physical and moral manhood.[13]

There was another reason. Historically women constituted the majority of the working class. According to statistics drawn up by Stefano Merli, the working class in 1876 was made up of the following percentages: women, 48.6 per cent; children, 23.2 per cent; and men, 28.2 per cent. Child labour would eventually be regulated in 1907. Women replaced these child labourers. The reasons were, according to Paola Lupo, quite obvious. Women are "more docile, go on strikes less, are paid less, and, in short, are easier to be taken advantage of … [A] woman doesn't complain and completes the most boring and harmful jobs. She stays in the factory longer – 14 to 16 hours a day – while men stay 10 to 12 hours a day."[14]

Candida acts in her own interest and is an antagonist against the state.[15] The young woman (*l'amica* – the two are not married yet live together) takes matters into her own hands and makes it clear that she would rather die than "procreate" another soldier. Consalvo, however, wants to keep the child. The predicament pits two distinct and opposing wills against each other. It is a hate-creating situation and is more dangerous, Aniante explains, than the sparks erupting from the blast furnaces of a steel mill. The next scene, in the couple's home, is presented as a surreal nightmare. Candida is tired from the procedure, and the aborted fetus is hidden in a coffee cup (a surrealist marker for the womb) placed on the fireplace mantel. Consalvo is visibly shaken and on unsure ground. Candida wants to keep the fetus, much like a child holds onto a doll. The couple looks down, together, into the cup at the fetus still breathing and hopeless. Consalvo does feel some responsibility for the act, but it is Candida who sticks the needle in the cocoon that is the unborn child.

The child resurrects with legs of steel. A terrible violence is perpetrated against the human form, and yet the child resurrects. Such is the commodified state of the body – a mechanized and militarized body – exhibited by fascist society during the *Decennale*: art cannot detach itself from the historical context in which it is produced. We can recall, as Bontempelli suggested in 1930, the need to "narrate the dream as realty, reality as a dream."[16] As a side note, Warren Goldstein explains that Benjamin's theory of dreams, much like those espoused by the Surrealists, synthesized Freud, Jung, and Marx, or rather, the unconscious with the collective unconscious. Goldstein interprets Benjamin in the following manner: "[I]f dreams are the product of the unconscious and if there is a collective unconscious there must also be collective dreaming and therefore a collective awakening." Goldstein refers to Marx in this way: "[T]he reformation of consciousness lies *solely* in the awakening of the world … from its dreams about itself." In other words, Goldstein explains that human beings, by becoming conscious of their own dreams, have the possibility of realizing them. Collective consciousness alternates between dreaming and awakening: the collective finds its expression in the dream and discovers meaning on awakening. Benjamin understood that living in a society meant living in a dream state and that society must wake up from this dream. This collective awakening found a parallel in both the redemptive nature of Messianism and in the revolution of Marxism. Collective dreaming was an act of "enchantment." The idea of collective awakening was an act of disenchantment. Benjamin's theory of dreaming and awakening is, in short, the dialectical theory of enchantment and disenchantment.[17]

Aniante engages with surrealist iconography. The short story depicts anti-fascism as a visceral force from within. The hybrid body represents the internalization of fascist aesthetics. It is a personal decision that gains meaning within the celebratory context of the *Decennale*. At a time when collective representations of the *Decennale* were initiating neophytes into fascist society, *Solaria*'s writers were instead presenting literature that took sacrifice to its extreme. Consalvo is faced with ethical questions: Was he complicit in the abortion? Is he a criminal? Who holds the truth? What follows is a depiction of mechanized reality that applied the reality of factory mechanization to the creation and exhibition of soldiers destined for war. Consalvo observes the reality of the street. It is Antonio Sant'Elia's tumultuously agile, mobile, and dynamic futurist city: *"cantiere tumultante, agile, mobile, dinamico, in ogni suo parte."*[18] Consalvo describes the city and its dynamism, velocity, and sequences. It is a modern city. The image represented by the author is that of a worker overcome by a factory, an emblematic image reminiscent of Charlie Chaplin's *Modern Times*. The society depicted is mechanized. The protagonist's assessment of modernity is far from positive. Rather, his is a feeling of alienation, despair, and perhaps even abandonment.

The mechanics of dehumanization lead to awakening and action. Consalvo reacts to the orderly chaos and proceeds to sabotage the war machine. At certain times in history change is necessary, even when it is imposed through violence. Consalvo is aware that he risks losing his job – his security – in this brief moment of resistance. And yet, these bourgeois concerns are but a trifle. The narrative sequences remind us of the Dadaist polemic against war as the result of a capitalist society. Art was, in this case, not meant to be expressed for art's sake but rather to critique the modern age. In the age of mass movements the Dadaist-inspired performance is clear: scandal, outrage, and shock effect are meant to instantiate a new narrative. The hero's experience uproots him from modern mechanized society. The ideal is best conceptualized through sabotage: a conscious act on behalf of the working class to reduce output of production in the military industrial complex. All work stops in the factory.[19]

Consalvo stands in for the proletarian who has become conscious enough to take his freedom. Candida's act violates the state's code of ethics. Both individuals struggle against society. Both engage in independent acts against the existing political and social order. Candida's abortion is a critique of fascist cultural imperialism and strikes at fascism's insistence on demographic growth and "prophecies of racial exhaustion."[20] In turn, the body that resurrects represents the modern body of the *Decennale*. It is the body of 1932: a preconfigured body genetically predisposed to the reality and needs of the fascist state. The shock value imposed on the reader by Aniante's narrative was meant to initiate an antagonistic chapter in the nation's narrative. Finally, as Bontempelli suggests, *"Consalvo e Candida"* presents the reader with an interesting mix of *immaginazione*, leaving our daily comfort zone, and *avventura*, a renewed aesthetic now modified according to our interior needs.[21]

Solaria had fully immersed itself in the reality of the *Decennale*.

October 1932

Solaria's Europeanism was likewise present in the writings of Renato Poggioli, a "mediator" for *Solaria* with the rest of Europe and especially Eastern Europe. For the September–October 1932 edition of *Solaria*, Poggioli submitted a review of the French translation of a novel, *The Good Soldier Švejk*, by Jaroslav Hašek, an author admired by Poggioli for his unconventional behaviour. The opening paragraph is a manifesto of sorts. Hašek is an anarchist and a drunken bohemian. His literature is an instrument of revolt:

> It was a monk from France and a warrior from Spain who gave Europe a gift – two great books of modern revolution, *Gargantua and Pantagruel* and *Don Quixote*. Their adventurous lives passed from the desk to the cloister and from the ship to the prison cell, traversing punishments and wounds, penance and jail breaks, but always maintaining a pure and uniform atmosphere of letters and literary scholarship. It was so essential to have in these a climate of culture and intelligence that one of them, in times more bleak and close, had the ambition of echoing their heroic iconoclastic laughter and reduced life to a simple and poor existence: of the humanist and man of letters. These adventures led to the discovery of rare books and research on style.[22]

Poggioli's heroes, François Rabelais and Miguel de Cervantes, are examples of historically determinant individuals who, notwithstanding trials and hardships, always maintained a coherent vision. The protagonist of Hašek's novel, *Chvéik* (or Švejk), is a fool, an aspiring soldier up to his neck in mediocrity, an inferior specimen of a man at his best and grotesque at his worse. Švejk is an idiot, a cretin living on the border between comedy and tragedy. He is unable to enter into the ranks of the army. Švejk however is an "original" character because his senselessness betokens his humanity. There is no spirituality, no religious mission, and no aura in this aspiring soldier. What redeem this fool are his utilitarian ways and his instinct. Nonetheless, Švejk regains his wits only when confronted with a truly dangerous situation. At that moment his idiocy morphs into intelligence, which allows Švejk to transform himself into an example for all to follow.[23] Hašek's novel was a far cry from the climate of the *Decennale*. Poggioli's intuition was ingenious: a rereading of an anti-war novel written by Hašek (at the time of the March on Rome) on the most militaristic of anniversaries.

In November 1932 *Solaria* published an article by Alberto Consiglio on Italo Svevo (another writer from Trieste, as was Stuparich) that also served as a critical assessment of the *Decennale*. Svevo had been discovered by James Joyce and Eugenio Montale. *Solaria* had dedicated ample space to Svevo, starting with the publication of *La burla* in 1928. Articles by Consiglio, Ferrata, and Debenedetti followed. In the opening paragraphs Consiglio speaks of the previous decade (note the temporal marker) as "intense" and "complex," an age in which men matured, perhaps "too soon," only to fall victim to their own defects.[24] The climate of the age, Consiglio notes, is useful in that it allowed individuals to confront themselves with the problems facing humanity. Svevo's novels (*Zeno, Senilità, Una vita*) contrast "moral solitude" with "social company" (*"contrasto tra solitudine morale e compagnia sociale"*). In *Zeno*, Consiglio writes, we learn to appreciate the dilemma between *"volontà"* ("will") and *"azione"* ("action"). In *Senilità* the author remarks instead on the mediocrity of individuals incapable of controlling their own lives (*"dominare la vita"*). And so, Consiglio concludes, the modern novel ought not to simply transcribe or objectively photograph reality but rather should be a description of reality mediated by a conscience. Svevo's writing represents not only the existential dilemma of the individual but also that of Trieste, a hybrid city, symbol of Europe.[25] Svevo therefore can now be reconsidered thanks to the climate of the age, the age of the *Decennale*. To summarize Consiglio: Svevo is a European novelist projected *towards* Europe. And Trieste best represents both the age and the existential dilemma of the individual. Trieste was *"terra travagliata"* – a land of travail and hardship. It is a city where intellectuals have never really experienced peace. Trieste is a border city, and we can include it in the same list as the Ireland of Yeats, Joyce, and Shaw; the Russia of Gogol and Dostoyevsky; or the Sicily of Verga, without forgetting Capuana, De Roberto, and Pirandello. The *Triestini* are *"popoli di confino"* ("border people") who don't possess a clear political consciousness. Rather, they are overwhelmed by political passion. They also best portray that "contrast" between the old century and the new. The *Triestini* who best exemplify this writing are Michelstaer, Saba, and Svevo. Consiglio adds another characteristic of the people of Trieste: *"un grano di spirit ebraico"* ("a grain of the Jewish spirit"). And, Consiglio writes, Svevo could turn out to be another Joseph Conrad.

A formal difference is immediately visible with the January 1933 issue of *Solaria*. The editorial board had eliminated the *Zibaldone* section reserved for critical essays and opted for a more direct presentation of these texts. Nicola Chiaromonte writes that Malraux's literature attempted to understand "Europe" through the eyes of "China" – the West through the eyes of the East.[26] He appreciates Malraux's criticism of individualism and, in its more "acute form," the will of power. Malraux writes "moral dialogues" of individuals who act and seek to understand the moral reasoning behind their actions. His characters create a dialogue with present-day events. They are thrown into history and forced to commit when confronted with their destiny.[27] Malraux is relevant because, according to Chiaromonte's unique review, Malraux critiques individualism. Malraux is an ideal writer. His novels *Les Conquérants* (1928) and *La Voie royale* (1930) bring to the forefront the true philosophy behind revolutionary events rather than just historical-political reasons. His writing underlines the moral significance of these gests. They represent the clash of ideas and a drama that is reduced to the bare minimum.

Civilizations were, at the time of the *Decennale*, heading towards the absolute negation of life: all of humanity was destined to be crushed by the mechanisms of modern society (similar considerations were seen in "Consalvo e Candida"). Chiaromonte's reading of Malraux presented an ideal opportunity to condemn "Supermen," Messianic figures, and the false religions they profess. True, Malraux's characters represent the epitome of Supermen. But at the same time they represent the absurdity of that myth. The vitalism that these characters portray, Chiaromonte explains, is but the substitution of "true reality" with the reality of "magic formulas." And we need not return to Nietzsche to understand that this delirium leads individuals to fail to grasp the reality in which they are living. At the time of the *Decennale*, individuals were seeking truth by attempting to find it in "abstract" symbols, a "sort of theology." Chiaromonte also focuses on modernity, the same modernity celebrated during the *Decennale*. Modernity, here read as the negation of life, had replaced reality with an artificial or false aesthetic ("*formule magiche*"). Modernity was not necessarily viewed as a negative concept. Rather what was negative, Chiaromonte notes, was its misuse.

In the same issue Chiaromonte reviewed [unfavourably in that he considered the book's "*avvertimenti*" ("notes") as "*imbarazzanti*" ("at times embarrassing")] Leo Ferrero's *Paris, dernier modèle de l'Occident*, which focused on Paris as a symbol of modernity. Chiaromonte explains that Paris is certainly representative, but the qualities Ferrero exalts are "typical of Western civilization since the time of Plato."[28] Ferrero had just moved to the United States thanks to a grant from the

Rockerfeller Foundation. He intended to study Native Americans in New Mexico, but regretfully died in a car accident in August 1933. According to Ferrero, Paris is "the last model of Western civilization" and a synthesis of Athenian and Roman qualities. Paris is a "creative" and an "orderly" city. The city is representative of "Europe." Paris is in love with "the social and intellectual values that make up a refined civilization." Ferrero's book described the ideal city "where multitude and elite, individual and society, intellect and life, law and life are beautifully united by an unwritten pact." Chiaromonte's review of Ferrero's book condemns the triumph of modernist aesthetics as celebrated during the *Decennale*. He agrees with the writer: perhaps a return to humanism, a religion of "the better things," could be the answer.[29] These essays, published in January 1933, are ideal examples of *Solaria*'s implicit strategy for dissent during the *Decennale*.

A couple of months later Chiaromonte wrote an article for *Solaria*, "Notes on Civilizations and Utopias."[30] In it he gives value to what he believes are humanistic ideals capable of overcoming the mechanistic systems of an artificial and false reality, and giving birth to a world in which "man" can finally exist as "man."[31] In the November–December 1933 issue, *Solaria* would return to Chiaromonte in "*André Malraux e 'La Condition Humaine.'*" Chiaromonte's review underlines the importance of the modern impulse present in the novel. This is especially seen in those pages where, for example, the character Kyo wanders through the city and perceives the landscape in practical terms. Malraux compels the reader to listen to his conscience and give meaning to life at times of incredible tension. Malraux's books represent ideas that confront themselves violently as moral dialogues. According to Chiaromonte the true test that a man must pass in order to prove his existence is the absolute destruction of himself: *pour avoir donné un sens à sa vie*.[32]

Il garofano rosso

Lo presi sottobraccio e ci incamminammo.

I took him by the arm and we set out.

The previous articles certainly left a mark on the young Elio Vittorini. Vittorini had been *presente* in virtually every issue of *Solaria*, starting with the publication in January 1933 of a short story titled "*Giorni di mare*" ("Days at the Beach"). In the end, the literature of Malraux (centred on "man," a theme at the core of Vittorini's writing) anticipated that same dilemma that many belonging to the new generation of fascists would experience when confronted with their destiny: war. In February 1933 *Solaria* began publishing episodes of Elio Vittorini's *Il garofano rosso* (*The Red Carnation*). The novel tells the story of a young man, Alessio Mainardi, and his political maturation from revolutionary fascism (the aura of 1922) to dissent and a utopian new order. The novel considers the circumstances surrounding the initiation of a new group of young men into society and the consecration of new ideas.

Equally important in *Il garofano* is the role of youth (*giovinezza*) in relation to literary criticism published in *Solaria* at the time. In an article on the literature of Alain Fournier, Consiglio reviewed *Le Grand Meaulnes* (*The Wanderer*) as a novel that remained in the imaginary realm.[33] The use of adolescence as a literary strategy allowed Fournier, Consiglio suggests, to distance himself *from* rather than participate *in* life. He explains that Fournier's protagonists do not orient their lives towards their studies but rather towards other forms of adventure. In Fournier's imaginary world the strong dispute power, and the weak side with the victor. Few, we infer, commit to an ideal. Consiglio concludes by considering narrative strategies. He writes that a memoir is a critical assessment of the past. It needs to be told within the context of those years and not from the point of view of the present age. This last strategy, Consiglio continues, leads to a less truthful and more utilitarian or practical approach. Fournier's writing is an example of a narrative style that reflects on the irrational, turbulent, and transitory nature of adolescence without, however, presenting a "mature reflection" by the narrator. *Le Grand Meaulnes* is, when considered within these parameters, "the poem about the desperation of living" as, we read between the lines, is *Il garofano rosso*.

The critic Maria Corti notes that the *Solaria* edition of *Il garofano rosso* contains more sequences, is linguistically more realistic, and includes a greater variety of secondary characters than the 1948 edition which is "memorialistic" and "lyrical." Other differences are relevant when considering the third episode published in *Solaria*. Corti explains that in this case Vittorini eliminates realistic language (of the *strapaesano* type) and opts instead for a more lyrical narrative.[34] The text is ambiguous and can be read as satisfying the ideological needs of revolutionary fascism. Anna Panicali defines this moment in the literary biography of Elio Vittorini as the author's attempt to project a "prophetic language."[35] At the time Vittorini developed an introspective or autobiographical element in his writing and presented his own solution to the crisis afflicting the modern age.[36] The author's strategy coincided with left-wing fascist (*fascisti di sinistra*) ideology that professed an anti-bourgeois spirit, encouraged the polemic against capitalism, and promoted a belief in the notion of "community." These so-called left-wing fascists were represented by four groups: (1) marginalized *ex-squadristi, ex-arditi, ex-futuristi, ex-rassisti,* and *ex-dissidenti*; (2) populists and intellectuals such as Malaparte, Maccari, and Ricci; (3) the generation of the *Giovani Universitari Fascisti* (GUF); and (4) union members (*sindacalisti*).[37]

Il garofano rosso is situated at the time of the Matteotti affair (1924). It tells the story of Alessio Mainardi's initiation into adult life. Alessio is a well-to-do student in love with Giovanna, the daughter of a high-ranking official. A red carnation is exchanged. Alessio then meets Zobeida, a prostitute who initiates Alessio into adulthood and teaches him a new moral, one that denies the legitimacy of the bourgeois values which defined the fascist (and Catholic) family.[38] Meanwhile, Alessio's friend Tarquinio grows up and takes his place with Giovanna. The conclusion of the first episode of *Il garofano rosso* published in *Solaria* (February 1933) is likewise indicative. The episode ends with the following words as Alessio and his older friend Tarquinio leave their room:

I took him by the arm and we set out.

The two leave together. Alessio begins his adventure towards adulthood. Likewise, Vittorini and *Solaria* also begin a new phase. In March 1933 Vittorini made a trip to Milan and, as a writer, began to transfer his thoughts from Milan to Sicily and from 1933 to 1920–4.

At the beginning of the novel Alessio identifies with the older generation that had participated in the March on Rome. Both he and Tarquinio believe in the fascist revolution and consider it an anti-bourgeois innovative force. Fascism is revolutionary and violent. Alessio keeps a diary (the "diary of a strategist"), although he has not written in it since the days following the March on Rome. The period coincides with the *biennio nero*, a moment that followed the *biennio rosso* and preceded the murder of Matteotti. The young men, and particularly Tarquinio, their leader, are keen on supporting revolutionary fascism. Tarquinio represents a model (the aura of the old generation), since he had participated in the March on Rome. He and Alessio meet at *la cava*, a place where they unite as a community and discuss politics,

Rosa Luxemburg (recall our flag in the previous chapter), and the theatrics of action.

Adolescence is seen here as an adventurous performance, and these young men intend to subvert the status quo as radicalized revolutionaries. The students "occupy" their school following the Matteotti affair. Alessio is suspended for the rest of the school year for his actions and decides to return home "to the countryside of the brick-making kilns." At home Alessio is considered a communist subversive ("*un comunista sovvertitore dell'Ordine Ristabilito dal Fascismo*") by his father's workers. He begins to develop a relationship with them. His main dilemma, concerning interest representation and political culture, is illustrative of the climate of the *Decennale* in that these issues were at the centre of discussion among union members: the *scuole sindacali*. These schools aimed to close the gap between workers and owners. These concerns were also at the centre of the corporativist solution, an idea that aspired to create a new order capable of giving a voice to those social classes traditionally excluded from participation in the state.[39] Alessio feels inferior to the workers. The words that Vittorini would later add to the text of *Il garofano rosso* in describing this specific event in the life of Alessio Mainardi, an awakening of consciousness, are equally important:

> If I had known then that my father's furnaces weren't the only furnaces, I would have imagined a life going from furnace to furnace. But I realized this at the same time as I realized everything else: that I was studying and would have studied for many years, that neither I nor my brothers would have grown up as labourers working under my father, and that there was a chasm of injustice between our father and the workers.[40]

The presence of the phrase "*un fossato di offesa*" ("a chasm of injustice") is a clear indication of Vittorini's strategy. *Il garofano rosso* can be read as a defining literary experience for Vittorini and eventually leads to the exploration of "*il mondo offeso*" in *Conversazione in Sicilia*. Alessio's experience with his father's workers leads to an awakening. The true meaning of youthfulness, of *giovinezza*, is to be found in the proletariat (and not in the aura of the soldier).[41] This awakening leads to a crisis that he tells Tarquinio about in letters. Tarquinio, a member of the generation that marched on Rome, responds that it takes much more than a simple "uprising" to redefine oneself as communist ("*Ma non fantasticare per questo che non sei fascista e che sei comunista*"). Tarquinio's concerns are representative of discourse specific to the reality of the

Decennale. In a sense, he is especially worried that Alessio is starting to lean more towards Moscow than Rome. He pledges to instruct the young man and help him discover what he is looking for. He even pledges to become his patron.

Seven new *camerati* arrive: Perez, Valente, Baiardo, Corsentino, Mattioli, Trovato, and Ahmed Cogia. Their arrival pits the "new generation" against the "old generation." At this moment Alessio distances himself from Tarquinio. Alessio is now acquainted with this group, the "sect" of the *Garofano rosso*. It is a new community that intends to unite the entire world population of youth. And so, after liberating himself from the prostitute Zobeida, Alessio heads out into the street and towards the masses. At the beginning of the last chapter (XV), Alessio follows a flag (a typical marker of revolutionary events – recall the flags exhibited at the 1932 exhibition) towards the funeral of a young girl, the funeral of *giovinezza*. Other flags and banners also arrive. Each represents a distinct group. They then move on to a *caffè*. There, an unknown child ("*un ragazzino dalla voce stridente*") appears as a mythical force calling for a new society. The child admonishes the young people gathered: the death of this young girl, of *giovinezza*, and of the aura of the original revolution is the partial responsibility of everyone. The child calls for the creation of a new civilization, indeed for the regeneration of society, complete with new protagonists and new ideas. The child acts as a spokesman (and symbol of redeemed *giovinezza*) for Vittorini's corporativist ideology.

The young girl's death was a suicide. If we consider the girl as a symbol of *giovinezza* – the rhetoric sustaining the fascist revolution – and recall the first footnote of the 1932 definition of fascism considered in the previous chapter, then we read her death as the regime's failed attempt to regenerate or radicalize the aura of the March on Rome. In short, the *Decennale*'s consensus-generating strategies had, at least for Vittorini, failed. Furthermore, the suicide of the girl is a pretext for imposing a series of rules destined to eliminate the free development of sentiments: all are now obligated, by force, to act for a greater "spiritualized" good.[42] A legal statute for love would punish, by death, prostitution and betrayal in all forms. Marriage unions would have to last at least five years so as to eliminate "frivolous" relationships. And each was free to begin at any age. The child's approach is intransigent.[43]

At the beginning of the novel Alessio is very much in awe of the aura of the March on Rome. His encounter with the new generation of fascists allows him to reconsider previously held ideological positions.

The shock value attributable to the death of the young girl, the passing of *giovinezza*, was meant to instantiate a new narrative, one that would regenerate society according to a greater will. Vittorini's activist response, via literature that presented new ideas and new protagonists, was a response to the climate of the *Decennale*. It set the stage for what was to come.[44]

In the spirit of the literature of Malraux, both Vittorini and *Solaria* chose to engage with reality. This was a distinct moment in the autobiography of the nation: an awakening of conscience ("*esame di conscienza*") and the belief in a cultural project focused exclusively on the ethics of truth, reason, and humanism. On the fascist front *Il garofano rosso* translated itself (in accordance with the *Duce*'s call to "go towards the people" and the strategies of the corporative state) into populist rhetoric. In the case of *Il garofano rosso*, Vittorini created a shock effect by staging the death of *giovinezza* so as to instantiate a new narrative, complete with protagonists (the new generation of fascists, now shocked out of a state of liminality) and ideas (essentially, a hybrid form of socialism and fascism).

A new generation of intellectuals was asked to confront history and emancipate itself. At the time of the *Decennale* Carlo Bernari was writing *I tre operai* (*The Three Workers*, 1934), a novel situated before the advent of fascism. In this novel, the protagonists are incapable of acting decisively on reality and committing to a project. At the same time a young Romano Bilenchi was working on *Il Capofabbrica* (*The Foreman*, 1935). The protagonist, Marco, experiences a transformation or awakening of sorts. A fascist hardliner (*squadrista*), Marco seeks redemption by "going towards the people" and understanding the working class. There, he meets and develops a friendship with a foreman named Andrea who has communist tendencies. The novel ends with both escaping reality and going towards a new city. Again, there is no commitment.

Notwithstanding these intentions, a new form of literature did not arise immediately, due to the lack of a catalyst. People and ideas needed to confront themselves with their destinies and, as Malraux (and Benjamin) would have it, with the reality of war and the finality of death. In the specific case of post-1932 fascist Italy, intellectuals had to deal with the Spanish Civil War and then the Ethiopian campaign.

In a letter to Silvio Guarnieri (25 July 1936) Elio Vittorini condemned the same war that had inspired thousands to go and fight for Franco in Spain.[45] Vittorini's epiphany was the consequence of his direct experience with the reality of a fascist war. In the letter to Guarnieri, Vittorini explained that he was still a *solariano* ("*Per noi, insomma, Dostojevskij è un grande scrittore*": *Solaria's* motto) and yet moving towards literature that was more explicitly engaged (and ideologically close to Marxism).[46] Vittorini was attempting to reconcile both fascist doctrine and Marxism in the name of a universalistic collective revolution.[47]

The Spanish Civil War had educated the masses. Vittorini later explained the relationship that these historical events would have on the completion of *Il garofano rosso* (*Solaria* version, 1935), the beginning (and interruption) of *Erica e i suoi fratelli*, and the beginning of *Conversazione in Sicilia* (1937). Ethiopia and Spain had educated an entire generation, especially the new generation which had been asked to march *from* Rome in 1932. It represented the political education of those Italians who eventually defeated fascism from within. The wars were a necessary path or stage for those wanting to create a new country, not by building on the experience of the previous generation (as the *Decennale* celebrations set out to do) but rather through direct contact with the brutal lesson of war. Vittorini's work was certainly representative of the generation of 1932.[48]

The Ethiopian campaign (the *Impero* was proclaimed on 5 May 1936) presented an ideal opportunity for the young men coming of age during the *Decennale* to search for new truths and experiences. Ben-Ghiat explains that at the time men such as Ruggero Zangrandi, Berto Ricci from *l'Universale*, and Luchino Visconti were enthusiastic supporters of the war. Vittorini attempted to enlist, but was unable to do so for bureaucratic reasons.[49] These members of the new generation, now intent on marching *from* Rome, aspired to carry out a renewed social revolution. War in Africa, "a practicum for the disciplinary education received in schools and fascist mass organizations," was to grant these young men the aura of fellowship experienced by their older *camerati*. It would also prepare them for total war.[50] Just as the *Decennale* had celebrated the beginning of a new age and called for a new form of culture that could write 1932, so too did the empire aspire to reform Italian culture. In November 1936 the journal *Riforma* was published along these lines. In the first issue we find an article, previously published in *Critica fascista* on 15 November 1935, titled "*Guerra fascista*." Here Bottai wrote that the empire had formally signified the end of the march *on* Rome and the beginning of the march *from* Rome,[51] while presenting a new prospective that needed to be reconciled within a larger European context. In abridged form, these were the circumstances (the massacres of the Spanish Civil War; the desperate poverty assailing the peasant now forced to become a soldier) in which Elio Vittorini began to write *Conversazione in Sicilia.*

The first instalment of the novel appeared in *Letteratura* (*Solaria*'s successor) between April 1938 and April 1939. The volume (textually almost identical to the version published in *Letteratura*) was first published in 1941 by Parenti (*Solaria*'s publisher). In *Conversazione* the protagonist, Silvestro, returns to his native Sicily after fifteen years to visit his mother. Along the way he meets a series of individuals with whom he engages in conversations. These characters offer us insight into the world of those "offended" – those who have been wronged by society. In part four, Silvestro encounters Calogero, a knife grinder who laments the absence of knives and scissors to be sharpened. Silvestro gives him his penknife, and Calogero attempts to overcharge him for his services. Read symbolically, Calogero laments the absence of a true revolutionary spirit (no knives to sharpen!), but although he is a cheerful worker he is still attached to bourgeois concerns. Calogero, the knife grinder with no knives to grind, symbolizes the incomplete Marxist. He introduces Silvestro to Ezechiele, a saddler, who explains that there is much injustice in the world but no one does anything about it – and neither does he. Ezechiele represents the disengaged intellectual living in an ivory tower. The three then move on to visit a cloth seller named Porfirio who refuses Calogero's knives and scissors and speaks of *acqua viva*, living water capable of washing away the world's sins. Porfirio is the voice of Christianity. The four continue to Colombo's tavern and inebriate themselves with wine and song, all except Silvestro.

In part five Silvestro encounters the ghost of his dead brother Liborio, a young man who enlisted "to see the world" and make a name for himself (and acquire, naturally, the aura of the soldier in battle). Liborio tells Silvestro that every night he witnesses in a dream a spectacle involving kings and their adversaries, the victorious and the defeated, or simply the protagonists of history. Although Vittorini does not include the representation, we do know that it is a historical one in that the protagonists are compelled to recreate forever the aura of those glorious actions. When Silvestro and Liborio first meet, Silvestro asks him if he is content. Liborio replies that he is miserable, especially since he lies dead in a field. It is a horrible ordeal for Liborio. We conclude that Liborio, dead in a field of blood and snow, is a victim of the Spanish Civil War. Liborio's disapproval is a linguistic abstract – *Ehm!* – so we are invited to read these final pages figuratively. Liborio's testimony denies the rhetoric of youthfulness, the *giovinezza* considered in the first two chapters of this book. He tells Silvestro that he weeps and suffers, a condemnation of the fascist glorification of the aura of war. Silvestro awakens from this dream and continues his conversation with his mother. News arrives of Liborio's death. The scene denounces the manner in which these young men are venerated in the annals of history for their sacrifice.

Vittorini condemns fascist demographic propaganda. Such propaganda insisted on the soldier-bearing function attributed to "fortunate mothers." Monuments celebrated these figures. And so, it is only fitting that at the end of *Conversazione in Sicilia*, the characters come together in front of the bronze monument of a woman. She is the mother of Italy. There, in a final act, the protagonist Silvestro experiences an epiphany by speaking up and pronouncing his word, *Ehm!*, just as the soldier Liborio had. A radicalized fascist revolution would have its heroes at all cost. The final act is to be read as a condemnation of fascist aesthetics, monumentality, and imperial triumphalism, those same intentions and aspirations exhibited and critically assessed in 1932.

Conclusion:
Illusion, the Highest Degree of Sacredness

But certainly for the present age, which prefers the sign to the thing signified, the copy to the original, representation to reality, the appearance to the essence … *illusion* only is sacred, *truth* profane. Nay, sacredness is held to be enhanced in proportion as truth decreases and illusion increases, so that the highest degree of illusion comes to be the highest degree of sacredness.

Ludwig Feuerbach[1]

This book has examined how the fascist regime and its cultural critics framed historical representation for concrete ideological and political purposes at the time of the *Decennale*. I have interpreted the *Decennale* as a collective representation situated halfway between the consensus years. The chapters of this book have looked "from a distance" at the literature, articles, speeches, documentaries, films, textbooks, and the 1932 Exhibition of the Fascist Revolution. I have considered the staging of the *Decennale* from "above" and from "below." I have analysed implicit and explicit response to the *Decennale* from the anti-fascists. As Guy Debord wrote, "All that was once directly lived [had] become mere representation."[2]

Representation encourages critical analysis and scepticism. A century and a half earlier, the political thinker Edmund Burke recorded his observations on the storming of the Bastille in a letter written to Lord Charlemont on 9 August 1789:

As to us here our thoughts of every thing at home are suspended, by our astonishment at the wonderful Spectacle which is exhibited in a Neighbouring and rival Country – what Spectactors, and what actors! England

gazing with astonishment at a French struggle for Liberty and not knowing whether to blame or to applaud! The thing indeed, though I thought I
saw something like it in progress for several years, has still something in it
paradoxical and Mysterious. The spirit it is impossible not to admire; but
the old Parisian ferocity has broken out in a shocking manner. It is true,
that this may be no more than a sudden explosion: If so no indication can
be taken from it. But if it should be character rather than accident, then
that people are not fit for Liberty, and must have a Strong hand like that of
their former masters to coerce them. Men must have a certain fund of natural moderation to qualify them for freedom, else it becomes noxious to
themselves, and a perfect nuisance to every body else. What will be the
event, it is hard still to say … In the meantime, the progress of the whole
affair is one of the most curious that was ever exhibited.[3]

There is much to learn from representations of the past. In our case
three generations of fascists were asked to participate in a spectacular
collective representation: the Great War generation that marched *on*
Rome, the generation of 1932 intent on marching *from* Rome, and finally,
the children born into the fascist regime. The *Decennale* presented an
ideal, unique, historically determinant opportunity for the fascist regime to radicalize itself. If we recall Emile Durkheim, "radicalization"
implies "long duration" and the creation of a state of "permanent revolution" linked to the aesthetic of an idealized, mythic past that looks
towards the future. What was once "implied as belonging to a pro-
found change in the religious and moral constitution of the individual"
(thanks to the March on Rome) was now able to "become an element of
this constitution" by means of a collective rite. This ceremony would
also have another consequence: "a transmission which at first was the
consequence of a rite" would be considered as "operating automatical-
ly from the nature of things and without the intervention of any human will."[4] Simply being present (*Presente!*) within the climate of the
Decennale would suffice. The *Decennale* was an experience "animated by
a common passion" meant to impart certain "acts and sentiments" that
would normally be impossible for the masses to achieve on their own.
The language, gestures, literature, and very force of the *Decennale* were
supposed to "shock" the collective and impose a new reality.[5] A "deity"
was celebrated as a "great god." It was a decisive moment in the history
of the cult of the *Duce*, as his name was "passed from one language to
another." The *fascio* was internationalized during this collective representation. The term "fascism" was defined for the first time.

Durkheim's theory of the social origins of religion drew attention from scholars such as Emilio Gentile. In this book I have analysed the *Decennale* within the theoretical frame of a political religion, for "political philosophy is the indispensable handmaid of theology."[6] I have focused on the rituals, myths, beliefs, and nationalist credo, and studied the religious dimension of fascism and the sacralization of politics as well as the role of technology, myth, and noble lies.

Political, religious, cultural, economic, and aesthetic ideologies function as normative forces that govern social relationships, aspire to be the truth, and are intimately linked to political realism. Public and private forms of worship arise from these. Spectacle, rituals, and literature, all manifestations of culture, react to ideology. These elaborate a comprehensive vision of the world and are particularly appreciated in times of crisis.

Roger Griffin's definition of fascism, a form of "palingenetic ultranationalism" has been especially appropriate in the context of this study. In an article published at the time of the *Decennale*, Mussolini wrote that all of Europe had entered a new phase.[7] The ideology of the previous century had collapsed, and no one was left to defend it. In 1932 new protagonists were needed. It was not a coincidence that party membership became available on 28 October 1932, a decision transforming the *Partito Nazionale Fascista* from an employment agency into a highly structured mass party.[8] The *Decennale*'s renewal was to be led by a new generation of fascists (neophytes) belonging to every class. The celebratory platform created an opportunity for three generations of fascists to participate in the liturgy of the state. The last group (date of birth, 1925–6) would become the protagonists of the civil war that ensued following 8 September 1943.

In 1932 new ideas were also needed (the term "fascism" was defined in 1932). The *Decennale* was an opportunity to exhibit an ideological template capable of guiding this transition. It was a collective religious experience intent on disciplining the nation (through compulsory party membership) and increasing national unity (official state-issued textbooks were implemented just before the *Decennale*; manifestations also increased). In short, people and ideas were incorporated into the fellowship of the state.

The *Decennale* was a stage in the nation's "rite of passage" ceremony on the path to complete totalitarianism. In the first phase Italy was separated physically (through the violence of the fascist squads) and symbolically (the March on Rome) from a previous form of existence. A liminal stage followed: a period corresponding to the state's transition from movement to regime. This second phase was marked by a period of preparation and ambiguity. A fascist secular religion provided the guidelines. Many individuals accepted its precepts, but others did not. The state understood this and worked harder to evangelize (*evangelizzare = fascistizzare*) its most stubborn citizens. This act of forgiveness and subsequent incorporation into fascist society after a period of internment and convalescence (note the biological metaphor) belonged to the third stage of the nation's rite of passage. It also involved a process of reintegration: a pardon was issued by the *Duce* at the time of the *Decennale*. Those who had once sinned were now able to read the sacred scripture, receive the Eucharist of the state, and become incorporated into the community. A collective prayer marked the moment of regeneration and rebirth. This was the *Decennale*. This book has studied aspects of this collective representation from a distance.

Anniversaries celebrating revolutionary events are collective celebrations. They recreate the aura of an original event, albeit from a safe temporal distance. These are inauthentic recreations of an event, and they lack originality. At times the original liturgical event is a staged deception. Just weeks before the March on Rome, Benito Mussolini famously stated: "A military march on Rome? A coup d'état? Preparatory organizations? Who has ever dreamed of these sorts of fantasies? It's true, very true that we talked about and are talking about a march on Rome but it's a march – even the profane should understand it – that's all spiritual and legal I'd like to say."[9] The March on Rome was therefore an illusion constructed on a mythical platform, a noble lie transformed into an aesthetic and conferred legal status. A common denominator is present, a "modern political spirit" that considers the state "as the outcome of reflection and calculation … as a work of art."[10]

The revolutionary status of the fascist revolution has been under scrutiny in the past. The revolution marked the beginning of a new age, and these circumstances served the fascists well. Mussolini was particularly set on acquiring power and, most importantly, creating a narrative. As Denis Mack Smith points out, the fascist squads were composed of 30,000 rather than 300,000 men, and twenty-four hours after Mussolini was asked to form a government on 29 October 1922 photographers were awaiting the arrival of these fascists marching on Rome (after General Pugliese allowed them through).[11] Mussolini then ordered his *squadristi* to destroy the printing presses of the opposition's newspapers and created his own reality: the myth of a civil war and

3,000 martyrs. The markets responded positively. Florists ran out of flowers. Authentic, original, historically spontaneous celebrations (for now) occurred. The fascists then organized the state according to their own intentions.

The *Decennale* was meant to "shock" the collective and impose a new reality.[12] Those who identified with fascism but belonged to other "clans" (representatives of fascist parties from abroad) partook in the celebrations. A "deity" was indicated as a sort of "great god." It was a decisive moment in the history of the cult of the *Duce*. The *fascio*, Durkheim's "totem," was internationalized during this collective representation, and ideas were consecrated. Universal fascism was also celebrated. The part was affected by the whole, like produced like, fellowships were formed, rites and collective recreations occurred, and the individual was annulled within the collective. The *Decennale* satisfied the people's "desire for a public identity."[13]

Rituals on both the macro and micro level celebrated these intentions. New protagonists and new ideas were consecrated, defined, and exhibited; an ideological manifesto set forth the strategy to be employed. Those who doubted, like the doubting Thomas of the Gospel, would see and finally comprehend. The *Decennale* was meant to write its own narrative, a new Book of Revelation.[14] The time was ideal. Crises dominated reality, thanks to a serious economic crisis sparked by a market crash and the subsequent weakening, in the eyes of the collective, of liberal democratic markets and parliamentary politics.[15] Similar circumstances appeared in 1932–3, a year that would eventually mark the height of the economic crisis. Stalinist Russia was celebrating the completion in 1932 (one year ahead) of the second five-year plan. In 1933 Hitler came to power on anti-communist fears (Boxheim papers).[16] Such circumstances allowed savvy *condottieri* to reformalize a mythic past in the present, take advantage of the general state of crisis, impose themselves in the political arena, and focus exclusively on the ideological. The results are clear to us today. The climate of the *Decennale* set out to revive the dynamism of the original March on Rome and transfer this energy into a new March *from* Rome. For example, the Ethiopian campaign (secret preparations would begin in 1933–4) was meant to redeem the *disfatta* (defeat) of Adwa in 1896 and was the result of specific normative measures meant to both enforce consensus and bring new blood into the movement. If we refer again to Paxton, these measures were meant to maintain the "fascist" element within the revolution, as opposed to the simply "authoritarian" element (as eventually happened in Spain, for example). The *Decennale* created the conditions for the state to exhibit the "permanent revolution" as an aesthetic, a lifestyle, linked to the events of 1922. In the case of Italian fascism, long-term radicalization would eventually be destabilizing and transform itself into a new aesthetic: the destruction of the nation from within.

Memory is constantly revised to conform to a specific identity project. The fascist aesthetic contained elements of modernity and the past, and so the inclusion of certain episodes along with the exclusion of others was meant to provide vigour to the permanent revolution the *Duce* was advocating.[17] This book has considered the Italian cultural sphere in 1932, a unit of time clearly defined by a celebratory event, the tenth anniversary of the March on Rome, as a system. We have mapped out specific discursive networks via an interdisciplinary approach and have focused on the year as a subject of analysis. The approach can be considered synchronic. It has examined distinct themes particular to this year in each chapter. It has discussed various forms of cultural manifestations and specific historical reality. In other words, how did various media engage with reality, deconstruct previously maintained meanings, and create or reconstruct new forms of meaning and new realities? In what way did the material engage with power and the dominant ideology to present a renewed reality? This approach is not necessarily limited to the written word. Discourse networks take into account discourse created by technology. This approach considers a discourse network as having the qualities of a technology in that, by the very nature of its existence and "exteriority," it creates a framework that, in turn, creates meaning. In times of crisis, groups huddle together. Networks are created and enhanced, and loyalties conflict with each other. These conclusions are particularly appropriate when applied to a critical reading of the climate of the *Decennale* in the concluding chapter of this book.

The study of one year has proven effective in the past. In an interdisciplinary study on expressionism titled *1910*, Thomas Harrison begins with a citation from the German expressionist poet Gottfried Benn: "1910, that is indeed the year when all scaffolds began to crack."[18] It's a relevant quote, when considered within the context of Harrison's study, in that his study considers the year as a moment of transition. Further questions are derived from this initial statement. Was the crisis specific to that year? Did it originate in the past? Did it look towards the future? Was it an expression of the fears of the present? Who were the protagonists of 1910? Was it a year in which an important literary work was published? Did the year represent the advent of a new age? A new aesthetic? Was it a year which inaugurated a new forum for cultural expression? Can some sort of "resurgence" be revealed meant to "liberate the human spirit from the pressures of material reality"? Did it represent a moment of decadence? Were the revelations of the year "meant to be read as warnings" or as "a call to arms"? Are wars staged in the private and the public sphere? These are some preliminary general questions that Harrison asks himself – ideal questions – when considering such a case study.

The *Decennale* presented itself as a platform on which fascism could exhibit and define the permanent revolution it was intent on creating. In contrast to other studies that take a broad approach towards the study of fascism, this book focuses on one specific year. Fascist ideology was never a constant, just as the interpretation that the regime had of 1922, with all its consequences, was never a constant.[19] Therefore, less is more.[20] This study has considered ritual, rhetoric, and spectacle, has engaged these elements in a conversation with ideas, and, most importantly, has avoided conceiving fascist intellectual or discursive content as a sort of complete ideology or theory univocally opposed to practice. Several considerations have been made. The fascist movement of 1922 did not entirely reflect the ideology, aspirations, and intentions of the fascist regime in 1932. In what way was the idea of youth different in 1932 from that of 1922? How did ritual engage with the aspirations of the fascist regime in 1932? How was rhetoric and spectacle related to the reality of 1932? In what fashion did the aesthetics of power differ in 1932? In these concluding remarks it is useful to recall Hans Ulrich Gumbrecht's study of the year 1926.[21] Gumbrecht does not provide a theoretical foundation for his analysis of the year but rather considers certain categories such as action versus impotence, authenticity versus artificiality, centre versus periphery, immanence versus transcendence, individuality versus collectivity, male versus female, present versus past, silence versus noise, sobriety versus exuberance, and uncertainty versus reality. In short, both works have proven extremely useful for a study of this sort.

This book (and especially the first three chapters) has examined the regime's intentions in reconsidering, refining, and exhibiting new people and new ideas on a renewed platform: the *Decennale*. Once I have looked at these elements and drawn the necessary conclusions, *then* I have presented appropriate dualisms: reason versus myth, collectivism versus individualism, fascist spiritual realism versus realism, and so forth. The fourth chapter of this book has focused on elements of implicit and explicit dissent in literature with psychological, social, or political overtones. It was not intended to be a postmodern reading of a little-known (at the time) literary review (*Solaria* never surpassed six to seven hundred copies). Rather, the chapter has considered the journal as a laboratory of sorts contributing to the transition from the *prosa d'arte* and *calligrafismo* typical of *La Ronda* (art for art's sake) to the modern neorealistic, politically engaged, and committed post-war novel. This book has aspired to exhibit its own main ideas: rationalism, humanism, a new relationship to be formed between the individual and the state, political commitment, cosmopolitanism, and a dialogue with Europe. The climate of the *Decennale* influenced a rethinking of ideas. This book has presented these conclusions and considered the protagonists and the literature belonging to the journal *Solaria*. The economic depression of the late 1920s, the poverty that ensued, the *Duce's* triumphant speeches, and the *Decennale*: these issues and events affected both fascist culture and the opposition.[22]

Avant-garde realism and radical culture emerged from the Soviet Union in the 1920s. In Italy technology was improving, and the futurists painted it. As a side note, the *Rex* episode in *Amarcord* was also considered in these pages. Romeo Bevilacqua celebrated the motorcyclist (recall *Amarcord* again) on glazed ceramic. Alessandro Bruschetti synthesized those years in a series titled *Sintesi fascista* (1935). Giacomo Balla glorified the new man, exemplified by Italo Balbo, in *Balbo and the Italian Transatlantic Flyers (Celestial Metallic Airplane)* in 1931. In Paris the literary scene renewed itself. Walter Benjamin wrote about it all.

Howard Eiland and Michael W. Jennings have recently presented a critical study of Walter Benjamin titled *Walter Benjamin: A Critical Life*.[23] Benjamin studied the scene that presented itself in the 1920s: popular culture (high and low), excluded groups, fashion, media, film, technology, and urban commodity capitalism. His writing was on the border: fiction, memoir, analysis, *Denkbild* (figures of thought), experience, historical remembrance, and art. Benjamin was a keen witness to European modernity. He contrasted the rituals of tradition and those of modernity. In order to draw relevant conclusions in these final pages a return to Benjamin's origins and biography is required. Walter Benjamin was born in 1892 into an "assimilated, secularized, wealthy, bourgeois German Jewish family."[24] The sounds of the ghetto would be replaced by the technology of the modern city, and a "reconfiguration of temporality and displacement as a result of technological transformations would later be joined by a more personal displacement, less the modern temporality, and more the tangible reality of flight as he [was] forced into exile with the rise of National Socialism."[25] It is likewise important to study the "complexities involved in the emancipation of the German-Jews from the ghetto," the "direct result of the absorption of enlightenment philosophy into European culture," and to look at the outcome of this emancipation: "[their] integration into European society and more secular studies." According to George Mosse, "this somewhat lopsided dialogue (German-Jews alone had to define themselves) was the desire to find a personal identity that superseded religion and nation."[26] Benjamin also met a young philosopher named Leo Strauss. Strauss was associated with the Jewish Academy (*Akademie fur die Wissenschaft des Judentums*) in Berlin, where he had just completed a book on Baruch Spinoza. Leo Strauss described the secular versus sacred dilemma as one that had emerged long ago in Spinoza's work. Benjamin's modern interpreters write that "the difference between enlightenment progress or the return to traditional values, on Strauss's reading, is essentially the difference between the secular and the sacred, between the rejection of prejudice and superstition, 'barbarism, stupidity, rudeness and extreme scarcity,' a rejection of the suffering embedded in a recollection of the past, in favour of future perfection produced not by God but by human endeavour, and repentance, return, redemption and restoration, that is a return to the beginning, to the perfection of 'old time.'"[27]

Benjamin completed his essay "Goethe's Elective Affinities" between December 1921 and February 1922. It is an important essay on the role of myth. The relationship between myth and truth is one of "mutual exclusion," and although Benjamin recognized myth as "a form of knowledge" he was to "recognize myth itself as the form in which the capitalist world presents itself to perception – as natural, as the only possible world." The task of criticism is the "differentiation of truth from myth, or rather the purging and clarification of the mythic element so as to intimate the true."[28] This book has been deeply influenced by the spirit of this statement.

In the period 1935–9 Benjamin refined one of his many ideas on modernity. An essay, "The Work of Art," was written. The process had its inception between May 1935 and February 1936. In June he participated in the International Congress for the Defense of Culture in Paris. Malraux also attended.[29] A notable outcome of the conference (the initial impetus had come from the Comintern in Soviet Russia): Stalinism was considered to be the only form of humanism capable of standing up and resisting the rise of fascism in Europe. The Paris congress also advanced an anti-fascist aesthetic. Fascism was taking Europe back to the Middle Ages, to myth and superstition. Communism represented the future.

Benjamin at the time was working on a new area of aesthetics: a "programmatic" piece. In the early 1930s he had written "Little History of Photography" (1931, an essay that examined "reproduction technology on the composition and reception of artworks"). The focus of the essay was the "fate" of art in the nineteenth century from the perspective of the present. These ideas influenced his aesthetic program. Benjamin mentioned the essay "The Work of Art" in a letter (9 October 1931) to Gretel Karplus. I'd like to present an excerpt from the letter, included in *A Critical Life*, edited by Howard Eiland and Michael Jennings:

> In these last weeks, I have come to recognize that hidden structural character of today's art – of the situation of today's art – which makes it possible to recognize what for us is decisive, but only now taking effect, in the "fate" of art in the nineteenth century. In this regard, I have realized my epistemological theory – which is crystalized around the esoteric concept of the "now of recognizability" (a concept that, very probably, I haven't shared even with you) – in a decisive example. I have found that aspect of nineteenth century art which only "now" is recognizable, as it never was before and never will be afterward.[30]

Eiland and Jennings then go on to explain that capitalism has destroyed the conditions necessary for an adequate human experience. Thus, *technik* – technology – was to be viewed as both a cause of impoverishment and its remedy.[31] Modern technology anaesthetizes human sensory capacities. At the same time technology liberates humans. Film can be reproduced. Film is a reproducible work of art and can shake the foundations of a cultural tradition on which the hegemonic class has depended for centuries to maintain its control. Film also causes change in the structure of the human sensory apparatus.[32]

In chapter one I surveyed the debate concerning the new generation of fascists. I looked at how the regime transposed the rhetoric of youth from the pages of literature to an exhibition. The identity and youth issue had not been specific to 1932. For Walter Benjamin school reform meant not just reform in the transmission of values, but educational reform going beyond the institutional framework. This kind of reform would concern a whole way of thinking.[33] Awakening youth was an idea common to nineteenth century German thought (Schlegel, Novalis, Nietzsche). Meaningful institutional change could take place only in the wake of cultural transformation. Youth was on the front line of this struggle for a "new humanity" and for a "radical new seeing." It would have to begin with education.[34]

We have read that in fascist Italy the debate on youth had begun with a 1928 editorial written by Camillo Pellizzi ("*Un regime di giovani*") in *Critica fascista*. The economic crisis of 1929 added further vigour to the conversation. In March 1932 *Il Saggiatore* invited its readers to an inquiry on the nation's youth. The debate on Italy's youth and engagement was also considered by other prominent journals such as *Vent'anni*, *Gioventù fascista*, *Camminare*, *Orpheus*, and *L'Universale*. *Il Saggiatore* published a series of fifty-seven essays between August and October 1932. The debate also made it to the pages of the populist *Il Selvaggio*. The identity issue espoused notions regarding collectivism and represented a new moment in the history of the fascist movement, one in which the individual's life affirmed itself in unity with the collective and the corporative state. If we refer again to a report issued by Carlo Scorza, the *Duce* necessitated an "armed religious formation ... capable of predicting the Leader's will even before he expresses it." Scorza advised the *Duce* that a myth-based illusion was needed, for "[i]n every age young Italians ... have had a flag, a belief, a myth."[35] In 1943 Scorza was called upon, once again, to "revitalize" the party. This time, Bosworth points out, Scorza concluded that "the most powerful weapon" that Italy possessed was "the figure, the thought, the person, the action of the *DUCE*."[36] The myth of the sacrifice of the first generation (the martyrs of the revolution and the Great War) had made way for the cult of the *Duce*, but in the end it still didn't work. If we return to Grandi's diary, it is a matter of record that fascism had become synonymous with the *Duce*. And the *Duce* was a man who lived his life as a work of art. Commenting on this point, Grandi wrote:

> You cannot play the dictator outside of your country. Unless you go to war ... In three years Mussolini never told me what was and what is his plan, his line, his command of foreign policy. Maybe he does not have a plan.
>
> He does not know, does not care, does not understand the difficult art of negotiation. He considers all negotiators as *furbi* – "clever" and nothing else. Mussolini is the decider. It is up to others to accept. In the same

way he often accepts what others decide. It's black and white. He does not know the difficult art of the market and of contract negotiations. He cannot know it. He is a Chief. In other words, a great Poet. But the country, next to a Chief, needs a good administrator capable of dealing with the affairs of the nation. Mussolini also considers the whole world, international affairs, etc., etc., an extension of himself. He is at the centre. Everything starts or comes to him or by him. No, the world is different. The proportions, the roads are different. It may be that direct contact with diplomatic affairs may give him a sense of reality, big and small – that reality of everyday life, the life of men. The life of a man and of a people without poetry is not life. But life is not made up only of poetry.[37]

Ideology cannot *be* foreign policy. In chapter two I investigated textbooks at the time of the *Decennale*: the pages presented the *Duce* as a cult figure, and they underscored the omnipresence of the *Duce* in both the private and the public spheres. These books introduced students to a new language. The pedagogy of *exempla* present in these *libri-unici* was clarified through didactic images and text. The short stories in the textbooks distilled a political agenda that was in tune with the exhibition value attributed to the new generation. These fascist textbooks celebrated the beginning of a new age, and in the chapter I considered nation-building and didactic materials made available in 1932. The textbooks analysed representations of the *Duce*, the myth of the March on Rome, and also rural life in fascist Italy, the *Risorgimento*, and the Great War within the context of the *Decennale*. In 1932 the regime sought to confer the aura of the revolution onto those members of the youth generation too young to appreciate macro-liturgies such as the *Mostra della Rivoluzione Fascista*. Rituals of initiation were also present on a micro-political level for neophytes born into the regime who had never experienced liberal parliamentary democracy. The classroom setting proved ideal. It was there that ideas were consecrated according to the precepts of sacred texts, a "great God" – the *Duce* – was introduced, and these children were initiated into fascist society. It was an experience that an entire generation clearly remembers to this day. The "aspirations and intentions" of the regime also need to be studied as part of the totalitarian method.[38] The words "aspirations and intentions" are indeed appropriate here, since the regime did not have the means to satisfy the demand for these textbooks. The responsibility was, instead, given to private publishing houses. These institutions were allowed a considerable amount of freedom in their editorial decisions. In short, the *libro-unico* genre was not exactly a success in assisting to realize the ambitions of the totalitarian regime.

In 1976 Luigi Meneghello published *Fiori Italiani*. The book begins with a question: *Che cos'è un'educazione?* What is an education? Luigi Meneghello first considered the issue in 1944 while hiding from the Nazi fascists as a member of the Resistance. There, selflessly assisted by peasants in the Valsugana Valley of the Trentino region, Meneghello questioned his own education as a young man coming of age within the fascist state. What evolved was a raising of consciousness, contrasting the simplicity and clarity of actually being "in action" with the artificially construed reality of ritual imposed by the regime. These pages have elaborated on the connection between the theory present in elementary school textbooks and the collective state that the fascists were intent on creating. Many truly believed in the idea such as, for example, a young man named Cesare Bolognesi.

In *Fiori Italiani* Meneghello remembers (I paraphrase his text here) Cesare, an adolescent originally from the Emilia-Romagna region. Cesare grew up in Schio. He arrived there around the age of twelve and thus spoke with a *schiota* r. He spoke Italian (as opposed to dialect) even at home. Meneghello writes: "'He was one of those creatures that the day that you discover them give to life a sense of great purity and beauty,' says M. Valgimigli in a letter dated January 1942." Meneghello continues: "We all felt that way. One had the sense of a privileged personality, something rare, lively and innocent, a fragile force that did not seem of this world … Being young seemed (I realize now) an adventure of supreme beauty: and being born Italian, and thus heirs of Rome." Cesare had cultivated a naive passion for historical research. In the personal history of his writings the theme of ritual sacrifice is well perceptible, but not in the sense that commemorations would have it. There is no "rise" or maturation. On the contrary. There is disruption, trauma, and tragedy. A real war had arrived and with it the sudden sense of having lived up to now among scenarios made up of words and cardboard. He wanted to justify the fascist war to himself with the cultural means that his education had given him … It was the myth of youth that was exploding in his hands.[39]

Cesare embodied the permanent revolution that the fascist regime aspired to maintain. Indeed, Cesare possessed a certain aura or transcendence that gave life meaning for those who experienced his presence. On 1 December 1941 Cesare was killed in battle at Sidi Rezegh, preferring death to the destruction of his own self (by becoming an anti-fascist). He had volunteered for the Libyan front, just as Mario Carli's hero Lucio had.[40] Cesare was the product of the collective state's educational program: an experiment that aspired to unite classroom instruction with the militarized nation at large. In September 1943, seventeen-year-old Franco Aschieri abandoned the classroom to enlist in the DECIMA MAS, an elite commando unit, which was part of the *Republica Social Italiana*. The DECIMA MAS deployed Aschieri behind enemy lines as a spy, where he was captured and executed on 30 April 1944 at Santa Maria Capua Vetere. Born in 1926, Aschieri belonged to the first generation of fascists born into the regime and indoctrinated with the state's textbooks, as he had most likely enrolled in elementary school in either 1931 or 1932.

The 10th Flotilla MAS is an exceptional case study in our final conclusion. Did the fascist educational system work? Was the indoctrination of the new generation of fascists – those that entered the school system at the time of the *Decennale* – effective? How did these men and women engage with the reality of war? Did the aura of the fascist revolution survive after the war? In what manner did the Borghese myth survive after the war?

In brief we can answer these questions thanks to declassified CIA files (readily available online since 2005).[41] The origins of the DECIMA MAS can be found in the *Arditi* (Shocktroops) of the Great War. The DECIMA was led by the "ambitious and ... able and energetic commander Prince Junio Valerio Borghese."[42]

Following 8 September 1943 soldiers who belonged to the 10th Flotilla MAS were sent on indefinite leave. In a dramatic move Borghese approached German authorities. Terms were stipulated, and an agreement was reached: The DECIMA would still exist and fight the Allies. It was to be free of any interference from the Germans. Personnel would not be sent to Germany for training. Granted these conditions, Borghese declared that he was willing to fight to redeem Italian honour. He met Admiral Doenitz in Berlin in October 1943. An agreement was stipulated. Some changes did occur. For example, the elite San Marco Regiment would constitute the land forces of the DECIMA and deal with sabotage, land operations, and anti-partisan activity. The situation was not always honourable. For example, in another declassified report written on 11 May 1944,[43] prisoner of war Freschi summed up the situation at La Spezia: "we have no food, no clothing, no supplies and no confidence." The report continues: "Freschi himself appears to have remained with the Flotilla owing to motives of misguided patriotism and personal dissatisfaction ... [W]hen asked, he said he had no scruples about throwing in his lot with the Germans, since he felt the King had let his country down, and his conscience would not let him fight the Germans after being Allies with them for so long. He added that, if released, he would go straight back to serve in the MAS again." Another prisoner of war, Garracione, presented a different story. Garracione had been given a choice: serve in the Italian Republican Navy or be sent off to a concentration camp in Germany. Garracione was "very much more cheerful and light-hearted than Freschi, whose recital was frequently punctuated by floods of weeping." Excerpts from the report read as follows: "internecine squabbling ... morale of the officers is definitively low as they know they are fighting for a lost cause ... ninety per cent of them had no choice, the remaining ten percent are hotheads (*esaltati*)." For prisoner of war Freschi, Mussolini still exists as a "force," but "he is never seen" and his "influence is taken for granted."

At the end of the war Borghese spent three years (the sentence called for twelve) in prison for collaborating with Nazi Germany. Shunned and isolated by the rest of Roman nobility, he was approached when agrarian reform laws were being considered by the Italian government. The landowners were headed by Prince Torlonia. The declassified documents likewise describe this personal moment. Borghese, "disgusted by this opportunism, did not accept their proposals and, in fact, has never re-established his former relationship with the Roman nobility, but has adopted instead a kind of splendid isolation."[44] A report issued on 10 July 1963 confirmed that "[Borghese] has led a politically insignificant life."[45] On 26 January 1970 Borghese was present at the American Embassy talking about his assessment of the political situation, his political movement, the *Fronte Nazionale* (National Front), and the Italian political system in general. It marked a turning point for the "Dark Prince." According to the report (not classified; for limited official use) titled "Italy 1969," Borghese stated: "[T]he public is utterly fed up with the government and party system, which is corrupt, inefficient and self-serving. They do not care about Lenin or Duce, or any other politician. Furthermore, the country is very rapidly sliding towards Communist control. The PCI now influences public policy to a considerable degree; in a short time it will be in absolute control."[46] Pages later we read: "The thought of a United Europe is no longer a source of hope. The massive entry of Communist and Socialist exponents into the political and economic structures of the building still under construction is not at all reassuring. There is a strong suspect … that the Reds want to partake in the said organizations only with a view to sabotage them." The report concludes that Italians are "getting deadly tired under the pressure of a heavy political situation, and begin to see no way out of the present tangle, unless the whole system is changed by some drastic means … a revolution, a civil war, a Communist coup de main in Parliament, or a military coup d'état … The dilemma now before the U.S. government is the following: either to abstain from every intervention, and leave Italy to slide inexorably into the Red Area; or to come to the rescue before it is too late, and sponsor the said concentration of Nationalist Forces, in a very efficient way." On 19 February 1971 the National Front was described as an "ineffectual right wing organization accused of planning a coup d'etat." The report continues: "The National Front (*Fronte Nazionale –* FN) is a right wing organization which bands together a limited number of members most of whom come from veteran and armed forces associations. Purpose … is to prevent the 'national drift to the left,' if necessary through a coup d'etat … The FN is the creature of former fascist Italian Social Republic (RSI) notable Junio Valerio Borghese … [W]ith its restricted following and limited financial resources and the comic opera stature of its leader, [the FN] lacks the potential to plan and carry though a coup."[47]

Further on, the report notes the FN's "alleged ability … and the presumed prestige of Borghese" but points out that "fantastic coup plans were discussed" in the FN meetings, giving them "comic opera aspects." According to the report, "the plotters' final session took place in a Rome restaurant where, flushed with the effect of wine, the conspirators closed the doors and windows and sang the fascist national hymn '*Giovinezza.*'"

These "comic opera" aspects were likewise noted during President Nixon's last visit to Italy. Borghese met with the presidential entourage and pointed out that a coup d'etat could provide the only solution. When he asked for US support, the US politicials are alleged to have replied, "Get moving, and once you have taken over the country, we will support you." Borghese's friends' comment on this story is that the Americans did not take Borghese seriously, and their reply was strictly a diplomatic one.[48]

An interview with James Angleton, director of the Office of Strategic Services (OSS) in Italy during the war and former head of CIA counterespionage, is also thought provoking. Angleton confirmed that hundreds of Italian prisoners of war had been recruited by the Soviet secret service to "lie low … until they had reached levels of prominence in the government." The story of Borghese's kidnapping by the OSS was, according to Angleton, true. Indeed, the OSS had contacted a certain Commander Marceglia, a member of the DECIMA who had just returned to Italy after a brief stay in a British prisoner camp in India. In February 1945 Marceglia presented Borghese with an offer: if he agreed to cooperate with the allies … he would be saved from the partisans who planned to gun him down in the streets of Milan and duly tried by his peers. Prince Borghese agreed.[49]

Young women also belonged to the autonomous women's section in the DECIMA. They certainly looked like soldiers, but in practice they had to resign themselves to support roles. The *Servizio Ausiliare Femminile* (Female Auxiliary Service) had 4,412 members. Some women participated in the rounding-up and torture of partisans. A few belonged to the infamous *Banda Koch*.

Anna Lisa Carlotti's anthology *Italia 1939–1945: Storia e memoria* mentions various case studies of those young women who adhered to the Italian Social Republic. Honour, loyalty, and betrayal are the most recurrent themes. Some joined the *Gruppi Fascisti Repubblicani Femminili* (GFRF – Fascist Republican Women's Groups), officially founded on 18 December 1943. Other young women enrolled in the *Servizio Ausiliario Femminile*, instituted on 18 April 1944, and defended the Republic of Salò. Fiamma Morini recalls the moment. She remembers why she continued to fight with the fascists:

> It was a strong desire to participate more in the war. I had seen in the immediate rear lines some auxiliary women fighters. For example, there were auxiliary women fighters with the "Lupo" who tended the wounded, were involved in the fighting, involved in what was the war. I already had a mother who had been a Red Cross nurse and therefore had treated the wounded … I wanted to do a little of what she had done, be more in contact with the fighters. Yet so far away from the front lines, it seemed that I wasn't doing enough. I wanted to do more; not that I wanted to pick up a gun and fight too, but I wanted to be closer to those who fought, those who suffered, who died … I would do anything, as long as I could be closer to those who fought. If I had been told, "You must die because you need to," I think I would not have pulled back. I was so convinced that I had to do something that would involve me completely, not only to a certain point. I have never been afraid of dying, much less of

suffering. Torture scared me, but death was not something that would bring me fear.[50]

Fiamma was born into a fascist family on March 1925 in Venice. Both of her parents had participated in the March on Rome. Fiamma's mother had volunteered as a nurse in the First World War. In this case the aura of the Great War had been projected onto the new generation: the indoctrination had worked.

In chapter three I studied the "writing" of the *Decennale*. The anniversary presented an ideal opportunity to define fascism in the pages of the most relevant and important literary and editorial "product" of the fascist period, the *Enciclopedia Italiana*. The document concluded by projecting fascism's future aspirations to build an empire. The *Decennale* also presented an official film titled *Camicia nera* that translated these ideas into images. *Camicia nera* projected a new truth onto spectators on a subconscious level. It recaptured selective moments of the past and legitimized them for the future. In the final image (the apotheosis of Mussolini), the *Duce* is projected as a new Caesar, leading the new generation as they march *from* Rome towards a new conquest. The regime's intentions in perfecting the totalitarian state were focused on militarizing the individual and, more importantly, annulling the individual within the reality of the collective state. Intellectuals were called upon to leave the ivory tower, participate in life, and study the new reality.[51] Intellectuals opposed to fascism viewed this strategy for cultural renewal and commitment as an opportunity to restore the dignity of the nation. Cultural renewal for them meant providing guidelines that reclaimed values such as equality, truth, and freedom and that inspired the new generation of intellectuals to elevate culture, within a European context, as a symbol and instrument of the formation of a new civilization. The intellectual was called upon to redefine himself as "committed": both parties (the hegemonic power and its opposition) were well aware of the opportunity.[52]

Not all were convinced that this renewal was possible. One issue at the centre of discourse in 1932 was the debate on literature and politics. A literary contest held by the journal *L'Italiano* was won by a peasant named Giuseppe Simone from Cassano delle Murge, Bari. The judges exalted the primitive and spontaneously generated verses of these new poets: poetic salvation, they wrote, could only be found in the ignorant, the *ignoranti effettivi*. At the same time, the contest honoured the verses of a young Mario Tobino. *L'Italiano* also published verses written in honour of Pascal D'Angelo, a virtually unknown Italian-American poet who had recently died in New York City. The *Duce*'s rhetoric at the time of the *Decennale* was naturally in tune with this project. In an editorial titled *"Ritorno alla terra"* ("Return to the Earth"), he explained:

> The true farmer detests those who want to stuff his head. It will be necessary therefore to celebrate the peasants in a serious way, in a way that is virile and such to make them proud of working the land.[53]

In times of crisis, ideology triumphs on both sides (the hegemonic power and the opposition), and social groups are reinforced. In this book I have argued that the rituals contributed towards a critical assessment of the reality of the *Decennale*. Those who chose to dissent often did so by collaborating within the confines of the regime. The result was implicit rather than explicit dissent as a reaction to a critical assessment of fascist aesthetics and the sacralization of its politics. The cultural studies approach has proven particularly effective when considering the ideological intentions of and resistance to fascism at specific periods. For example, in 1932 a young man named Mario Dogliero (a worker at Fiat) was encouraged by his supervisors to join the Fiat choir as a way of atoning for his anti-fascist relapses. His son Giovanni, born in 1922, tells the story:

> By chance, the Fiat choir had to go to Rome for a concert, right? And so my father's friends say to him: "Look … you'll see it's a good idea – this is his friend speaking – "Join the choir, come and sing and maybe" … because they saw that he was in for trouble for what he'd, that's why, it was at the height of the Fascist period, right? And, in fact, he joined the choir, and then they sent him to Rome. Listen, he had two months to learn the whole score for the Apostles Supper to sing in Rome … and then … ah, if I think about that! When Mario told this story! [Laughter] By the way, it was at the time they put on the Exhibition of the Revolution in Rome, you see; the Fascist one, when they showed you what happened to the Fascist martyrs, one thing and another, all the epic deeds, just as if it were now, let's say, from the Liberation to the present day, no? And then at the end there was something like … a sort of … let's say … a sort of Pantheon, there were all the names, weren't there? And then every time the lamp was lit that illuminated the name of a fallen Fascist, they played the anthem *Giovinezza* very softly and *Presente!*, *Presente!*, *Presente!*. Well, my father, who in the

meanwhile, was going round, it was then they had published all Mussolini's unpublished letters, well, he says that he stood there with his hands behind him – Is Mario still there? He tells them this even now when he goes to the club – and he went round like this and then a militiaman came up behind him and said, "What are you looking for?" And he replies in Piedmontese, "I'm looking." "But what for?" And he replies again in Piedmontese, "I'm looking." You see what's happening? So, in the end, this fellow got fed up … But Mario then says, "I'm looking for the salary he gets now." [Translator: Mussolini's salary] Then they start tailing him. You should hear him tell it! … "I got out of there with my hair standing on end" … It's really something to hear him telling the story. Mario still tells it now when he goes to the club: "I'm having a good look! I'm looking for something!"[54]

Giovanni's story, taken directly from Luisa Passerini's cultural studies–based book *Fascism in Popular Memory*, is, Passerini explains, a perfect example of Freud's "functioning wit," which brings together two different types of *materiale inedito* (unpublished material): Mussolini's letters and his salary. The lightness of his *motto* with which he exposes fascism as a sham is likewise particularly relevant. Mario joins the choir, hence giving in to the regime's intent on channelling dissent, but at the same time uses his Quixotesque wit to mock fascism's sacred space within a sacralized temporal space, the *Decennale*. The 1932 Exhibition of the Fascist Revolution, and in particular the last hall to be visited (Hall U), was meant to regenerate the minds and souls of the Italian people through song and religious choreography. It aspired to enforce a new reality looking back to the Great War and the March on Rome of 1922. Ever the materialist, Mario is capable of seeing through the pseudo-mythic nonsense exhibited and dissenting. In this instance the young man (a not-too-convinced *camerata*) was capable of critically assessing the regime's ideas: rhetoric/ideology of the past that was once constricted to the literary page and now exhibited as a modernist spectacle. In short, the collective representation of the *Decennale* provided an ideal platform upon which to regenerate, celebrate, exhibit, critically assess, and dissent.

This book also seeks to make a useful contribution to the reception of the *Decennale* by anti-fascists in Italy. The fact that fascism had been defined and new members were being initiated into the fellowship of fascist society also clarified what the anti-fascist movement was confronting. Several groups reacted: the most intransigent anti-fascists living abroad and represented by the newly printed *Quaderni di Giustizia e Libertà*, "institutionalized" anti-fascists such as Benedetto Croce, marginalized intellectuals best represented by the journal *Solaria*, and left-wing fascists such as Elio Vittorini. In exile Carlo Rosselli expressed his own concerns:

> Whoever lives will see. Notwithstanding the recent waves I hope in the Left's victory. 1932 will be decisive. Either we'll exit from this deadlock or we'll wrap ourselves up in it in an unsolvable manner. I remain, as always, an optimist. The world doesn't end, and from the greatest evils often comes something good. In this sense, the crisis is working towards peace. If you work for something else it's more dubious.[55]

Cultural renewal was based on the celebration of the fellowship of humanity or, generally speaking, "Europe" (as opposed to "fascist Italy"), morality as ontology, and freedom as a religious construct. The main idea: a united Europe. In abridged form we can summarize the major proponents of this idea. In the United States William Penn wrote "An Essay towards the Present and Future Peace of Europe, by the Establishment of an European Dyet, Parliament, or Estates," published in 1693–4. The conclusion he reached is as follows: "By the same *Rules of Justice and Prudence … Europe* may obtain and preserve *Peace among Her Soveraignties*."[56] Many years later Mazzini called for a United States of Europe. The main principles behind this movement would be national self-determination, democracy, and thus the civic education of its individuals. Mazzini would eventually inspire patriotic and anticolonial movements all over the world: the early Zionists read him, as did Gandhi, Nehru, and Sun Yat-Sen. Woodrow Wilson was inspired by Mazzini: "On the way to attend the 1919 peace conference in Paris, Wilson visited Genoa and paid tribute in front of Mazzini's monument. The American president explicity claimed on that occasion that he had closely studied Mazzini's writings and 'derived guidance from the principles which Mazzini so eloquently expressed.' Wilson further added that with the end of the First World War he hoped to contribute to 'the realization of the ideals to which his [Mazzini's] life and thought were devoted."[57]

In his opening speech pronounced on 21 August 1849 at the Second General Peace Congress held in Paris, Victor Hugo focused on creating a united Europe.[58] Hugo remarked in his speech (I paraphrase) that a day is coming when war between Paris and London, between Petersburg and Berlin, and between Vienna and Turin will be absurd and impossible, just as war between Boston and Philadelphia is unthinkable. One day France, Russia, Italy, England, and even Germany, all the nations of the continent, will unite without losing their own distinctive qualities and individualities, and will merge together in a higher form of unity and brotherhood. And on that day bullets and bombs will be replaced by votes and universal suffrage. A day will come when guns are exhibited in museums, just as today museums exhibit instruments of torture.

In 1923 Leon Trotsky also participated in the discussion on a united Europe. An article titled "The United States of Europe" appeared in *Pravda* on 30 June 1923. The Great War had been, for Trotsky, an imperialist war. And although the United States had participated marginally in the effort, Trotsky believed that the United States was encouraging the destruction of Europe. Such a danger could encourage the people of Europe to unite the proletarian class in the "United States of Europe."[59] Gaetano Salvemini would also discuss Mazzini's legacy. For Salvemini, humanity meant Europe – he did not give much importance to the United States of America. He summarized Mazzini's thought as follows:

If the law of progress brings us to the constitution of Humanity, and Humanity is the association of single nations and of free peoples, it follows "that Humanity will not be truly constituted until all the peoples that form it, having won the free exercise of their sovereignity, are united in a republican federation. Nationhood is sacred." "The Pact of humanity cannot be signed by individuals, but by free and equal peoples with a name, a flag and a consciousness of their own life." "Without a recognition of free and spontaneously constituted national states, we shall never have the United States of Europe."[60]

Benedetto Croce's *Storia d'Europa*, published on the eve of the *Decennale*, likewise proposed a united Europe. The volume marked the beginning of a new path for the philosopher, one that saw Croce engaged in a *"lotta da clerc,"* as Gianfranco Contini wrote: less the moralist and more concerned with ethical issues.[61] Croce interpreted history only to determine, as Gobetti did, relevant strategies for the present political struggle.[62] Gobetti likewise referred to words as a "mythic force." Fascism's words remained stale. D'Annunzio was capable of penetrating reality and transforming it. De Vecchi on the other hand was not. For Gobetti, an objective of the anti-fascist struggle was not the immediate fall of fascism. Rather, he saw the struggle as setting out to renew the character of Italians intellectually, ethically, and morally. Croce's epilogue was a true prophecy. Read at the time of the *Decennale*, it summed up the pedagogical intent of the *Storia d'Europa*. In the last paragraph the author explained his writings were not to be considered as prophecy but, rather, as a strategy for those who, like himself, had made a choice.

> Meanwhile, in all parts of Europe we are watching the growth of a new consciousness and of a new nationality ... This process of a European union, which is directly opposed to nationalist competition and has already set itself up against it and one day will be able to liberate Europe from it altogether, tends at the same time to liberate Europe from the whole psychology that clings to this nationalism and supports it and generates kindred manners, habits, and actions. And if this thing happens, or when it happens, the liberal ideal will be fully restored in men's minds and will resume its rule.[63]

Benedetto Croce's *"antifascismo europeo"* was at the centre of Piero Gobetti's strategy.[64] The strategy critically assessed fascist reality and opposed competing nationalisms of various European nations with a unified front in the name of humanism. Croce's indications continued Gobetti's hope for a cultural revival that defined anti-fascism as a "matter of style" meant to awaken the consciousness of those enslaved by the rhetoric of fascism.[65] It was a call towards assuming responsibilities and accepting one's life as a political struggle, and the only way to modernize and save freedom in Italy.[66] And it meant living anti-fascism as the struggle to create a new society, to paraphrase Gobetti.[67]

The best life, Leo Strauss reminds us, is a life dedicated to understanding and contemplation. This type of life is distinguished from the practical or political life. Prudence and moral virtues are key elements of this life. To lead a good life, one deserves to be one's own master. In other words one has to make the right decisions. And in order to make these decisions one has to possess a certain "goodness of character." These virtues present themselves only to the "morally good man," and the "morally good man is the properly bred man, the well-bred man. In short, the sphere of prudence is thus closed by principles evident only to gentlemen."[68] These men represent the elite. They do not lack pride or manliness, for those who are lacking in these qualities usually "obey a stronger man."[69]

Solaria represented this elite. It was the ideal *polis*. The assumption that this marginalized group of gentlemen had no effect on the anti-fascist movement is absurd. A renewed program for *Solaria* gave a slanted character to the journal. Readers were asked to read between the lines. The literature presented was to have a mythic force. Readers were asked to read in an esoteric manner. The renewed editorial strategy was to be read as implicitly anti-fascist, and several examples have been presented in these pages. In reading Stuparich, Gadda applauded his realism and objectivity.[70] Gadda's appreciation for "truth" in Stuparich was a critical assessment of fascist reality. Here, Gadda defined his opposition: truth versus fascist war rhetoric as a guide for true patriots in the nation-building process. In another article, this one written by Garosci on Beccaria and considered in these pages, Garosci clarified that Beccaria's outrage was directed against a "system of abuses," the by-product of the transformed relationship between society and the individual. Garosci implicitly criticized absolutist political systems, the dangers of absolute power, and a "system of abuses" that had shocked the relationship between society and the individual. A by-product of the advent of imperialism was a lack of faith in society. Capital punishment was seen as the "war of a nation towards a citizen."[71]

In the age of mass movements, the Dadaist-inspired performance recounted in *"Candida e Consalvo"* was clear: scandal, outrage, and shock effect were meant to instantiate a new narrative. The hero's experience uprooted him from modern mechanized society. Chiaromonte appreciated Malraux's criticism of individualism and, in its more "acute form," the will of power. Malraux wrote "moral dialogues" of individuals who act and seek to understand the moral reasoning behind their actions. His characters created a dialogue with present-day events. They were thrown into history and forced to commit when confronted with their destiny. According to both Malraux and Chiaromonte, the true test that a man must pass in order to prove his existence is the absolute destruction of himself.

The *Decennale* celebrations radicalized and interpreted the needs of the fascist movement. The intentions and aspirations of the regime did not always correspond to the reality of the situation. Thanks to the *Decennale* millions of people had seen and understood the intentions and aspirations of the regime. The *Decennale* was meant to satisfy the people's "desire for a public identity."[72] The event, a new cycle in the history of the fascist movement, was a revelation. Millions of visitors from all countries had seen, witnessed, and understood.[73]

It is not the primary objective of this book to consider whether or not the *Decennale* actually worked and why or why not. However, certain conclusions can be drawn. Bosworth points out that "regime propagandists loved to cite the *Duce* as the inspiration of the schemes – he had provided the slogan, 'To reclaim the land, and with the land the man, and with the man, the race.'" But the actual truth was that even the campaign against malaria "succeeded only fitfully because the processes involved were top-down and authoritarian, easily manipulated to the benefit of wealthy locals, and obscure and costly to those actually afflicted by the disease." As a result of the African war, Bosworth remarks, the regime began to cut down on medical welfare, and by 1945 malaria had returned to those same areas that had once been afflicted by it; "for all the talk about a return to the land … the *Duce* failed to suture the traditional gap in wealth, influence, status and understanding between city and countryside."[74]

I have also considered fascist textbooks and presented a comparative approach with Soviet textbooks. There was a certain amount of affinity between fascism and bolshevism. In 1932 Emilio Bodrero, editor of *Bibliografia fascista*, wrote that as a "direction" fascism and bolshevism were essentially identical. Both set out to do away with the previous century and make a clear break with the past. Both of these political systems, furthermore, were born from the war. Both wanted to return to "man." Nonetheless a striking difference does exist between the two. Bolshevism set out to return man to his natural state, whereas fascism wanted to return man to Rome, the *civitas*.[75]

This attitude had successively lost its vigour, starting from the late 1920s. Soviet state planning, Soviet cinema, Soviet theatre, and Soviet literature were appreciated and read as models of modernity. Even in architecture and urban planning, both fascist Rome and Soviet Moscow shared similar opportunities. Unlike Rome, Soviet Moscow was a new centre that stimulated ambitious transformations from the old imperial rule (in St. Petersburg) to a new socialist urban canvas. Even in Soviet Moscow, the bolshevik vision of urban planning demolished emblematic structures such as the Chudov monastery, the Ascension convent, the cathedral of Our Lady of Kazan, the Resurrection Gate on Red Square, and the cathedral of Christ the Redeemer.[76]

Rome or Moscow? The debate that occurred in the leading journals (and especially in *Critica fascista* and in the literature of Ugo Spirito), which we have considered in the previous pages, opened up to a certain predisposition (*disponibilità*) towards the Soviet experience. However, the end of the Ethiopian war, the Italian effort in Spain, and the Stalinist purges allowed Mussolini to reconsider the fascist stance as a movement set to become even *more* revolutionary than Soviet Russia. "Supercapitalism," be it private or state-sponsored, was not fascist and would never be fascist; this was a rallying cry for the new generation of fascists, university students (GUF), and left-wing fascists. For example, in his book *Mussolini il duce* De Felice cites two authors we have already become acquainted with in these pages, Romano Bilenchi and Berto Ricci (in 1937). He mentions both of them in reference to the economic systems. According to Bilenchi:

[W]e have already fought communism and reject it as a technique; we oppose the immediate destructive violence of the old capitalist world with a gradualism in both destruction and rebuilding. As a doctrine we not only reject communism because we have a history and a conception of the individual different from the Russians, but we take on the serious task of overcoming Communism by opening the gate to the human, true civilization of labour. So we, the Italian people, assume the responsibility for having started a revolution against super-capitalism.[77]

For Ricci this new phase in the history of the fascist movement implied renewal and emancipation from the accumulation of wealth. In a "just" regime citizens would be at the mercy of government. And government would restore justice and establish a new order:

There are and there must be many ways to overcome Moscow thanks to the sincerity, intensity, humanity, and universality of the fascist revolution. For example: by not abolishing property, which once severed is reborn just like the tail of a lizard, but by abolishing the proletariat – those without property. And by recognizing that property, and with it the development of all the powers of the human personality, is an inseparable attribute of the producer. Furthermore, we can overcome Moscow by not eliminating individual initiative but rather by eliminating the indefinite accumulation of private wealth. We can overcome Moscow by removing, from ourselves and from our habits and customs, every vestige of anti-historical and old-fashioned materialism – the true opium of the people and the true religion for the bourgeoisie. We can overcome Moscow by progressively uniting the people in the name of the Empire, which is the only possible and righteous *International*. We can overcome Moscow by not fornicating with worldwide capitalism but rather knowing that we have it against us.[78]

What is often viewed as "ideological incongruity" can, in fact, be explained through foreign policy and was "consonant" with Mussolini's realpolitik. It has been demonstrated that similarities did exist between the two movements. Mussolini recognized Soviet Russia via treaty on 7 February 1924. Italian newspapers and magazines had numerous correspondents in Russia. *La Stampa* sent Pietro Sessa, Curzio Malaparte, Corrado Sofia, and Corrado Alvaro. *Il Tevere* sent the poet Vincenzo Cardarelli. Both fascism and communism were united in their denounciation of capitalism. On 2 August 1930 fascist Italy and Soviet Russia signed a commercial treaty. Another trade treaty was signed on 28 April 1931. Both countries signed a pact of non-aggression on 2 September 1933. Good relations with Russia were important to keep the German menace in check and to lessen French influence. The accord that Mussolini signed with French Foreign Minister Pierre Laval in January 1935 led the nation towards the Ethiopian campaign. The very notion of empire associated the fascist movement with dynamism and vitality. These qualities were considered spiritual and moral expressions. The fascist way of life, characterized by discipline and sacrifice, allowed the Italian people to redeem themselves from centuries of abandonment and foreign occupation. It also allowed fascism to redeem the world from its economic and moral crisis. *Gerarchia* published a series of articles dedicated to the topic in 1932. The journal's editor, Margherita Sarfatti, believed that Mussolini's universalistic aspirations were meant to defend the racial integrity of the West.[79] The salvationist theory espoused by universal fascism was deemed credible by the simple fact that the crisis sparked by the market crash of 1929 had made many people question the validity of liberal democracies.[80] Fascism, in turn, presented a romanticized form of anti-capitalism that sought to combat the alienation and social divisiveness created by the capitalist state.[81] This crisis, as is known, reached its peak in 1933 during *Anno X*.[82]

De Felice had once suggested, Bosworth reminds us, that the Ethiopian campaign was instigated by a failed domestic policy. Bosworth likewise reminds us, this time by referring to Falasca-Zamponi, that Mussolini's "totalitarian culture," which was built on the spectacle of war, was what drove Mussolini to Africa in 1935. Meanwhile, in 1935 police had dismantled a *Giustizia e Libertà* cell in Turin, and in November 1936 Mussolini remarked that hostility towards the Ethiopian war was largely due to the large number of Jewish journalists reporting. In 1938 the anti-Semitic campaign was set into action for practical and political reasons. For practical reasons it would have been impossible to have

Italian fascist Jews and anti-Semitic Nazis sitting at the same table for talks. For political reasons it allowed Mussolini to form an alliance with Hitler without explicitly having to sign one. In the arenas of culture and propaganda the eternal Italian problems of patronage and *clientelismo* "continued to exist despite the puffing of a mystical national and, soon, racial unity."[83] Bosworth then points out that in March 1938 Italy "lost its independence and the history of 'real' Fascism came to an end." In October 1938 the Italian masses rejoiced that peace had finally arrived.

What was the connection between the 1932 celebrations and the reactions to these celebrations and the transition from Italian fascism's conservative phase to its totalitarian, imperialistic, and racist phase? The revolution now needed to be revitalized once more *after* Ethiopia. And so, Bosworth concludes, "it was time for Italy to go racist."[84] Alexander De Grand mentions Gian Galeazzo Ciano's diary as an important primary source to understand this moment. Ciano writes that in 1938 Mussolini was irritated

> at these factions of the bourgeoisie that were always ready to sit on their hands. He spoke of a third wave, to begin in October, resting on the peasant and worker masses. He intends to create concentration camps with the harshest police restrictions. A foretaste of this turning of the screws will be given by the torching of Jewish, Masonic, Francophile writings. Jewish writers and journalists will be banned from any activity ... The revolution must start to affect the comportment of Italians. They must learn to be less tenderhearted, to become hard, implacable, hateful. That is to say, masters.[85]

According to Alexander De Grand, Italian fascism entered into crisis between 1935 and 1940 because the regime had created a series of fiefdoms between 1926 and 1933. Furthermore, from 1922 to 1934 Mussolini inherited a colonial program that predated the March on Rome. Mussolini revealed himself as a master of realpolitik. De Grand confirms that the colonies emerged as a laboratory for a renewed fascist totalitarian experiment that would create a new society and then, if possible, export the totalitarian tendencies of late fascism to Italy.[86] In 1937 the Third Colonial Congress led to the racial exclusion laws for the empire. In 1938 Mussolini ordered a census of the African population of Italy, just as he ordered one for the Jewish population. The threat to Italian purity came from seventy-two African individuals.[87] In 1938 the anti-Semitic legislation excluding Jews from public life was enacted in Italy.

De Grand points out that until recently historians have not "integrated" the imperialist-colonialist phase into the history of the regime. His article titled "Cracks in the Facade: the Failure of Fascist Totalitarianism in Italy, 1935–9" allows us to understand what fascism didn't do and didn't accomplish. Fascism was not a party dictatorship but a bureaucracy that created an alliance among "economic power centres [to transform them] into a military-industrial complex." Furthermore, towards the end of the 1930s the regime lost control of its cultural agenda. By this time, writes De Grand, fascism "was an ideological and cultural blank filled in by various constituencies." Mussolini was dependant on a "traditional conservative (non-totalitarian) establishment that questioned many of the new policy directives."[88] These compromises, lessons in realpolitik, brought the *Duce* even more trouble. The masses had become passive, and conformity was enforced not by conviction but rather by intimidation. "[A]ny attempt to interfere in private conduct, not only in matters of race, only increased passivity and alienation."[89] At times these measures bordered on the ridiculous, such as the abolition of the "effeminate" *lei* form, which was to be replaced by *voi*. By the late 1930s the same old divisions existed in society, the corporative state had failed, talent was being misused, and passive resistance was the norm.

Able men such as Bottai, Grandi, and Balbo (Gobetti famously wrote in his program manifesto, "The new man is Balbo") were not allowed to emerge as leaders. The *Duce* took every measure to ensure this was so, entangling everyone in a series of compromises.[90] Giuseppe Bottai's diary is an accurate and haunting read that depicts these years. In recollecting the moment preceeding the Great War, Bottai wrote that he *"volli la guerra"* (wanted war) as something that came from within and that he had to "pass" through it (*dovevo "passare" di là*). The need for war was visceral.[91] In his diary entries on the African front, Bottai remembered his own entrance into the Great War. For Bottai, war was a poetic event. The fascist movement was a poetic moment (*"Poesia vissuta è stata per me tutta la mia partecipazione al movimento fascista ... poesia da vivere è questa Guerra"*). Bottai never chose fascism. Fascism chose Bottai, just as a dream takes hold of those who sleep (*"finita la guerra, il fascismo m'à preso, come i sogni prendono i dormienti"*).[92] Nonetheless, in an entry written on 10 December 1935 he confirmed that fascism's revolution was an incomplete one (*"una rivoluzione mancata"*).[93] Even Asvero Gravelli, editor of *Ottobre* (previously mentioned in this book), failed to make the cut. Gravelli had been seen at Asmara crying, beat up, and reduced to pieces.[94] Days later Bottai concluded that the propaganda schemes (just like commercials) set up by the regime had been effective to a certain point but had essentially failed.[95]

Bottai's *Diario* documents the promulgation of the anti-Semitic race laws. On 10 August 1938 he noted that the press was especially interested in demonstrating a certain continuity in the thought process of the *Duce*. Other instances were brought to light. Mussolini had confided in Ludwig (of Jewish origin) for his 1932 conversation-dialogues (mentioned in this book). Several senators nominated by Mussolini were Jewish. Mussolini's first biographer, Margherita Sarfatti, was Jewish.[96] On 27 August 1938 Bottai received notice that Mussolini was intent on excluding Jewish teachers from the school system. Bottai remarked that such actions were mad and precipitous ("*i fatti folli e precipitosi*").[97] Italo Balbo was furious. Nonetheless, these orders were meant to be followed. On 1 September 1938 another proposal was made: transfer Italian Jews to Africa, near Kenya. On 2 September 1938 Bottai went ahead and presented his proposal excluding Jews from public life, which became law on 5 September 1938 and confirmed the policy of exclusion.[98]

By the end of the 1930s, propaganda fed exclusively off the cult of the *Duce*, empire, and race. Film, the most celebrated means of propaganda, wasn't faring too well either. As De Grand points out, an official Directorate for Cinema had been created in 1934, but American movies were not restricted until 1938. The LUCE documentaries fared a bit better. Party membership, which had become mandatory in 1932, was likewise also becoming increasingly irrelevant. By 1937 it was decided that party membership was not obligatory if you had been employed by the state before 1932.[99] In August 1938 "Mussolini found himself in a testy exchange with the Vatican over racial policy."[100] Living conditions also worsened. Men were given preferential treatment in the public sector, and in 1933 women were excluded from state exams. The demographic program was directly connected to a "negative stand on women's rights … [P]rocreation and child rearing were set forth as the exclusive functions of all women … [Y]et despite all these efforts, the birth rate declined. In the 1921–25 period, there were 29.9 live births per thousand; by the years 1936–40, this figure had fallen to 23.1."[101] Laws had been enacted and schools had been reformed, but to no avail. The regime's efforts to organize the masses (and especially those coming of age in 1932) had failed. On 20 January 1941, just days before leaving for the Albanian front, Bottai wrote in his diary that he feared he no longer had faith in his leader.[102]

To conclude: the problem was Mussolini. On 21 September 1941 Bottai visited the inferno that had become Dachau:

> Visit to a camp of Italian workers, on the way towards the sad Dachau concentration camp. Dachau is also sad. A series of wooden shacks that look like barracks and a hospice. The barracks house these poor lost Italians, nostalgic Italians. When I'm about to get back in my car and leave, they tighten around me calling for *"pasta! pasta!"* This call for help also makes me feel sorry for them.[103]

On 10 April 1942 Bottai wrote in his diary that "myths were changing … they change, they confuse themselves with other myths, and eventually disappear."[104] On 19 May 1943 Bottai confirmed that Carlo Scorza's new propaganda movement was all talk and no action. Talk at breakfast meetings among fascists focused on negotiating a "separate peace." Mussolini had become a *"capro espiatore"* – a scapegoat.[105] In the days that followed 8 September 1943 Bottai would reflect on the destiny of Italy: impending defeat that was too often masked in brief moments of victory:

> [E]ven the lie of propaganda reveals the national genius. The Italians tell lies and they listen to lies pretending to believe them. Italians will go so far, in their daily Machiavellian lives, as to not even believe in the truth any more.[106]

On 3 January 1943 Bottai assessed the situation after the Allies reached Tripoli: "Who will win this war? This is a war of religion, a war of ideas. Of land as well, but above all of ideas. And this war demands soldiers who are fanatics. Look at Russia. The Russians fight because Russia is communist. Russian soldiers hear about communism and about the homeland, maybe more about communism than the homeland."[107]

At dawn on 16 October 1943 the SS raided the Jewish ghetto in Rome. Bottai wrote: "The Germans are at work in the Jewish Ghetto and are about going here and there looking for isolated Jewish professionals or merchants. There's talk of entire truckloads full of families. This *pogròm*, happening right under the eyes of the Vatican, must be inebriating our number one ally."[108]

The politics of exclusion were now finalized. Two decades earlier Piero Gobetti had written "Elogio della ghigliottina" ("In Praise of the

Guillotine"), an article already mentioned in these pages.[109] To paraphrase, Gobetti spoke about "pessimism" – indeed an Old Testament type of pessimism – that lacked any palingenetic rebirth. This pessimism was at the core of Mussolini's program. Fascism, Gobetti continued, was a catastrophe. But fascism was something else. Fascism was the autobiography of a nation. And Mussolini was nothing new under the sun. After all, one could not ask a country of D'Annunzio followers to sacrifice themselves. Gobetti and his group opposed fascism, and there was something that seemed slightly mad about it all. Indeed Gobetti bore the mask of an "anti-fascist Don Quixote." In "Questioni di tattica" ("A Question of Tactics") Gobetti explained that his group's retreat had a purpose: Mussolini and fascism had to fulfil fascism's parabola and its mission so that the *Duce* could not blame his lack of success on others.[110]

No alibis. Italians were uneducated, ignorant, and in all essence, slaves, and not capable of ruling themselves. Mussolini, myth and all, could therefore be useful for teaching Italians what tyranny was all about. After all, Italians had never been able to celebrate reason as the Reformation had encouraged. Italy's Reformation had instead been best exemplified by Machiavelli, "a pragmatist," Gobetti declared. National regeneration had not been possible by means of a religious revolution (Antonio Gramsci would dedicate pages in his notebooks to the topic).

The only type of regeneration on the table – a philosophical reformation – would be the one inspired by Benedetto Croce. In 1942, exactly ten years after the *Decennale* celebrations and the publication of the *Storia d'Europa*, two decades after the March on Rome, and in the middle of a devasting world war, Benedetto Croce published the essay "Perché non possiamo non dirci cristiani" ("Why We Cannot Not Call Ourselves Christians").[111] The essay merits attention. In August 1942 Benedetto Croce received a copy of the New Testament from a friend, Maria Curtopassi. Croce counterposed his reading of the New Testament to the pre-Hellenic, pre-Eastern, barbaric hoards of violence. The essay brings to light truth and human action. There is no conversion to Christianity on Croce's behalf. Rather, he remarked again on the triumph of secular liberalism, which has integrated the lessons of the Renaissance, the Reformation, and the Enlightenment. Croce's essay also coincided with a period in which the church began to explicitly dissent from fascism. Croce explained that "Christianity is the greatest revolution that humanity has ever completed." All other revolutions are "specific and limited ... Christianity's primacy is that it maintains the original impulse." According to Croce, Christianity developed thanks to myths – the myth of the reign of God, the myth of the resurrection of the dead, the myth of baptism, the myth of atoning for one's sins. These myths were effective because Christianity does not distinguish between race, class, those who are free or those who are enslaved, and looks towards a world created by God as an act of love. The philosopher studies this mystery.

Bottai recorded, amused, the *Duce*'s reaction to Croce: "In any case, Cristianity is not a revolution, it's a revelation."[112]

The problem, Salvemini wrote (in 1932), was Mussolini:

> Now, reading certain journals published by the dominant party in Italy or even certain articles in which some of the militant youth express their ideas and state of mind, it could even be said that in the fascist movement some good seeds could even grow. If only they would not be suffocated by *Mussolinismo* or rather by this despicable conglomerate of lies, of low class servitude, of histrionic contortions, something like a bluff – that of an ignorant presumptious man as is personified in the *Duce* and is thickened in the official cult worship that he demands from his followers.[113]

The *Duce*[114] promoted a "dangerous life," but only as a way of dissimulating his own fears. Violence, incarceration, and exile for dissidents, along with an amnesty for all those who had committed crimes in the name of the state, only contributed to the state of crisis. After 8 September 1943 the fascist regime broke apart from within. On the run, Bottai wrote on 23 October 1943 that new slogans had appeared on the walls of buildings, "Down with all," and he asked himself: "Are we nearing the 'long-live death' cries of the Spanish Civil War?" On the run, Bottai read from Psalm 56 in the Scripture: "Be merciful to me, my God, for my enemies are in hot pursuit; all day long they press their attack. My adversaries pursue me all day long; in their pride many are attacking me ... I put my trust in you."[115]

The time had arrived for the anti-fascist movement (and the "new generation") to indicate the *quid agendum*, two decades or so after the first March on Rome, in order to redeem the nation *from* its current state of sin.[116] Dissent, it is clear, was beginning to stir, perhaps as a reaction to the pomp and splendour of the *Decennale*, the creation of an empire, and the politics of exclusion. Perhaps also as a critical reaction to the "artificial aura" imposed on the new generation through the rhetoric of the regime celebrated during the *Decennale* and studied in these pages. This book has explained the role that the *Decennale* played in this process.

Civil war followed the armistice of 8 September 1943; as the ancients teach us, civil war is a period following peace. Civil war affected both judgment and action like never before. Depravity ensued. It was caused by civil war, a "man-made plague that resembles the depravation caused by the plague proper" and a moment when Italians would forgo the fear of the gods, piety, and human law.[117]

Appendix: Antonio Aniante, "Consalvo e Candida," *Solaria* (June 1932): 23–7

Entro le mura dell'ospedale ci si sente protetti: mura basse ma solide che arrestano ai loro orli il nervosismo della strada: davvero fuori è l'inferno; di colpo, qui dentro, quasi un peso cade dall'anima, e tutto invita al riposo: i padiglioni, gli alberi, le aiuole sono semplici, irriducibili, piani, chiari, inoffensivi; le suore, i medici, gli infermieri, i custodi, i giardinieri vanno pacifici; prudente è l'oriolo della cappella.

Consalvo dovrà rientrare fra mezz'ora in officina; rimane al capezzale di Candida soltanto dieci minuti; le ha portato un'arancia, due franchi di fiori, un romanzo. Si parla a voce bassa. Anche stasera rincaserà solo; da una settimana si rifà il letto alla meglio. "L'ospedale ci ha rinconciliati; le direbbe- stai bene e ritorna: un nonnulla ci aveva fatto diventare nemici." "Ci siamo odiati, -risponderebbe Candida, -e la nostra compagnia ci è sembrata a volte insopportabile." Ma quei giorni sembrano lontani, e non ne son trascorsi che sette appena dalla notte paurosa, che non dovrà più ripetersi. "Chi di noi due lo ha ucciso? Si direbbe che gli infermieri leggano nei nostri occhi il segreto che tu e io nascondiamo. Senza dubbio abbiamo anima di criminali. I buoni non calpestano nemmeno una formica. Chi ti ha dato tanta forza, tanto coraggio? Forse un giorno ne riparleremo, Candida, facendo lite, e ci accuseremo a vicenda."

In un quartiere operaio della città, un casamento, appuntellato ai quattro angoli, non era stato ancora demolito. I suoi sette piani erano abitati da gente equivoca. In alto, all'ultima porta stava la levatrice. Consalvo insistette: "Sono l'amico di Candida, se non aprite sfondo la porta, o chiamo la polizia." Una vecchia, che aveva le mani lunghe e pulite, aprì con mezz'ora di ritardo. "Ho settant'anni- gli disse più tardi- e da mezzo secolo che non ho fatto altro mestiere. In tutto questo tempo non c'è stata una sola cliente che abbia voluto denunciarmi. Non ricordo il minimo incidente." Consalvo le guardava le mani dalle dita lunghe e nervose: "Hanno impedito- pensava- a centinaia di innocenti di venire al mondo." "Le donne che non vogliono figli non sono poche e non hanno tutti i torti. Non sempre si deve nascere. La legge è ingiusta. Il mondo è cattivo. Il governo vuole folla a tutti i costi. Ma i motivi per i quali una donna si oppone a creare sono anche importanti. Quando ero giovane, l'epoca era un'altra; da qualche anno il mio lavoro è più che raddoppiato. La povertà, l'infelicità, le guerre, le malattie costringono le donne di migliore volontà a non dar soldati alla patria." Consalvo considerava più attentamente le parole della vecchia. "Nascondetevi," gli disse, e andò all'uscio. Entrò una ragazza dal viso sciupato, mal vestita. "Chi vi manda?," "Un'amica." "Che volete? Ho capito,- continuò la vecchia- cercate altrove." L'altra insistette, la supplicò. La vecchia la mise alla porta. "Questa vita mi è insopportabile," disse la ragazza, congedandosi. Consalvo uscì. "Perché la avete cacciata via?" Dal pianerottolo del settimo piano si udiva il pianto della visitatrice. "Ferma, -gridò Consalvo, trattenendola per la veste- che fate? Un salto a terra? da questa altezza?"

Se la disgraziata si fosse gettata dalle scale non una ma due creature avrebbero trovato la morte. In questi casi- pensava Consalvo- chi dovrebbe perire? Nessuno, né la madre né l'innocente; i buoni giudici risparmiano la vita di chi è già al mondo.

Si trovò così suo malgrado complice di Candida, la notte del delitto. Il figlio era stato nascosto in una tazza da caffè, sul marmo del camino. Seduto sul letto, Consalvo fumava per distrarsi; poi gli sembrò di poter dormire ma un sonno guasto più nocivo della veglia, e si rialzò. Candida al suo fianco, assopita, aveva il respiro pesante di dolore e di stanchezza. Una mano le passò sui capelli, come a una bestiola. Il ricordo gli andò alla casa di suo padre ove una gatta aveva mangiato i suoi piccini. Le idee si confondono di fronte a un fatto così mostruoso: allora uomini e animali sono una stessa cosa. "Candida, dormi?" Il pensiero che la donna dormisse lo rendeva maggiormente nervoso, gli dava più dolorosa una sensazione di solitudine. Fuori della stanza incombeva la città immensa, come un naufragio permanente di navi lo circondava da tutte le parti. La chiamò, affettuoso, le strinse una mano, raccolse nelle sue labbra un sorriso. L'amica non dormiva. La luce della luna si posava sul marmo del camino e sulla tazza. "Che ne facciamo del piccino?" Inattesa fu la risposta di Candida. "Lo conserveremo." "Come?" le chiese stupito. Non era una donna ma una bambina che non vuole separarsi dalla bambola. Consalvo si ritrovò in piedi, dinnanzi la tazza; aveva acceso la luca. "Vediamo se vive ancora." Sedettero in mezzo al letto, sotto la lampada. L'innocente sembrava un giocattolino di celluloide, ma tanto piccolo da osservarsi con una lente di ingrandimento. L'involucro, più che trasparente, era tuttavia intatto, e là ove si era staccato dal grembo della madre era venato di sangue. "Piccino, che fai?" Graziose e puerili le domande di Candida simulavano stupore, paura, rimorso. L'esserino agonizzante nella tazza faceva contrasto con la potenza e la superficie dell'universo, essendo ancora vivo, muovendo le dita, aprendo e chiudendo la bocca. Candida appuntò uno spillo sul bozzolo: il delitto era compiuto.

Nel resto della notte, durante un sonno angoscioso, il morticino resuscitò e si fece uomo e si piantò in mezzo alla stanza, saldo sulle sue gambe d'acciaio. Consalvo e Candida si svegliarono, accesero la luce: a un angolo della stanza uno scarafaggio saliva e scendeva da una pallottola di concime.

Seduto al capezzale di Candida, guardava l'orologio dell'ospedale: "Fra dieci minuti debbo tornare all'officina." I malati si vedevano dalla finestra passeggiare nel giardino. Indimenticabili sono i loro occhi, spenti e rassegnati. Un infermiere passò portando una gamba di gesso e di garza intrisa di sangue. Una dopo l'altra due barelle attraversarono la sala. Grazioso e verde era il recinto delle malattie contagiose, che seguiva i padiglioni del cancro e il laboratorio dei raggi ultravioletti. Consalvo si alzò: "Ritornerò domani alla stessa ora." Lontana era l'uscita, e l'ambiente lo esortava alle meditazioni severe. "Chi ha torto e chi ha ragione? Ho veramente partecipato a un delitto aiutando Candida alla soppressione dell'innocente? Se fosse stata, la mia, azione lodevole? Nulla forse di tutto ciò. Ciascun uomo ha la sua idea in proposito. Fatalisti e ottimisti: i primi mi assolverebbero, i secondi mi darebbero l'ergastolo. Gli altri direbbero che nulla di straordinario è avvenuto fra me e Candida. Chi ha la verità in mano? Ma quel che è certo è che io non sono più un uomo tranquillo; e se mi trovassi di fronte alla giustizia rimarrei a testa bassa."

Fuori dell'ospedale, i veicoli tagliarono netta la sua requisitoria. Biciclette, *camions*, vetture, *tramwais*, pedoni, agenti: non gli fu facile attraversare la strada, e si ritrovò sul marciapiede opposto con il cuore scosso. Era un giorno come un altro ma sembrava festa, di lavoratori, di gente sana che non ha peccato. Un uomo forte portava sulle spalle un quintale di farina, un altro guidava la sua macchina come se fosse in pista; nella piazza due lottatori appassionavano la folla; un carro alto e massiccio, trainato da due bei cavalloni bianchi, era condotto da due giovani superbi; ciascuno di questi esseri all'inizio della sua vita era stato minuscolo involucro di celluloide; e raggiunse la porta dell'officina che era l'ora precisa della ripresa pomeridiana del lavoro; corse allo spogliatoio, indossò il camice, iniziò la vita precisa della civiltà meccanica, al cospetto di una gigantesca ruota dentata che veniva mossa da una larga banda di cuoio lucido; e infallibile come numeri i compagni iniziavano la musica precisa dei motori; gigantesche e potenti le macchine erano messe in moto senza sforzo; questo mistero l'uomo stesso l'ha creato per ridurre l'uomo un minuscolo oggetto inutile, tanto semplice e puerile è la sua mansione, tanto miracolosa e complessa è la funzione degli organi meccanici; così come nulla alla fine della giornata la produzione, dalla quantità prestabilità. è un fatto compiuto: in fila, come soldati centinaia di obici son fabbricati e stanno lì pronti per un domani di guerra.

Consalvo aveva lavorato parecchi anni alla costruzione del materiale bellico, ma soltanto quella volta ci pensò davvero al significato della sua fatica; e al pensiero della strage, si arrestò, un attimo, il minimo bastevole per produrre un grave guasto. I compagni sopraggiunsero, attirati dal rumore insolito degli ingranaggi; vennero gli specialisti e i superiori, e il lavoro fu sospeso.

Gli operai uscivano contenti e lui solo andava per le strade, triste al pensiero di poter essere un disoccupato. Fuori, i boscaioli del municipio davano gli ultimi colpi di ascia agli alberi sterili, e scavavano buchi per trapiantare alberelli teneri e fecondi; e a strappare e a elevare ci mettevano tutta la loro violenza. Comprò un giornale e lesse la cronaca della città: parecchie persone nelle dodici ore si erano uccise; gli *autobus* avevano sfracellato pedoni distratti; alle porte si segnalava una catastrofe ferroviaria; un areoplano si era bruciato in cielo; migliaia di morti e di feriti si registravano in una guerra lontana; tutte queste notizie in poche pagine, a breve distanza l'una dall'altra, davano del mondo una idea paurosa; ma anche, fra una tragedia e un tracollo di industrie, lieti eventi si annunciavano con le parole più belle. Proprio allora Consalvo imboccava la strada del Macello Centrale, e nella calma della sera il rassegnato appello alla vita del bestiame da sacrificare riempì l'aria.

Qualche ora dopo, incontrò una donna e ballò fino al mattino, e fu lei che lo accompagnò all'officina. Consalvo riprese il lavoro, questa volta cantando una canzone che dalla sconosciuta aveva imparato, di soldato innamorato che va in guerra.

Antonio Aniante

Consalvo and Candida

Within the walls of the hospital one feels protected. The low but solid walls stop at their edges the nervousness of the street. It's really hell out there. All of a sudden, here, a weight almost falls from the soul, and everything leads us to rest. The halls, trees, flower beds are simple, irreducible, plain, clear, harmless; nuns, doctors, nurses, janitors, gardeners go about peacefully. Prudent is the oriole of the chapel.

Consalvo must return in half an hour to the factory; he remains at Candida's bedside only ten minutes and has brought an orange, two francs worth of flowers, and a novel. He speaks in a low voice. Even tonight he will return home alone. It's been a week since he's been making his bed as best as he can. "The hospital has reconciled us," he would say to her. "You're fine and you'll return; a trifle had made us enemies." "We hated ourselves," Candida answered, "and our company at times was unbearable." But those days seem far away, and only seven have passed since the fearful night, which will not happen again. "Which one of us killed him? It seems that the nurses can read in our eyes the secret that you and I hide. No doubt we have the souls of criminals. The good can't even step on an ant. Who gave you so much strength, so much courage? Maybe one day we'll talk about it, Candida, in an argument, and we will accuse each other."

In a working-class neighbourhood of the city stood a tenement that had not yet been demolished, held up by beams in the four corners. Its seven floors were inhabited by questionable people. On the top floor, last door, lived the midwife. Consalvo insisted, "I am Candida's friend. If you don't open the door I'll break it down. Or I'll call the police." An old woman with long clean hands opened the door half an hour later. "I'm seventy," she told him, "and for half a century I have not done any other job. In all this time there has only been one customer who wanted to turn me in. I don't remember any other incident." Consalvo looked at her long-fingered and nervous hands. Those hands have prevented hundreds of innocent children from coming into the world, he thought. "Women who don't want to have children are not rare," said the old woman, "and the fault does not lie only with them. A child doesn't always have to be born. The law is unfair. The world is bad. The government wants an army of children at all costs. But the reasons why a woman resists creation are also important. When I was young, it was another era. In a few years my work has more than doubled. Poverty, misery, wars, diseases compel women to refuse to give soldiers to the homeland." Consalvo considered the words of the old woman carefully. "Hide yourself," she then said, and went to the door. A badly dressed girl with a worn out face entered. "Who sent you?" "A friend." "What do you want? I understand," continued the old lady, "look elsewhere." The girl insisted and pleaded with her. The old woman accompanied her to the door. "My life is unbearable," the girl said, and she left. Consalvo came out. "Why have you have thrown her out?" From the landing of the seventh floor you could hear the visitor's cries. "Stop," Consalvo shouted, holding on to her dress. "What are you doing? Jumping to the ground? From this height?"

If the wretched girl had thrown herself down from the stairs, not one but two creatures would have died. In these cases, he thought, who should perish? Nobody, neither the mother nor the innocent child. Good judgement saves the lives of those who are already in this world.

Consalvo found himself becoming Candida's accomplice the night of the murder. They hid their son in a coffee cup on the marble fireplace. Sitting on the bed Consalvo smoked to distract himself until he seemed able to sleep. But it was a sleep more harmful than a vigil, and so he stood up. Candida was at his side and asleep. Her breathing was heavy with pain and fatigue. He passed his hand through her hair, like one would with an animal. In his memory he went back to his father's house, where a cat had eaten its young. He felt all mixed up and confused faced with something so monstrous. So, he mused, humans and animals are the same. "Candida, are you asleep?" The thought that she was asleep made him more nervous and gave him a painful feeling of loneliness. Outside the room the immense city loomed as a permanent sinking ship, surrounding him on all sides. He called her affectionately and squeezed her hand. He set his lips in a smile.

His girlfriend was not asleep. The moonlight rested on the marble fireplace and on the cup. "What should we do with the baby?" Candida's response was unexpected. "We'll save him." "How?" he asked in amazement. It was not a woman who had replied, but a girl who does not want to separate herself from a doll. Consalvo found himself standing before the cup and turned on the light. "Let's see if he still lives." They sat up in bed under the lamp. The innocent looked like a toy made out of celluloid, but was small enough to to need a magnifying glass to see him. The membrane, rather than being transparent, was intact, and there, where the child had detached himself from his mother's womb, it was tinged with blood. "Little one, what are you doing?" Candida's gracious and puerile questions simulated astonishment, fear, and remorse. The creature dying in the cup contrasted with the power and the surface of the universe. Still alive and moving his fingers, he opened and closed his mouth. Candida stuck a pin in the cocoon: the crime was committed.

During the night while the two slept fitfully, the little corpse resurrected itself. It became a man who planted himself in the middle of the room, steady on legs of steel. Consalvo and Candida woke up and turned on the light. In the corner of the room a cockroach went up and down from its bullet-sized deposit of fertilizer.

Sitting at Candida's bedside, he looked at the hospital's clock. "In ten minutes I have to go back to the factory." Through the window, he saw patients strolling in the garden. Their eyes were unforgettable, dull and resigned. A nurse came carrying a cast and gauze soaked with blood. One after the other, two stretchers crossed the room. Charming and green was the barrier separating infectious diseases, the halls of cancer, and the laboratory of ultraviolet rays. Consalvo stood up, "I will return tomorrow at the same time." The exit was far, and the environment gave rise to heavy brooding thoughts. "Who is wrong and who is right? Did I really participate in a crime by helping Candida destroy an innocent? But what if my action was commendable? Perhaps nothing of all this. Each man has his own views about it. Fatalists and optimists: the first would absolve me, while the latter would give me a life sentence. Others would say that nothing extraordinary has happened between me and Candida. Who has the truth in hand? What is certain is that I am no longer an untroubled man, and if I were to find myself in front of justice I would keep my head down."

Outside the hospital vehicles cut out his indictment. Bikes, trucks, cars, tramways, pedestrians, agents: it was not easy to cross the street, and he found himself on the opposite sidewalk with his heart shaken. It was a day like any other day, but it seemed like a workers' holiday – a holiday for healthy people who have not sinned. A strong man carried a ton of flour on his shoulders; another drove his car as if it were on the track; in a *piazza* two wrestlers captivated the crowd; a tall and massive coach, pulled by two beautiful white horses, was led by two arrogant young men. Each of these beings had once been a tiny shell of celluloid. He reached the door of the factory at the precise time in the afternoon when they resumed work. He ran to the locker room, put on his coat, and stepped into a precise mechanical civilization in the presence of a giant gear, driven by a broad band of polished leather and infallible as numbers. The music of the precise engine began, effortlessly setting gigantic and powerful machines into motion. Men themselves have created this mystery to reduce man to a tiny useless object: so simple and childish is his job, yet so miraculous and complex is the function of the mechanical organs. By the end of the day the production quota has been met. On the production line, hundreds of howitzers have been manufactured like soldiers and stand waiting, ready for tomorrow's war. Consalvo had worked for several years in the manufacturing of war materials, but only then did he really think about the meaning of his work and about the possibility of a massacre. He stopped work for a moment, just enough to create a serious breakdown. His fellow workers arrived, attracted by the unusual noise of the gears. Specialists and line managers came, and work was suspended.

The workers left work happy, and only he walked the streets sad at the thought of being unemployed. Outside, the woodcutters of the town hall were chopping down the barren trees and digging holes for transplanting seedlings, tender and fruitful. They put all their violence into ripping open and elevating the trees. He bought a newspaper and read what had happened in the city. Several people had been killed during the previous twelve hours: a bus had smashed distracted pedestrains; at the edge of the city, a train catastrophe had occurred; an airplane had burned up in the sky; thousands of deaths and injuries were recorded in a distant war. All these reports were all contained in just a few pages, printed close together, and created the impression of a scary world. But among the tragedies and the collapse of industries, happy events were announced in the most beautiful words. Just then Consalvo entered the road leading to the central slaughterhouse. In the calm of the evening, the air was filled with the resigned appeal to life by the cattle about to be led to sacrifice.

A few hours later, he met a woman and danced until morning. It was she who accompanied him to the factory. Consalvo went back to work, this time singing a song he had learned from his unknown friend, a song of a soldier in love who goes to war.

Antonio Aniante

Notes

Introduction

1 Benito Mussolini, "Discorso alla camera per il Decennale," in *Scritti e discorsi dal 1932 al 1933* (Milan: U. Hoepli, 1934), 139–40. All citations in this study are presented in their original format (caps, italics, etc.). All translations, unless otherwise indicated, are mine.

2 Renzo De Felice, *Fascism: An Informal Introduction to Its Theory and Practice – An Interview with Michael Ledeen* (New Brunswick, NJ: Transaction Books, 1976), 44. "De Felice: [F]ascism as movement is a constant in the history of fascism; a constant that loses importance as time progresses, it loses hegemony and becomes secondary; but it is always present. Fascism as movement is the 'red thread' that connects March 1919 with April 1945; fascism as regime, fascism as party, is something quite different. As far as fascism as movement is concerned, there are certain phases, periods, elements, but they are a continuum, notwithstanding their diversity. Within fascism as regime there are fractures of a more fundamental sort. Fascism as movement is that part of fascism that has a certain vitality. With this I do not want to present a positive evaluation of it, an evaluation of merit; I simply want to make a statement of fact about the vitality of fascism, while the party, the regime, represents its negation in certain respects. / Ledeen: Could you please expand on this? / De Felice: Fascism as movement is the impulse to renew, to interpret certain needs, certain stimuli, and certain themes of renovation. It is that spark of revolutionary fervor that there is within fascism itself, and that tends to construct something new. It is a collection of elements, above all cultural (conscious and unconscious) and psychological, which in part belong to the intransigent fascism that predates the march on Rome, but in part represent

something new and different, which developed only afterward. These
elements represent the self-representation of fascism projected into the
future, above and beyond the actual conditions it brought about, the fears,
the defeats imposed by the regime, above and beyond the life of Mussolini
itself. In this context it is the fundamental component for the understanding of the consensus; it is the moral component, alongside the material one
(that of security, which I analyzed in my last volume). Fascism as regime,
on the other hand, is the politics of Mussolini, it is the result of a political
program that – whether desired or not – tended to make fascism just the
superstructure of the personal power of a dictatorship, of a political line
that in many ways became merely the inheritance of a tradition. Hence-
forth, whenever I utilize the term 'fascism' I intend Italian fascism." See
also Renzo De Felice, *Mussolini il duce: Gli anni del consenso 1929–1936*
(Turin: Einaudi, 1974).

3 Emilio Gentile, *La Grande Italia: The Myth of the Nation in the 20th Century*
(Madison: University of Wisconsin Press, 2009). See chapter 12. See also
Alexander De Grand, "Reflections on Italian Nationalism," *Journal of
Modern Italian Studies* 15, no. 3 (2010): 458–61.

4 See De Felice, *Mussolini il duce*, 38–44 (on Spengler); Charles S. Maier,
"Some Recent Studies of Fascism," *Journal of Modern History* 48, no. 3
(September 1976): 506–21. See especially page 510. It is true that De Felice
placed too much faith in official documents and in the language employed
in these documents (and that these documents, at times, cannot be found
in the archives). Nonetheless, his method is important.

5 Patrick Finney, *Remembering the Road to World War Two: International
History, National Identity, Collective Memory* (New York: Routledge, 2010).

6 Patrick Bernhard has most recently presented a brief review of the latest
scholarship. I object to his assertion on popular support and Italian
fascism: a "contested and difficult question." Fascism was a quintessential
Italian political phenomenon, a typical product of a country that has
never experienced the Protestant Reformation but, rather, the Counter-
Reformation. Italy will always be subjected and enslaved to myth,
superstition, and "spectacle." Bernhard also brings up other typical
statements such as "Fascist Italy" was harmless compared to the dictator-
ships of Stalin and Hitler. These too are dangerous statements. There
was *no* Nuremberg trial in Italy; in fact Italy was immediately enlisted in
the Cold War. See Patrick Bernhard, "Renarrating Italian Fascism: New
Directions in the Historiography of a European Dictatorship," *Contemporary European History* 23, no. 1 (2014): 151–63. See also the research
conducted by Filippo Focardi: Filippo Focardi and Lutz Klinkhammer,

"The Question of Fascist Italy's War Crimes: The Construction of a Self-Acquitting Myth (1943–1948)," *Journal of Modern Italian Studies* 9, no. 3 (2004): 330–48.

7 Zeev Sternhell, *The Birth of Fascist Ideology: From Cultural Rebellion to Political Revolution* (Princeton, NJ: Princeton University Press, 1994), 6.

8 Gaetano Salvemini, *Mussolini diplomate* (Paris: Grasset, 1932).

9 R.J.B. Bosworth, *Whispering City: Modern Rome and Its Histories* (New Haven, CT, Yale University Press, 2011); Aristotle Kallis, "The 'Third Rome' of Fascism: Demolitions and the Search for a New Urban Synthax," *The Journal of Modern History* 84, no. 1 (March 2012): 43.

10 John Coverdale, *Italian Intervention in the Spanish Civil War* (Princeton, NJ: Princeton University Press, 1975).

11 Finney, *Remembering the Road*, 128.

12 Constantin Fasolt, "History and Religion in the Modern Age," *History and Theory* 45, no. 4 (December 2006): 18–19.

13 Oswald Spengler, *The Decline of the West* (New York: A.A. Knopf, 1928).

14 Emilio Gentile, *The Sacralization of Politics in Fascist Italy* (Cambridge, MA: Harvard University Press, 1996).

15 Emilio Gentile, *La via italiana al totalitarismo: il partito e lo stato nel regime fascista* (Rome: Carocci, 1995), 65–9.

16 Dante Germino, *The Italian Fascist Party in Power: A Study in Totalitarian Rule* (Minneapolis: University of Minnesota Press, 1959), 16.

17 Emile Durkheim, *The Elementary Forms of the Religious Life*, 2nd ed. (London: Allen and Unwin, 1976), 10.

18 Emilio Gentile, *Politics as Religion* (Princeton, NJ: Princeton University Press, 2006), xiv.b.

19 See Ruth Ben-Ghiat and Alice A. Kelikan, eds., "Reflections on Italian Nationalism and Fascism: Essays for Alexander De Grand," special issue, *Journal of Modern Italian Studies* 15, no. 3 (2010). See also Christopher Duggan, "Francesco Crispi, the Problem of the Monarchy, and the Origins of Italian Nationalism" in the above special issue, pages 336–53.

20 Jeffrey T. Schnapp, *Anno X: La Mostra della Rivoluzione Fascista del 1932* (Pisa-Rome: Istituti editoriali e poligrafici internazionali, 2003), 19.

21 Walter Benjamin, *The Work of Art in the Age of Its Technological Reproducibility, and Other Writings on Media*, ed. Michael W. Jennings et al., trans. Edmund Jephcott et al. (Cambridge, MA: Belknap Press, 2008).

22 Roger Griffin, *Modernism and Fascism* (Basingstoke, UK: Palgrave Macmillian, 2007), 24.

23 Leo Strauss, *Thoughts on Machiavelli* (Chicago: University of Chicago Press, 1958), 81–2.

24 See Warren S. Goldstein, "Messianism and Marxism: Walter Benjamin and Ernst Bloch's Dialectical Theories of Secularization," *Critical Sociology* 27, no. 2 (2001): 246–81. See especially Goldstein's excellent summary of Benjamin's essay (summarized here) on page 261.

25 See photographs in Archivio Centrale dello Stato Roma (ACS). MRF. CD 2a.

26 Rainer Stollmann, "Fascist Politics as a Total Work of Art: Tendencies of the Aesthetization of Political Life in National Socialism," *New German Critique* 14 (Spring 1978): 58–9.

27 See Leo Strauss, *The City and Man* (Chicago: University of Chicago Press, 1978).

28 John R. Gillis, "Memory and Identity: The History of a Relationship," in *Commemorations: The Politics of National Identity*, ed. John R. Gillis (Princeton, NJ: Princeton University Press, 1994), 5.

29 R.J.B. Bosworth, *Mussolini* (London: Bloomsbury, 2010), 9.

30 Ibid., 121.

31 See Martin Blinkhorn, "Afterthoughts. Route Maps and Landscapes: Historians, 'Fascist Studies' and the Study of Fascism," *Totalitarian Movements and Political Religions* 5, no. 3 (2004): 508–17. See also John Pollard, "'Clerical Fascism': Context, Overview and Conclusions," *Totalitarian Movements and Poltical Religions* 8, no. 2 (2007): 444.

32 David Forgacs and Robert Lumley, eds. *Italian Cultural Studies: An Introduction* (Oxford, New York: Oxford University Press, 1996), 2–3.

33 Jan Nelis, "Italian Fascism and Culture: Some Notes on Investigation," *Historia Actual Online* 9 (2006): 141–51, http://www.historia-actual.org/Publicaciones/index.php/haol/article/view/142/130.

34 Jeffrey T. Schnapp, *Staging Fascism: 18BL and the Theatre of Masses for Masses* (Stanford, CA: Stanford University Press, 1996).

35 Ruth Ben-Ghiat, *Fascist Modernities: Italy, 1922–1945* (Berkeley: University of California Press, 2001).

36 Dino Grandi, quoted in De Felice, *Mussolini il duce*, 372, 374.

37 Simonetta Falasca-Zamponi, *Fascist Spectacle: The Aesthetics of Power in Mussolini's Italy* (Berkeley: University of California Press, 2000), 27.

38 Ibid.

39 Claudio Fogu, "Il Duce taumaturgo: Modernist Rhetorics in Fascist Representations of History," *Representations* 57 (Winter 1997): 24–51.

40 Franco Moretti, "Conjectures on World Literature," *New Left Review* 1 (January–February 2000): 57.

41 R.J.B. Bosworth, *The Italian Dictatorship: Problems and Perspectives in the Interpretation of Mussolini and Fascism* (London, New York: Arnold, 1998).

42 Bruno Wanrooij, "The Rise and Fall of Italian Fascism as a Generational Revolt," *Journal of Contemporary History* 22, no. 3 (July 1987): 411. He quotes from De Felice, *Mussolini il duce*, 3–4, 218.

43 Carlo Rosselli, "Mussolini e i giovani," *Quaderni di Giustizia e Libertà* 2, no. 35 (30 August 1935). See especially the Biblioteca Gino Bianco online: http://www.bibliotecaginobianco.it.

44 Frank Burke, "Federico Fellini: Realism /Representation/Signification," in *Federico Fellini: Contemporary Perspectives,* ed. Frank Burke and Marguerite R. Waller (Toronto: University of Toronto Press, 2002), 33.

45 The reference is, of course, to Guy Debord, *The Society of the Spectacle*, first published in 1967 (and especially the opening quotation from Feuerbach).

46 Central to my approach is Schnapp, *Anno X*; Gentile's scholarship as presented in *The Sacralization of Politics*; Falasca-Zamponi, *Fascist Spectacle*; Ruth Ben-Ghiat, *Fascist Modernities*; Marla Stone, *The Patron State* (Princeton, NJ: Princeton University Press, 1998); Tracy Koon, *Believe, Obey, Fight: Political Socialization of Youth in Fascist Italy* (Chapel Hill: University of North Carolina Press, 1985). Also consult "The Aesthetics of Fascism," special issue of the *Journal of Contemporary History* 31, no. 2 (April 1996), as well as two special issues on "Fascism and Culture" in *Modernism/Modernity* (September 1995) and (January 1996). The previous represents the bibliographic minimum. Other bibliographical references will be included with each chapter. See also R.J.B. Bosworth, *The Oxford Handbook of Fascism* (Oxford: Oxford University Press, 2009).

47 Roger Griffin, *The Nature of Fascism* (London, New York: Routledge, 1993), 26.

48 Emilio Gentile, cited in Stanley G. Payne, introduction to *A History of Fascism, 1914–1945* (Madison: University of Wisconsin Press, 1995), 5–6.

49 Payne, *A History of Fascism.*

50 Guy Debord, *The Society of the Spectacle*, trans. Donald Nicholson-Smith (New York: Zone Books, 1994), http://www.cddc.vt.edu/sionline/si/tsotsoo.html. See Chapter IV, thesis 109.

51 Robert Paxton, "The Five Stages of Fascism," *Journal of Modern History* 70, no. 1 (March 1998): 1–23.

52 Adrian Lyttelton, *The Seizure of Power: Fascism in Italy, 1919–1929* (London: Scribner, 1973), 85. In 1923 Mussolini had a role in *The Eternal City*, an American film starring Lionel Barrymore and directed by George Fitzmaurice for Samuel Goldwyn Company. The film is presumed lost.

53 Denis Mack Smith, *Mussolini* (New York: Alfred A. Knopf, 1982), 54.

54 Giulia Albanese, *La marcia su Roma: violenza e politica nella crisi dello stato liberale* (Rome-Bari: Laterza, 2006). See also Michael R. Ebner, *Ordinary*

Violence in Mussolini's Italy (New York: Cambridge University Press, 2011), 35–41.

55 Jeffrey T. Schnapp, Olivia E. Sears, and Maria G. Stampino, eds. *A Primer of Italian Fascism* (Lincoln: University of Nebraska Press, 2000), 304.

56 Benito Mussolini, "Discorso dell'Ascensione," in *Opera omnia*, ed. Edoardo and Duilio Susmel, 44 vols. (Florence: La Fenice 1951–1980), 28: 60–1.

57 Ebner, *Ordinary Violence*, 44–7; See also De Felice, *Mussolini il duce*, II, 146–52.

58 Lutz Klinkhammer, "Was There a Fascist Revolution? The Function of Penal Law in Fascist Italy and in Nazi Germany," *Journal of Modern Italian Studies* 15, no. 3 (2010): 390–409.

59 The crisis was manipulated as a consensus-generating strategy. See Zeev Sternhell, "Modernity and Its Enemies: From the Revolt against the Enlightenment to the Undermining of Democracy," in *The Intellectual Revolt against Liberal Democracy, 1870–1945*, ed. Zeev Sternell (Jerusalem: Israel Academy of Sciences and Humanities, 1996), 11–29; Zeev Sternhell, *The Birth of Fascist Ideology: From Cultural Rebellion to Political Revolution*, with Mario Sznajder and Maia Asheri, trans. David Maisel (Princeton, NJ: Princeton University Press, 1994).

60 Martin Blinkhorn, *Mussolini and Fascist Italy* (New York: Routledge, 2006), 63.

61 See http://csmt.uchicago.edu/glossary2004/shock.htm. The reference is to Benjamin's essay "On Some Motifs in Baudelaire," in *Illuminations*, ed. Hannah Arendt (New York: Shocken Books, 1968), 155–200.

62 Benito Mussolini, "Decidersi," in *Scritti e discorsi dal 1932 al 1933*, 10–11.

63 Documentaries and newsreels from the Archivio LUCE are easily accessible online: www.archivioluce.com/archivio/.

64 Kallis, "The 'Third Rome' of Fascism, 40, 40–79.

65 Ibid., 41.

66 Ugo Spirito, *Memoirs of the Twentieth Century*, trans. from Italian and ed. Anthony G. Costantini (Amsterdam: Rodopi, 2000), 112–13.

67 Istituto Luce Cinecittà, 1932. "Il Duce nelle trionfali giornate del decennale," D063801. Please refer to this clip for the quotes that follow.

68 Ibid.

69 Ibid.

70 See the Gospel according to Mark (14:22–5): "Et manducantibus illis, accepit Jesus panem: et benedicens fregit, et dedit eis, et ait: Sumite, hoc est corpus meum. Et accepto calice, gratias agens dedit eis: et biberunt ex illo omnes. Et ait illis: Hic est sanguis meus novi testamenti, qui pro multis effundetur. Amen dico vobis, quia jam non bibam de hoc genimine vitis usque in diem illum, cum illud bibam novum in regno Dei."

71 Istituto Luce Cinecittà, 1932. "Il Duce nelle trionfali giornate del decennale," D063801.

72 Benito Mussolini, *Talks with Mussolini*, interviews by Emil Ludwig (New York: AMS Press, 1982). In December 1931 Ludwig had interviewed Josef Stalin.

1. Exhibition Value

1 Mario Carli, *L'Italiano di Mussolini: romanzo dell'era fascista*, 2nd ed. (Milan: Mondadori, 1936), 41–3.

2 Piero Meldini, *Sposa e madre esemplare: ideologia e politica della donna e della famiglia durante fascismo* (Florence: Guaraldi, 1975), 39.

3 Ferruccio Vecchi, *Arditismo civile* (Milan: Libreria de L'Ardito, 1920), 10.

4 Giovanni Papini, *Maschilità* (Florence: Libreria della Voce, 1915).

5 Mario Carli, *L'ardito futurista* (*Manifesto*), in "*Vittorio Veneto*" numero unico, 1919. See http://www.alterhistory.altervista.org/Documenti/testiGET.php?titolotesto=ArditoFuturista.

6 Manlio Pompei, "Educazione virile," *Critica fascista* 16 (1932): 306–7.

7 George L. Mosse, *Nationalism and Sexuality: Respectability and Abnormal Sexuality in Modern Europe* (New York: Howard Fertig, 1985).

8 Carli, *L'Italiano*, 266–7.

9 See Wanrooij, "The Rise and Fall of Italian Fascism."

10 *Archivio Centrale dello Stato, Segretaria particolare del* Duce, *carteggio riservato (1922–1943)*, fasc. 242/R, Riunione del Direttorio del PNF, sottofasc. 2, in Giuliano Manacorda, *Letteratura e cultura del periodo fascista* (Milan: Principato Editore, 1974), 162–3.

11 Manacorda, *Letteratura e cultura*, 164–5.

12 Strauss, *Thoughts on Machiavelli*, 44–5.

13 The *Scuola* has been studied but in a limited way. See, for example, Michael Ledeen, *Universal Fascism: The Theory and Practice of the Fascist International, 1928–1936* (New York: Howard Fertig, 1972), mentioned already in this study, and Mario Isnenghi, *Intellettuali militant e intellettuali funzionari* (Turin: Einaudi, 1979). See also the official documents from the *Scuola*: AA.VV. *Quaderni della Scuola di Mistica Fascista Sandro Italico Mussolini*, Roma, *Dottrina Fascista*, anni 1938–1942. Julius Evola represents an interesting case study. In 1931 Evola published the first edition of *La tradizione ermetica* with the publishing house Laterza. Benedetto Croce's mediation was essential for this publication to occur.

14 Indro Montanelli, "Noi Giovani," *L'Universale* (December 1933).

15 Ibid.

16 S.D. Ross, "Beauty: Conceptual and Historical Overview," in *Encyclopedia of Aesthetics*, ed. M. Kelly (New York, Oxford: Oxford University Press, 1998), 1:237.

17 The debate is clearly summarized by De Grand in Alexander J. De Grand, *Bottai e la cultura fascista* (Bari: Laterza, 1978), 137. The new generation's dissent was essentially limited to (1) the past/old generation, (2) Gentile's idealistic philosophy, and (3) the failed implementation of the corporativist state.

18 Giuseppe Bottai, "Funzione della gioventù," *Critica fascista* (1 March 1933); Ugo de Vita, "Funzione della gioventù. 1. Impiego dei giovani," *Critica fascista* (15 April 1933).

19 "Sulla nuova generazione," *Occidente*, (January–March 1933). These themes would eventually be incorporated in the novel of the *Decennale*: *Il garofano rosso* (see chapter 4).

20 Ben-Ghiat, *Fascist Modernities*, 107.

21 Ibid., 109–12.

22 Emilio Gentile, "Fascism as Political Religion,"*Journal of Contemporary History* (May–June, 1990): 231–2.

23 Giuseppe Mazzini, "Une nuit à Rimini," in *Scritti politici editi ed inediti di Giuseppe Mazzini* (Imola: Cooperativa Tipografia Editore Paolo Galeati, 1907), 2:4–5.

24 Mazzini, "Manifesto della 'Giovine Italia,'" in *Scritti politici*, 80–1.

25 Mazzini, "Della Giovine Italia," in *Scritti politici*, 106, 110.

26 Mazzini, "D'alcune cause che impedirono finora lo sviluppo della libertà in Italia," in *Scritti politici*, 165–8, 178.

27 Benito Mussolini, "Audacia!," *Il Popolo d'Italia* (15 November 1914).

28 See Emilio Gentile, ed., *Mussolini e La Voce* (Florence: G.C. Sansoni, 1976); Emilio Gentile, *La Voce e l'età giolittiana* (Milan: Pan, 1972).

29 Filippo Corridoni, "Avantguardia," 5 December 1914, in Renzo De Felice, *Mussolini il rivoluzionario* (Turin: Einaudi, 1965), 293.

30 Giulio Santangelo, "Unità della rivoluzione italiana," *Occidente* (October 1932): 104. Santangelo quotes Bodrero in *900* (1927).

31 De Felice, *Mussolini il rivoluzionario*, 560–1.

32 Renzo De Felice, *Sindacalismo rivoluzionario e fiumanesimo nel carteggio De Ambris-D'Annunzio (1919–1922)* (Brescia: Morcelliana, 1966), 327–30.

33 Alceste De Ambris, *La Carta del Carnaro. Nei testi di Alceste De Ambris e di Gabriele D'Annunzio*, ed. Renzo De Felice (Bologna: Il Mulino, 1974), 99–100.

34 Hans Ulrich Gumbrecht, "I redentori della vittoria: On Fiume's Place in the Genealogy of Fascism," in "The Aesthetics of Fascism," special issue, *Journal of Contemporary History* 31, no. 2 (April 1996): 255.

35 Gabriele D'Annunzio, "Il sudore di sangue," in *Prose di ricerca* (Milan: Mondadori, 2005), 1:812–13.

36 Gabriele D'Annunzio, "Messaggio del convalescente agli uomini di pena," in *Prose di ricerca*, 1:562–3.

37 Margherita Sarfatti, "L'Universalità della politica italiana," *Gerarchia* (1 January 1932).

38 Giuseppe Bottai, "Totalità, perennità, universalità della rivoluzione fascista," *Quadrante* (December 1933).

39 Virginio Galbiati, "Il Convegno della Giovane Europa," *Ottobre* (15 March 1933).

40 Asvero Gravelli, no title, *Ottobre* (15 January 1933).

41 Asvero Gravelli, "Verso il convegno della Giovane Europa. Quesiti da discutere," *Ottobre* (15 March 1933).

42 Volantino di propaganda, a firma di Luigi Biscottini, caduto fascista, pubblicato dall'Avanguardia Giovanile di Fano ACS *Mostra Rivoluzione Fascista* DOPO MARCIA PNF 13138.

43 For a complete bibliography regarding the exhibition, see Alessandra Capanna, *Roma 1932: Mostra della Rivoluzione Fascista* (Turin: Testo & Immagine 2004), 83.

44 See Joseph T. Durkin, "Early Years of Italian Unification as Seen by an American Diplomat, 1861–1870," *Catholic Historical Review* 30, no. 3 (October 1944): 271–89, 283n37. See also *Cathechismo Garibaldino; istruzioni da farsi ai giovanetti italiani dai 15 anni* (Pesaro: Tipografia Fratelli Rossi, 1866).

45 Quoted in William Kilborne Stewart, "The Mentors of Mussolini," *The American Political Science Review* 22, no. 4 (November 1928): 843–69, 856n1.

46 Claudio Fogu, "Fascism and Historical Representations: The 1932 Garibaldian Celebrations," in "The Aesthetics of Fascism," special issue, *Journal of Contemporary History* 31, no. 2 (April 1996): 317–45. See also Luigi Freddi, *Traccia Storico-Politica per la Mostra del Fascismo* (Rome: Tipografia della Camera dei Deputati, 1932), 97; *Atti del terzo congress degli Istituti Fascist di Cultura: Milano 24–25 aprile 1933* (Rome: Istituto Nazionale Fascista di Cultura, 1933), 114.

47 Dino Alfieri and Luigi Freddi, eds., *Mostra della Rivoluzione Fascista: Guida storica. 1. Decennale della marcia su Roma* (Rome: Partito nazionale fascista, 1933).

48 Schnapp, *Anno X*, 16.

49 Ibid., 18.

50 Ibid., 47.

51 Giornale LUCE A1019; Giornale LUCE A1033; Giornale LUCE B0150; Giornale LUCE B0156; Giornale LUCE B0160 (for the inauguration);

Giornale LUCE B0171 (for the King's visit); Giornale LUCE B0198; Giornale LUCE B0210 (for the ritual of the changing of the guard).

52 Steven Heller, *Iron Fists: Branding the 20th Century Totalitarian State* (London, New York: Phaidon Press 2008). In 1932 *Bibliografia fascista* likewise dedicated a series of articles to modernism and typography. See also Sergei M. Eisenstein, Yves-Alain Bois, and Michael Glenny, "Montage and Architecture," *Assemblage* 10 (December 1989): 110–31.

53 See Eisenstein, Blois, and Glenny, "Montage and Architecture," 110–31.

54 Ada Negri, "Madri di Martiri," *Corriere della Sera* (11 March 1933), in Schnapp, *Anno X*, 99–101.

55 Giuliana Bruno, *Public Intimacy: Architecture and the Visual Arts* (Cambridge, MA: MIT Press, 2007), 26.

56 Alfieri and Freddi, *Mostra della Rivoluzione Fascista: Guida storica*, 79–80.

57 Ibid., 120.

58 Bruno, *Public Intimacy*, 22.

59 I borrow the phrase from Richard Trexler. See Roberta Suzzi Valli, "The Myth of Squadrismo in the Fascist Regime," *Journal of Contemporary History* 35, no. 2 (2000): 131–50. Suzzi Valli mentions Alessandra Staderini, "La 'Marcia dei martiri': la traslazione nella cripta di Santa Croce dei caduti fascisti," *Annali di storia di Firenze*, III (2008).

60 Robert R. Shanafelt, "The Nature of Flag Power: How Flags Entail Dominance, Subordination, and Social Solidarity," *Politics and the Life Sciences* 27, no. 2 (September 2008): 14–15.

61 Ebner, *Ordinary Violence*, 46. Ebner quotes from Alberto Aquarone, "Violenza e consenso nel fascism italiano," *Storia contemporanea* 10, no. 1 (1979): 147. See also Questura di Latina to DGPS, 21 March 1959, in ACS, *confinati politici*, b. 178, "Camarra, Natale."

62 *Un'altra Italia nelle bandiere dei lavoratori. Simboli e cultura dall'Unità d'Italia all'avvento del fascismo.* (Turin: Centro Studi Gobetti, 1980).

63 Alfieri and Freddi, *Mostra della Rivoluzione Fascista: Guida storica*, 127,136.

64 *Un'altra Italia nelle bandiere dei lavoratori*, 8–12.

65 See Ebner, *Ordinary Violence*, 23. Ebner quotes from Guido Crainz, *Padania: il mondo dei braccianti dall'Ottocento alla fuga dalle campagne* (Rome: Donzelli 2007), 188.

66 Bruno, *Public Intimacy*, 3.

67 Alfieri and Freddi, *Mostra della Rivoluzione Fascista: Guida storica*, 191, 216.

68 Capanna, *Roma 1932: Mostra della Rivoluzione Fascista*, 55.

69 Mazzini, "Manifesto della 'Giovine Italia,'" in *Scritti politici*, 80–1.

70 Schnapp, *Anno X*, 61–2.

71 Ben-Ghiat, *Fascist Modernities*, 97. "By 1932, the year the Exhibition of the Fascist Revolution was inaugurated in Rome with great fanfare, intellectuals of the war generation such as Bontempelli and Camillo Pellizzi were warning that the gap between rhetoric and reality would eventually alienate the brightest members of the new generation. The government was playing a dangerous game by preaching change and demanding continuity, these men intoned, since 'one cannot serve the cause of the revolution and reaction at the same time.'" See especially Camillo Pellizzi, "Terza lettera," *Il Selvaggio* (31 March 1932); Massimo Bontempelli, "Scuola dell'ottimismo," *Occidente* (November–December 1932).

2. Textbooks for *Il balilla Vittorio*

1 Francesco Giuseppe Graceffa, *La politica scolastica nell'Italia fascista* (Lamezia Terme: Fratelli Gigliotti, 1995), 68.
2 The texts considered in this chapter are the first set of *libro-unici*: Dina Belardinelli-Bucciarelli, *Sillabario e piccole letture* (Rome: La Libreria dello Stato, A. IX); Ornella Quercia Tanzanella (Ornella), *Sillabario e prime letture* (Rome: La Libreria dello Stato, A. VIII); Ornella Quercia Tanzarella, *Il libro della II classe* (Rome: La Libreria dello Stato, 1930); Grazia Deledda, *Il libro della terza classe elementare, letture* (Rome: La Libreria dello Stato, 1930); Angelo Silvio Novaro, *Il libro della IV classe elementare* (Rome: La Libreria dello Stato, 1930); Roberto Forges Davanzati, *Il libro della V classe elementare: Il balilla Vittorio* (Rome: La Libreria dello Stato, 1932).
3 ACS Gabinetto 1931–33 fasc 5.1 n. 9880.
4 This chapter was inspired by Clive Foss, "Teaching Fascism: Schoolbooks of Mussolini's Italy," *Harvard Library Bulletin* 8 (1997): 5–30. See also Tracy Koon, *Believe, Obey, Fight: Political Socialization of Youth in Fascist Italy* (Chapel Hill: University of North Carolina Press, 1985); Monica Galfré, *Il regime degli editori. Libri, scuola e fascismo* (Rome-Bari: Laterza, 2005).
5 Galfré, *Il regime degli editori.*
6 Ignazio Silone, *La scuola dei dittatori* (Milan: Mondadori, 1974), 138.
7 Tanzarella, *Il libro della II classe,* 112.
8 See Luigi Salvatorelli and Giovanni Mira, *Storia d'Italia nel periodo fascista* (Milan: Mondadori, 1972).
9 Novaro, *Il libro della IV classe elementare,* 154.
10 Ibid., 157.
11 Ibid., 158–9.
12 Ibid., 159.

13 Ibid., 160–1.

14 Ibid., 75–6.

15 Ibid., 76.

16 Novaro, *Il libro della IV classe.*

17 Forges Davanzati, *Il balilla Vittorio,* 20.

18 Ibid., 117.

19 Fogu, "Fascism and Historical Representations, 337.

20 Roberto Forges Davanzati was the author of a *libro-unico: Il balilla Vittorio.* See also Alexander De Grand, *The Italian Nationalist Association and the Rise of Fascism in Italy* (Lincoln: University of Nebraska Press, 1978).

21 Deledda, *Il libro della terza classe elementare,* 34.

22 Ibid.

23 Archivio Centrale dello Stato Roma (ACS), Alto Commissariato per le sanzioni contro il fascismo (ACSCF), titolo XVII, volume 1, fascicolo 581.

24 Liliano Faenza believes that *Cuore* and *Testa* (Paolo Mentegazza) were the literary models behind *Il balilla Vittorio.* See Liliano Faenza, *Fascismo e ruralismo nei testi di G. Deledda, A.S. Novaro, R. Forges Davanzati* (Bologna: Alfa, 1975).

25 Marcella Bacigalupi and Piero Fossati, *Da plebe a popolo: l'educazione popolare nei libri di scuola dall'Unità d'Italia alla Repubblica* (Florence: La Nuova Italia, 1986), 207–12.

26 Forges Davanzati, *Il balilla Vittorio,* 236.

27 Ibid., 239–42.

28 *I fasci femminili,* 20, in Piero Meldini, *Sposa e madre esemplare,* 68.

29 James Bowen, *A History of Western Education,* vol. 3 (New York: St. Martin's Press, 1981), 406–7.

30 Bowen, *History of Western Education,* 506–14. Bowen refers to an article by George Counts ("Education in the USSR," *New Republic* 13 [February 1935]). The first decade of the Soviet educational experiment had been "progressive." Around 1931–2 resolutions adopted by the Central Committee of the Communist Party of the Soviet Union restored "discipline" and "authority" in the schools.

31 See www.iisg.nl/collections/sovietchildren/ and http://digital.library. mcgill.ca/russian/default.htm.

      The bibliographic references mentioned here (the original Russian has not been translated) and scanned textbook pages are taken from the McGill website.

32 Partito Nazionale Fascista, *Foglio d'Ordini,* in *Atti del Partito Fascista,* quoted in Mabel Berezin, *Making the Fascist Self: The Political War of*

Interwar Italy (Ithaca and London: Cornell University Press, 1997), 64. The *Decennale* celebrations lasted the entire month of October 1932.

33 Berezin, *Making the Fascist Self*, 114–15.

3. "Writing" 1932

1 Arturo Cattaneo, *Chi stramalediva gli Inglesi* (Milan: Vita e Pensiero – Largo A. Gemelli, 2007), 20.

2 Ibid., 10–11.

3 Archivio Centrale dello Stato Roma (ACS), Alto Commissariato per le sanzioni contro il fascismo (ACSCF), titolo XVII, volume 1, fascicolo 226.

4 Ibid., fascicolo 236; Ibid., fascicolo 554.

5 Ibid., fascicolo 589.

6 Ibid., fascicolo 588.

7 ACS. MRF Serie Espositiva. b. 112 f.16036, f.16037.

8 Ibid., b. 112 f.16044.

9 Ibid., b. 112, n. 16486.

10 ACS, ACSCF, titolo XVII, volume 1, fascicolo 338.

11 ACS, MRF, Serie Espositiva. b. 112, n. 5745.

12 Ibid., n. 5744.

13 Elio Vittorini, "Il mio ottobre fascista," in Elio Vittorini, *Le opere narrative*, ed. Maria Corti (Milan: Mondadori, 1974), 127.

14 Giuseppe Bottai, "Impegni per l'Anno Decimo," *Critica fascista* (1 November 1931): 101.

15 Sergio Pannunzio, "La fine di un regno," *Critica fascista* (15 September 1931).

16 Roberto Fiorini, "A proposito dell'antitesi Roma o Mosca," *Critica fascista* (15 October 1931): 385.

17 Mario Rivoire, "Affinità ed antitesi fra Roma e Mosca," *Critica fascista* (1 November 1931): 414. See also Giulio Santangelo, "La Russia: questione di civiltà," *Occidente* (July–September 1933); Luciano Inganni, "Roma e Mosca: Nettissima antitesi," *Critica fascista* (1 December 1931).

18 Anton Giulio Bragaglia, "La impaginazione geometrica," *Bibliografia fascista* (February–March 1932): 99.

19 Anton Giulio Bragaglia, "Architettura tipografica," *Bibliografia fascista* (February–March 1932): 286.

20 See especially Gherardo Casini, "Esortazione al realismo," *Critica fascista* (15 February 1932); Gherardo Casini, "Esortazione ad una letteratura," *Critica fascista* (15 September 1932); Gherardo Casini, "Appello al coraggio," *Critica fascista* (15 October 1932).

21 Sergio Pannunzio, "Contribuiti per una nuova cultura," *Saggiatore*
   (August–October 1933). See also Pannunzio's articles: "Del romanzo"
   (January 1932); "Narciso o dello scrittore" (March 1932); "Necessità del
   romanzo" (June 1932); "Discorso sulla pittura" (August–September 1932);
   "Del cinema italiano" (November 1932); and "Sulle arti figurative" (March
   1933).
22 "Introduzione," *Il Saggiatore* IV, no. 6 (August–October 1933): 7–8, in Vito
   Santoro, *Letteratura e tempi moderni. Il lungo dibattito negli anni Trenta* (Bari:
   Palomar, 2005), 15.
23 Berto Ricci, "Manifesto Realista," *L'Universale* (1 January 1933).
24 An English translation can be found online at http://www.worldfuture
   fund.org/wffmaster/Reading/Germany/mussolini.htm. See also *1925–*
   1995: la Treccani compie 70 anni: mostra storico-documentaria, presentazione
   di Rita Levi-Montalcini (Rome: Treccani, Istituto della enciclopedia
   italiana, 1995), 119.
25 See Gabriele Turi, *Il mecenate, il filosofo e il gesuita"l'Enciclopedia Italiana,"*
   specchio della nazione (Bologna: Il Mulino, 2002), 135.
26 *1925–1995: la Treccani compie 70 anni*, 196.
27 For a history of the entry, see Emilio Gentile et al., *Il Fascismo nella Treccani*,
   prefazione di Giorgio Galli (Milan: Terziaria, 1997); Turi, *Il mecenate, il*
   filosofo e il gesuita, 133–67.
28 Leo Longanesi, "Breve storia del cinema Italiano," *L'Italiano* (January–
   February 1933): 19–28.
29 Philip Cannistraro, *La fabbrica del consenso: fascismo e mass media*, prefazione
   di Renzo De Felice (Rome-Bari: Laterza, 1975), 286–91. Mystery surrounds
   the existence of the documentary.
30 ACS PCM, Gabinetto, 1931–1933, fasc 5.1 n. 7843.
31 See C.E.J. Griffiths, *The Theatrical Works of Giovacchino Forzano: Drama for*
   Mussolini's Italy (Lewiston, NY: Edwin Mellen Press, 2000).
32 Leo Longanesi, "L'occhio di vetro," *L'Italiano* (January–February 1933): 54–5.
33 The concept was developed by Rudolf Otto in his book *Das Heilige,* first
   published in 1917. The young child's experience "engages man's sentiments, drives him to 'industrious fervor' and fills him with a boundless
   dynamic tension both in terms of asceticism and zealousness against the
   world and the flesh, and in terms of heroic behavior by which the inner
   excitement erupts into the external world." Rudolf Otto, *The Idea of the*
   Holy: An Inquiry into the Non-Rational Factor in the Idea of the Divine and Its
   Relation to the Rational [1917] (London and New York, 1958), 33. See also
   Leo Longanesi, "L'occhio di vetro," 37–8. "Per accorgersi del volto della
   realtà, noi dobbiamo provare qualche emozione straordinaria che ci sollevi

e ci distacchi da noi stessi; sotto la scossa di un'emozione uomini e cose ci appaiono diversi, come dicevo dianzi, in una luce bianca, in una realtà insospettata, strana, autonoma, ferma al di sopra di tutto. Ma la realtà ha sempre questo aspetto di visione, è sempre al di fuori del nostro tempo e del nostro spazio, anche se l'abitudine ha creata una intimità con lei, un velo che copre i nostri occhi. Il cinematografo, superata la pittura in movimento, la letteratura, le bizzarrie tecniche e l'operetta, cercherà sempre più una maggiore aderenza al vero, portando sullo schermo i segreti che solo *una macchina* sa rapire alla realtà."

34 All references to Benjamin refer to "The Work of Art in the Age of Mechanical Reproduction," in *Illuminations: Essays and Reflections*, ed. Hannah Arendt, trans. Harry Zohn (New York: Schocken Books, 1968). The essay is available at https://www.marxists.org/reference/subject/philosophy/works/ge/benjamin.htm.

35 Ibid.

36 Benito Mussolini, "Il primo discorso presidenziale," in *Scritti e discorsi*, 3:8.

37 Luigi Sturzo, *Idolatria collettiva*, 286–7, in Gentile, *Politics as Religion*, 99–100. The quote is taken from Gentile's translation of Sturzo's article "Idolatria collettiva" (which appeared in *El Matì*, 19 December 1933) published in Luigi Sturzo, *Miscellanea londinese* (Bologna: Zanichelli, 1967), 2:286.

4. Critical Dissent

1 Gioacchino Volpe, *L'Italia in cammino: l'ultimo cinquantennio* (Milan: Treves, 1927).

2 For the letter references, see the introduction to Benedetto Croce, *Storia d'Europa* (Milan: Adelphi, 1991). See also Croce-Mann, *Lettere. 1930–1936*, introduzione di E. Cutinelli Rèndina, pref. di E. Paolozzi (Naples: Pagano, 1991).

3 Benedetto Croce, *Storia d'Europa* (Bari: Laterza, 1931), 29. I quote from the first edition in this case.

4 Ibid, 45.

5 Ibid, 67.

6 Marco Gervasoni, *L'intellettuale come eroe. Piero Gobetti e la cultura del Novecento* (Florence: La Nuova Italia, 2000).

7 Piero Gobetti, "Elogio della ghigliottina," *La Rivoluzione Liberale* (23 November 1922).

8 Renato Poggioli, "Classicità e barbarie di Svejk," *Solaria* (September–October 1932): 46. The context and meaning of Poggioli's words will be considered further on in this chapter.

9 Leo Ferrero, "Perché l'Italia abbia una letteratura europea," *Solaria* III, no. 1 (1928): 32–3. "Si chiama letteratura europea quella che dipinge il proprio paese, sottintendedo gli altri. Lo scrittore europeo non deve quindi esiliarsi per amore del forestiero ma acquistare, conoscendo il mondo, quell sottinteso. Ogni libro è il frutto di un paragone; e in ogni libro che dipinge grandiosamente l'Italia si deve avere il presentiment del mondo." See also Luisa Passerini, *Love and the Idea of Europe* (New York and Oxford: Berghan Books, 2009).

10 Giuliano Manacorda, ed., *Lettere a Solaria* (Rome: Editori Riuniti, 1979).

11 Carlo Emilio Gadda, "Review of Giani Stuparich, *Guerra del '15*," *Solaria* VII (1932): 2.

12 Demographic politics was a constant for the *Duce*. See Benito Mussolini, "Rilievi demografici," 29 November 1927, in *Opera omnia* 23: 70–2; "Discorso ai medici," 22 November 1931, in *Opera omnia* 25: 58–62; "Il numero è forza," 16 September 1933, in *Opera omnia* 26: 52–3. See also Ebner, *Ordinary Violence*, 172; Victoria De Grazia, *How Fascism Ruled Women: Italy, 1922–1945* (Berkeley: University of California Press, 1992); Anna Treves, *Le nascite e la politica nell'Italia del Novecento* (Milan: LED Edizioni Universitarie, 2001).

13 Benito Mussolini, "Macchina e donna," *Il Popolo d'Italia* (31 August 1934).

14 See Stefano Merli, *Proletariato di fabbrica e capitalism industrial. Il caso italiano: 1880–1900* (Florence: La Nuova Italia, 1972), 112; Paola Lupo, "La condizione femminile nel primo proletariato di fabbrica," *Quaderni piacentini* 53–4 (1974): 206, in Meldini, *Sposa e madre*, 43.

15 De Grazia, *How Fascism Ruled Women*, 58. See also Carl Ipsen, *Dictating Demography: The Problem of Population in Fascist Italy* (Cambridge: Cambridge University Press, 1996), quoted in Ebner, *Ordinary Violence*, 14.

16 Massimo Bontempelli, *L'avventura novecentista*, ed. R. Jacobbi (Florence: Vallecchi, 1974), 161.

17 Goldstein, *Messianism and Marxism*, 259.

18 See Antonio Sant'Elia, "Manifesto of Futurist Architecture," http://www .unknown.nu/futurism/architecture.html.

19 See Arturo Giovannitti, 1912, Essex Co. Jail, Lawrence, MA: "Does sabotage hurt the worker? The workers' movement? How about public opinion? But the worker is isolated in his struggle. It is a delicate operation that requires skill. Saboteurs are the eclaireurs, the scouts of the class struggle, they are the 'sentinelles perdues' at the outposts, the spies in the enemy's own ranks. They can be executed if they are caught (and this is almost impossible), but they cannot be disgraced, for the enemy himself, if he be gallant and brave, must honor and respect bravery and daring."

20 De Grazia, *How Fascism Ruled Women*, 48.

21 Bontempelli, *L'avventura novecentista*, 352, in Luigi Fontanella, *Storia di Bontempelli* (Ravenna: Longo, 1997), 65. Fontanella: "'Uscire dal quotidiano' vuol dire, in ultima analisi, fare della propria esistenza un'avventura permanente in cui vita reale e vita riflessa siano continuamente interscambiabili, in cui i gesti che l'accompagnano non hanno né fine, né si pongano, al pari del sogno, un obiettivo utilitaristico."

22 Poggioli, "Classicità e barbarie di Svejk," 46.

23 Ibid.

24 Alberto Consiglio, "Italo Svevo," *Solaria* (November 1932): 30.

25 Alberto Consiglio, "Italo Svevo. II – Un'opera," *Solaria* (December 1932): 33. See also "Caratteri di Svevo," *Solaria* (March–April 1929).

26 Nicola Chiaromonte, "Idee e figure di André Malraux," *Solaria* (January 1933): 18.

27 Ibid.

28 Nicola Chiaromonte, "Parigi come modello," *Solaria* (January 1933): 62.

29 Ibid.

30 Nicola Chiaromonte, "Nota sulla civiltà e le utopie," *Solaria* (April–May 1933): 15.

31 Ibid.

32 Nicola Chiaromonte, "André Malraux e '*La condition humaine*,'" *Solaria* (November–December 1933): 80–5.

33 Alberto Consiglio, "Alain Fournier," *Solaria* (June–July 1933).

34 Maria Corti, "Prefazione," in Elio Vittorini, *Le opere narrative*, LII, LIII.

35 Anna Panicali, *Il primo Vittorini* (Milan: Celùc libri 1974), 143. These pages intend to read *Il garofano rosso* as a novel that describes a moment in the autobiography of a writer at a time in which the regime had decided to "go towards the people" (*Andare al popolo*). Furthermore, the following paragraphs intend to illustrate Vittorini's populist, anti-bourgeois, and corporativist stance within the general context of the *Decennale* as a strategy of dissent through collaboration. See "Per lo stato corporativo," in Benito Mussolini, *Scritti e discorsi dal 1932 al 1933*, 7, 272–3. On 14 November 1933 the corporative state became reality.

36 Giuseppe Langella, "Il romanzo a una svolta," in *Dai Solariani agli ermetici. Studi sulla letteratura italiana degli anni venti e trenta*, ed. Francesco Mattesini (Milan: Vita e Pensiero, 1989). As for the quotes from Vittorini, see Elio Vittorini, rec. a *Una Vita*, 54–8, in *Antologia di Solaria*, ed. Enzo Siciliana (Milan: Lerici, 1958), 168–73.

37 Giuseppe Parlato, *La sinistra fascista. Storia di un progetto mancato* (Bologna: Il Mulino, 2000), 17–18.

38 See Lorenzo Greco, "La censura del *Garofano rosso*," in *Censura e scrittura: Vittorini lo pseudo-Malaparte, Gadda* (Milan: Il Saggiatore, 1983).

39 Ben-Ghiat, *Fascist Modernities*, 101–2. "Ultimately, corporativism served the regime best by functioning as a symbol of fascism's revolutionary will to forge an antileftist, antiliberal 'third way' to modernity … This public relations success owed much to Bottai, who served as the patron saint of a burgeoning corporativist subculture that encompassed institutes, academic programs, and publications that exposed a new generation of Italians to the ideas of leftist thinkers such as Marx, Stalin, Arturo Labriola, and Sidney Webb. Corporativist propaganda, with its promises to 'eliminate the economic ruling class,' convinced many younger intellectuals of the regime's political good faith and its commitment to anticapitalist agendas. For this generation, corporativism meant more than the attainment of specific economic goals such as the regulation of production and the redistribution of wealth. It promised a new relationship between the individual and the State and the triumph of a new code of values that would underwrite fascism's programs of collective transformation." See also Parlato, *La sinistra fascista*, 83–5. The quotes can be found in "Quaderno '37," *Il Ponte* (31 July–31 August 1973): 1135–6.

40 Elio Vittorini, *Il garofano rosso* (Milan: Mondadori, 1997), 67. The episode was not included in the *Solaria* version of *Il garofano rosso* but added later on (probably ca. 1935–6), as we have already read above.

41 Vittorini, *Il garofano rosso*, 70–1.

42 Tarquinio, a "static" representative of the old generation of fascists, is now seen as "an enemy" of the *ragazzino*, symbol of a redeemed and radicalized *giovinezza*. The *ragazzino* is not only introduced to the community but represents the future protagonist of a utopian society. See Vittorini, *Il garofano rosso*, 161, 165.

43 Ben-Ghiat mentions the program of the editors of the youth review *Cantiere*: "The corporative revolution knows no compromises … [I]t touches everything in our lives, transforming our way of thinking, our moral and social relationships as well as economic ones … No reformism, no reaction, just revolution. This is fascism." "Rivoluzione di popolo," *Cantiere* (10 March 1934), in Ben-Ghiat, *Fascist Modernities*, 101. Ben-Ghiat later explains: "The antibourgeois sentiments expressed in *Cantiere* and *Il garofano rosso* unsettled intellectuals of the war generation such as Pellizzi, who had been warning government officials for some years that encouraging the radical tendencies of youth would impede the formation of a new ruling elite. In a spring 1934 issue of *Critica fascista*, Pellizzi urged Bottai to punish those who were trying to relive the atmosphere of the early 1920s. Ben-Ghiat, *Fascist Modernities*, 117.

44 In 1948 Vittorini justified himself. See "Appendice," *Il garofano rosso*, 191.

45 Letter to Silvio Guarnieri (25 July 1936), in *I Libri, la città, il mondo: Lettere 1933–1943*, ed. Carlo Minoia (Turin: Einaudi, 1985), 58–9.

46 The note on Dostoyevsky can be read in the "manifesto" found in the first issue of *Solaria* (1926). As Bonsaver points out: "This mixture of literature and politics is a good indicator of Vittorini's personal approach to politics." The year was 1937, which suggests that it was probably the events in Spain which spurred Vittorini to explore Marxist ideology. This suggestion is confirmed by the memories of Romano Bilenchi, who remembers that soon after the beginning of the Civil War, "Elio, Vasco [Pratolini] e io, ormai inseparabili, cominciammo a leggere *Le lotte di classe in Francia* e altri scritti di Marx che Vittorini aveva avuto segretamente in prestito da un funzionario della 'Nazionale.'" Romano Bilenchi, "Vittorini a Firenze," *Il Ponte* 7/8 (1973), in Guido Bonsaver, *Elio Vittorini: The Writer and the Written* (Leeds, UK: Northern Universities Press, 2000), 68.

47 Elio Vittorini, "La rivoluzione culturale," *Il Bargello* (January 1937): 3. "Si è voluto con queste rivoluzioni, la nostra e la marxista, rispondere in qualche modo a un'ansia antica delle masse: l'ansia di raggiungere una migliore condizione umana, l'ansia di elevarsi," in Bonsaver, *Elio Vittorini*, 69.

48 Elio Vittorini, "Un'educazione politica. (Guerra di Spagna)," *Il Politecnico* (October 1945): 1, in Elio Vittorini, *Diario in pubblico* (Milan: Bompiani, 1957), 189–90.

49 Ben-Ghiat, *Fascist Modernities*, 127.

50 Ibid.

51 Giuseppe Langella, *Il secolo delle riviste* (Milan: Vita e Pensiero, 1982), 140.

Conclusion

1 Ludwig Feuerbach, Preface to the second edition of *The Essence of Christianity*, quoted in Guy Debord, *The Society of the Spectacle*, trans. Donald Nicholson-Smith (New York: Zone Books, 1994), http://www.cddc.vt.edu/sionline/si/tsotsoo.html.

2 Debord, *The Society of the Spectacle*, thesis 1.

3 "Edmund Burke," *Blackwood's Edinburgh Magazine* 34 (1833): 485.

4 Durkheim, *Elementary Forms*, 177. Robert Paxton cites Giuseppe Bottai, "La Rivoluzione permanente," *Critica fascista* (1 November 1926): the revolution must be permanent. For further bibliographical information, see Robert Paxton, *The Anatomy of Fascism* (New York: Alfred A. Knopf, 2004), 289.

5 Durkheim, *Elementary Forms*, 210–11. "There are periods in history when, under the influence of some great collective shock, social interactions have

become much more frequent and active. Men look for each other and assemble together more than ever. That general effervescence results which is characteristic of revolutionary or creative epochs. Now this greater activity results in a general stimulation of individual forces. Men see more and differently now than in normal times. Changes are not merely of shades and degrees; men become different. The passions moving them are of such an intensity that they cannot be satisfied except by violent and unrestrained actions, actions of superhuman heroism or of bloody barbarism. This is what explains the Crusades, for example, or many of the scenes, either sublime or savage, of the French Revolution. Under the influence of the general exhaltation, we see the most mediocre and inoffensive bourgeois become either a hero or a butcher."

6 Strauss, *The City and Man*, 3.

7 On 22 August 1933 the *Duce* published "Fra due civiltà" in *Il Popolo d'Italia*: "Non v'è dubbio, che l'episodio della fronda socialista francese ha un valore di sintomo e va messo in rapport con tutto il movimento d'idee che la Rivoluzione fascista ha provocato durante questi primi undici anni della sua storia e anche con le profonde trasformazioni delle costituzioni politiche e sociali che si sono effettuate in grandi Paesi d'Europa. Siamo entrati in pieno in un periodo che può chiamarsi di trapasso da un tipo di civiltà e un altro. Le ideologie del secolo XIX stanno crollando e non trovano più difensori. Non è sintomatico che ci siano dei socialisti stanchi del socialismo quale era stato imbalsamato dalla dogmatica marxista? Così ci sono dei democratici che non vogliono più saperne di democrazia e dei liberali che considerano trapassata la fase demoliberale negli Stati dell'Occidente." Mussolini, "Fra due civiltà," in *Scritti e discorsi dal 1932 al 1933*, 7, 229.

8 C. Giglio, "Sono aperte le iscrizioni," *Critica fascista* (1932): 27.

9 Benito Mussolini in 1922: "Marcia militare su Roma? Colpo di Stato? Organizzazione preparatoria? Chi ha mai sognato fantasie di questo genere? È vero, verissimo, che noi abbiamo parlato e parliamo di Marcia su Roma, ma si tratta di una Marcia – lo dovrebbero capire anche i più profani – del tutto spirituale, vorrei dire legalitaria." Mussolini, "Che cosa significa la 'marcia su Roma' secondo il segretario del fascio," *Corriere della Sera* (6 October 1922). In short, the 1922 March on Rome was an illusion constructed on a mythical platform, an illusion transformed into an aesthetic and conferred legal status.

10 Jacob Burkhardt, *The Civilization of the Renaissance in Italy* (New York: Penguin, 1990), 20.

11 Mack Smith, *Mussolini*, 54. "On 29 October, the king accepted this advice and Mussolini, at the age of only thirty-nine, became the twenty-seventh

prime minister of Italy. But the fascist leader was not satisfied with something so unspectacular as a royal appointment. He needed to develop the myth of a march on Rome by 300,000 armed fascists to enforce the 'ultimatum' he had given the king, and eventually a legend was invented of Mussolini on horseback leading his legions across the Rubicon. In reality there were fewer than 30,000 fascist militiamen ready to march, many of whom had no arms at all and would have been quite unable to stand up to the garrison troops in Rome … [I]ndeed 400 policemen proved sufficient to hold up the fascist trains long before they reached Rome. Mussolini subsequently admitted this in private with amused satisfaction. His fascist squads did not arrive in Rome until twenty-four hours after he had been asked to form a government and only after General Pugliese had orders to let them through. But the photographers were waiting to picture their arrival and the myth was launched of fascism winning power by an armed insurrection after a civil war and the loss of 3,000 men. These fictitious 3,000 'fascist martyrs' soon took their place in the government-sponsored history books."

12 Durkheim, *Elementary Forms*, 210–11.

13 Ibid., 129, 213, 356, 380–3.

14 Mussolini, "Fra due civiltà," in *Scritti e discorsi dal 1932 al 1933*, 7, 231. "Questi ultimo quattro anni di crisi hanno accentuate i caratteri di questa situazione. Ma le nuove idée fasciste che agitano ogni Nazione del mondo, non avrebbero raggiunto lo sviluppo attuale, senza l'intervento di quelle che chiamerò cause positive. Milioni di uomini di tutti i paesi hanno visto e finalmente compreso. Tre cose hanno, soprattutto, colpito l'intelligenza: la Mostra della Rivoluzione, la Via dell'Impero, la bonifica delle Paludi Pontine. Storia di un recente passato e creazione di vita. Il decennale è stato una rivelazione."

15 Revolutionary events occur especially when states experience an internal form of crisis. See Charles S. Maier, "Political Crisis and Partial Modernization: The Outcomes in Germany, Austria, Hungary and Italy after the First World War," in *Revolutionary Situations in Europe, 1917–1922: Germany, Italy, Austria-Hungary*, ed. Charles S. Maier (Montreal: Interuniversity Centre for European Studies, 1977), 119–31.

16 Paxton, *Anatomy of Fascism*, 105. "In Germany after 1930 only the communists, along with the Nazis, were increasing their vote. Like the Nazis, the German communists thrived on unemployment and a widespread perception that the traditional parties and constitutional system had failed. We know from Nazi party documents captured by the German police in 1931 – the 'Boxheim papers' – that Nazi strategists, like many

other Germans, expected a communist revolution and planned direct action against it. The Nazi leaders seemed convinced in 1931 that forceful opposition to a communist revolution was their best route to broad national acceptance." See also Silone, *Scuola dei dittatori*, 247. "Prof. Pickup: A Berlino ci è stato assicurato che nel febbraio del 1933 la polizia scoprì nei sotterranei della casa 'Karl Liebknecht' quintali di material cospirativo, provante che i comunisti preparavano una rivolta per i giorni seguenti."

17 In 1922 Mussolini stated: "Ma se Mazzini, se Garibaldi tentarono per tre volte di arrivare a Roma, e se Garibaldi aveva dato alle sue camicie rosse il dilemma tragico, inesorabilmente di 'O Roma o morte' questo significa che negli uomini del Risorgimento italiano, Roma ormai aveva una funzione essenziale di primissimo ordine da compiere nella nuova storia della Nazione italiana. Eleviamo, dunque, con animo puro e sgombro da rancori il nostro pensiero a Roma che è una delle poche città dello spirito che ci sono al mondo, perché a Roma, tra quei sette colli così carichi di storia, si è operato uno dei più grandi prodighi spirituali che la storia ricordi, cioè si è tramutata una religione orientale, da noi non compresa, in una religione universale che ha ripreso sotto altra forma quell'impero che le legioni consolari di Roma avevano spinto fino all'estremo confine della terra. E noi pensiamo di fare di Roma la città del nostro spirito, una città, cioè, depurata, disinfettata da tutti gli elementi che la corrompono e che la infangano, pensiamo di fare di Roma il cuore pulsante, lo spirito alacre dell'Italia imperiale che noi sogniamo." In 1932 Rome was again the protagonist: this time of both nation-building and empire. Benito Mussolini, "Il discorso di Udine," 20 September 1922, in *Opera omnia* 2: 311.

18 Thomas Harrison, *1910: The Emancipation of Dissonance* (Berkeley: University of California Press, 1996).

19 Albanese, *La marcia su Roma*, 197, 199, 203. "L'immagine proposta della marcia restava insomma in bilico tra continuità e rottura … Nella stessa rappresentazione dell marcia su Roma erano insite delle contraddizioni: la difficoltà di abbandonare il mito fondatore della marcia, fonte della legittimità di Mussolini al governo e della sua rafforzata autorità rispetto ai presidenti del Consiglio precedenti, e al tempo stesso l'esigenza di normalizzare l'immagine dell'evento, unico modo per garantire la stabilità futura del governo fascista. Tali ambiguità, perciò, si riproponevano nell'altalenarsi di riflessioni differenti che sull'evento furono elaborate nell'intera storia del regime fascista in Italia. Alla fine del mese di ottobre 1923, i preparativi del primo anniversario della marcia su Roma rivelano quanto fosse necessario per il governo ribadire l'importanza di questo mito fondatore. Era questo un tentativo inedito di costruzione di una

religione politica che era stata propria del fascismo fin dalle origini, ma
che con l'ascesa al governo si era senz'altro rafforzata. La marcia su Roma,
come altre feste fasciste, diveniva a poco a poco una celebrazione di Stato
… il modo in cui si parlava della marcia, e anche gli eventi che si sceglieva
di enfatizzare o di dimenticare, dipendeva soprattutto dalla fase politica
attraversata dal governo e dal regime, e dal tipo di legittimazione neces-
saria per garantire il consenso."

20 David D. Roberts, "How Not to Think about Fascist Ideology, Intellectual
Antecedents, and Historical Meaning," *Journal of Contemporary History* 35,
no. 2 (April 2000): 185–211, as well as Roger Griffin, "The Reclamation
of Fascist Culture," *European History Quarterly* 31, no. 4 (October 2001):
609–20. See also John Passmore, "The Objectivity of History," in *The
Philosophy of History*, ed. Patrick Gardiner (Oxford: Oxford University
Press, 1974), 153–4. "Very often, the historian does not seem to know *what*
he is doing; his instinct leads him to select a single problem for consideration, and yet he feels uneasily that since he is purporting to write about
the 'History of England,' he ought to say something about its literature,
or its social life. So a good book is marred by perfunctory and irrelevant
chapters; and the historian cannot defend himself against the charge of
arbitrariness, since his selection is not determined by the structure of the
work he has undertaken. History books, indeed, ought commonly to be
more, not less, selective than they are; greater selectivity would be a step
towards objectivity, not away from it. What the historian calls 'general
history' is a fraud – resting for its plausibility upon the metaphysical
notion that there is something called 'the whole community' which moves
in the manner of a single man. If this point be granted, the question still
arises: how exactly is the historian to choose among his material? The
determining factor, I have suggested, must be the nature of the problem
from which he sets out, just as it is in the case of the physical scientist.
There is, however, an important difference in the character of his problems; historical problems are more like a certain type of problem in
applied science than they are like problems in pure science."

21 Hans Ulrich Gumbrecht, *In 1926: Living on the Edge of Time* (Cambridge,
MA: Harvard University Press, 1997).

22 Langella, *Il secolo delle riviste*, 106–7. "Tuttavia, se questi erano i riferimenti
nominali e culturali, certamente non estranea alla svolta solariana deve
essere stata la situazione complessiva che si era venuta a creare in Italia
all'inizio degli anni trenta. I termini salienti della quale si possono
riassumere nell'incrocio contraddittorio tra la grave depressione economica
sopravvenuta dopo il 1929, che provocò un progressivo impoverimento

nella popolazione urbana e rurale i cui punti di massima si registrano proprio tra il '32 e il '33; e il crescente trionfalismo politico dei discorsi ufficiali, che toccò il suo culmine nell'ottobre del 1932, a un passo dalla svolta di 'Solaria,' in occasione delle celebrazioni per il decennale della marcia su Roma, quando Mussolini assicurò nel giro di un decennio la completa fascistizzazione dell'Europa. Un simile quadro generale era destinato ad avere dei precisi riflessi intellettuali, all'interno della cultura fascista ma anche al di fuori. In primo luogo, il decennale aggiungeva nuovo vigore, se ce ne fosse stato bisogno, alla convinzione dell'imbattibilità del regime; rimetteva in ogni caso questa convinzione al centro della riflessione intellettuale; e poneva semmai il bisogno, per gli oppositori del regime, date le contraddizioni, le inadempienze e i risvolti inaccettabili presentati dalle dittatura mussoliniana, di inventare una nuova strategia per avviare il fascismo, dall'interno e per via legale, verso una sua progressiva trasformazione in senso liberale e democratico."

23 Howard Eiland and Michael W. Jennings, eds., *Walter Benjamin: A Critical Life* (Cambridge, MA: Belknap Press, 2014).

24 Kathleen Kerr-Koch, *Romancing Fascism: Modernity and Allegory in Benjamin, de Man, Shelley* (London: Bloomsbury Academic, 2013), 28.

25 Ibid.

26 Ibid. Kerr-Koch refers to Mosse here.

27 Ibid.

28 Eiland and Jennings, *Walter Benjamin: A Critical Life*, 166.

29 Ibid., 503. See also http://www.gisele-freund.com/international-congress-for-the-defense-of-culture-hall-of-the-mutualite-paris-21th-of-june-1935/.

30 Eiland and Jennings, *Walter Benjamin: A Critical Life*, 501.

31 Ibid., 513.

32 Ibid.

33 Ibid., 38–9.

34 Ibid., 40–1. In 1914 Walter Benjamin wrote an essay titled "The Life of Students," a call to arms and a manifesto.

35 Manacorda, *Letteratura e cultura*, 162–5.

36 Bosworth, *Mussolini*, 322.

37 Dino Grandi, *Diario*, agosto 1932, in Archivio D. Grandi, b. 25, fasc. 90, sott. 40, in De Felice, *Mussolini il duce*, vol. 2, 342–3.

38 Galfré, *Il regime degli editori*, xv. Gentile is mentioned in Galfré's introduction.

39 Luigi Meneghello, *Fiori Italiani* (Milan: Rizzoli, 1976), 340. I paraphrase Meneghello's text here.

40 Manara Valgimigli, "Scolaro caduto in guerra," in Cesare Bolognesi, *Quattro libelli inediti di Arnaldo Fusinato. Saggio sulla vita giovanile del poeta e quattro appendici* (Vicenza: Officine Grafiche STA, 1967), 13.

41 The document concerning the 10th Flotilla MAS is available at http:// www.foia.cia.gov/sites/default/files/document_conversions/1705143/ BORGHESE%2C%20JUNIO%20VALERIO_0001.pdf.

42 In March1942 Borghese was awarded l'Ordine Militare di Savoia with the following note: "Comandante di sommegibile assegnato alla Xa Flottiglia MAS per operazioni con mezzi d'assalto, dopo aver compiuto con successo tre audaci e difficili imprese, studiava e preparava con tecnica perfetta e sagacia una quarta operazione per il forzamento di altra base nemica. Con il suo sommergibile si avvicinava al munitissimo porto affrontando con fredda determinazione i rischi frapposti dale difese e dalla vigilanza del nemico per mettere i mezzi d'assalto nelle condizioni migliori per il forzamento della base nemica. Lanciava quindi i mezzi d'assalto nell'Azione che era coronate da brillante successo avendo portato al grave danneggiamento di due corazzate nemiche." http:// www.foia.cia.gov/sites/default/files/document_conversions/1705143/ BORGHESE%2C%20JUNIO%20VALERIO_0006.pdf.

43 The 11 May 1944 report can be found at http://www.foia.cia.gov/sites/ default/files/document_conversions/1705143/BORGHESE%2C%20 JUNIO%20VALERIO_0002.pdf.

44 The account of Prince Boghese's life after the war can be found at http:// www.foia.cia.gov/sites/default/files/document_conversions/1705143/ BORGHESE%2C%20JUNIO%20VALERIO_0022.pdf.

45 Ibid.

46 This document on the National Front and the Italian political situation can be found at http://www.foia.cia.gov/sites/default/files/document_ conversions/1705143/BORGHESE%2C%20JUNIO%20VALERIO_0028.pdf.

47 The 19 February 1971 report on the National Front can be found at http:// www.foia.cia.gov/sites/default/files/document_conversions/1705143/ BORGHESE%2C%20JUNIO%20VALERIO_0036.pdf.

48 Ibid.

49 The interview with James Angleton can be found at http://www.foia.cia .gov/sites/default/files/document_conversions/1705143/ BORGHESE%2C%20JUNIO%20VALERIO_0040.pdf.

50 Anna Lisa Carlotti, ed., *Italia 1939–1945: Storia e memoria* (Milan: Vita e Pensiero, 1996), 332. "Era forte il desiderio di partecipare di più alla Guerra. Io avevo visto delle ausiliarie nelle immediate retrovie, ad esempio con il 'Lupo' c'erano le ausiliarie che curavano I feriti, erano più coinvolte nel

combattimento, in quella che era la guerra; avevo già avuto la mamma che
era stata crocerossina e perciò aveva curato feriti … Io desideravo un poco
fare quello che aveva fatto lei, essere più a contatto con il combattente,
mentre invece così a distanza mi sembrava di fare qualche cosa che non
era sufficiente, volevo fare di più; non è che volessi prendere in mano un
fucile e combattere anche io, però essere più vicina a chi combatteva, a chi
soffriva, a chi moriva … Fare qualsiasi cosa, ma essere più vicina a chi
combatteva. Se mi avessero detto: 'Tu devi morire perché è necessario'
penso che non mi sarei tirata indietro. Ero talmente convinta che dovevo
fare qualche cosa che mi coinvolgesse completamente, non solo fino ad un
certo punto. Non mi ha mai fatto paura morire, molto meno della soffer-
enza, Cosa come la tortura potevano spaventarmi, però il morire non era
una cosa che mi facesse paura, che mi preoccupasse."

51 Benito Mussolini, "Discorso al convegno dei dirigenti della
   Confederazione Nazionale dei Sindacati Fascisti Professionisti ed Artisti,"
   1 October 1932, in *Opera omnia* 44: 29–30. See also "Discorso per il cinquan-
   tenario della società italiana degli autori ed editori," 28 April 1933, in
   Opera omnia 44: 50–1.

52 The term itself was relatively new and born out of the Dreyfus affair.
   Christophe Charle, *Naissance des intellectuels, 1880–1900* (Paris: Ed. de
   Minuit, 1990).

53 Benito Mussolini, "Ritorno alla terra," *Il Popolo d'Italia* (4 July 1933).

54 Luisa Passerini, *Fascism in Popular Memory Memory: The Cultural Experience
   of the Turin Working Class*, transl. Robert Lumley and Jude Bloomfield
   (Cambridge: Cambridge University Press, 1987), 88.

55 Carlo Rosselli alla madre, Parigi 7 febbraio 1932, in *I Rosselli. Epistolario
   familiar*, ed. Zeffiro Ciuffoletti (Milan: Mondadori, 1997), 528.

56 William Penn's essay is available through the Online Library of Liberty in
   the collection *The Political Writings of William Penn*, http://oll.libertyfund
   .org/titles/893.

57 Giusseppe Mazzini, *A Cosmopolitanism of Nations: Giuseppe Mazzini's
   Writings on Democracy, Nation Building and International Relations*, ed.
   Stefano Recchia and Nadia Urbinati (Princeton, NJ: Princeton University
   Press, 2009). See especially the introduction.

58 Victor Hugo, "Opening Address to the Paris Peace Congress, 21 August
   1849," www.ellopos.net/politics/hugo-addresses-europe.asp.

59 Leon Trotsky, "Is the Time Ripe for the Slogan: 'The United States of
   Europe'?" The article is available at https://www.marxists.org/archive/
   trotsky/1923/06/europe.htm.

60 Gaetano Salvemini, *Mazzini: A Study of His Thought and Its Effect on 19th Century Political Theory*, trans. I.M. Rawson (Stanford, CA: Stanford University Press, 1957), 56.

61 Gianfranco Contini, *La influenza culturale di Benedetto Croce* (Milan-Naples, 1967), 48–52.

62 "Piero Gobetti nella storia del pensiero italiano," *Belfagor* II (1951): 130–48. See especially Piero Gobetti, "Il nostro protestantesimo," *Rivoluzione liberale* (17 May 1925) and "Dall'esilio," *Rivoluzione liberale* (28 June 1925); Marco Gervasoni, *L'intellettuale come eroe. Piero Gobetti e le culture del Novecento* (Florence: La Nuova Italia, 2000), 407. See also Piero Gobetti, "Lo spirito piemontese," *Rivoluzione liberale* (19 April 1925) and "Croce oppositore," *Rivoluzione liberale* (6 September 1925).

63 Contini, *La influenza culturale di Benedetto Croce*, 48–67.

64 Gervasoni, *L'intellettuale come eroe*, 163.

65 Piero Gobetti, "Croce oppositore," in Gervasoni, *L'intellettuale come eroe*, 163.

66 Piero Gobetti, "La nostra cultura politica," *Rivoluzione liberale* (8 March 1923).

67 Piero Gobetti, *La Rivoluzione liberale*, prefazione di Umberto Morra (Turin: Einaudi, 1948).

68 Strauss, *The City and Man*, 24–5.

69 Ibid., 23.

70 Gadda, "Review of Giani Stuparich."

71 Aldo Garosci, "Note sull'eloquenza di Beccaria," *Solaria* VII (1932): 4.

72 Durkheim, *Elementary Forms*, 129, 213, 356, 380–3.

73 Mussolini, "Fra due civiltà," in *Scritti e discorsi dal 1932 al 1933*, 7, 231. "Milioni di uomini di tutti i paesi hanno visto e finalmente compreso. Tre cose hanno, soprattutto, colpito l'intelligenza: la Mostra della Rivoluzione, la Via dell'Impero, la bonifica delle Paludi Pontine. Storia di un recente passato e creazione di vita. Il decennale è stato una rivelazione." The article was originally published in *Il Popolo d'Italia*: Mussolini, "Fra due civilta," *Il Popolo d'Italia* (22 August 1933).

74 Bosworth, *Mussolini*, 236–7.

75 Emilio Bodrero, "La fine di un'epoca," *Bibliografia fascista* (January 1932).

76 Kallis, "The 'Third Rome' of Fascism," 58.

77 Romano Bilenchi, "I nemici della rivoluzione," *Critica fascista*, cited in De Felice, *Mussolini il duce*, 304.

78 Berto Ricci, "Del 'più' e del 'meno,'" *Critica fascista*, cited in De Felice, *Mussolini il duce*, 304–5.

79 Margherita Sarfatti, "L'Universalità della politica italiana," *Gerarchia* (1 January 1932); Giuseppe De Lorenzo, "Ghandi," *Gerarchia* (1 January 1932).

80	Agostino Nasti, "Civiltà collettivistica," *Critica fascista* (15 August 1933): 302.
81	Mark Antliff, "Fascism, Modernism and Modernity," *The Art Bulletin* 84, no. 1 (March 2002): 148–69.
82	Bosworth, *Mussolini*, 212–13.
83	Ibid., 239–40. Please refer to these pages for this paragraph.
84	Ibid., 269–70.
85	Alexander De Grand, "Mussolini's Follies: Fascism in Its Imperial and Racist Phase, 1935–1940," *Contemporary European History* 13, no. 2 (2004): 137; Galeazzo Ciano, *Diario 1937–1943*, ed. Renzo De Felice (Milan: Rizzoli, 1980), 156. De Grand quotes from the entry for 10 July 1938.
86	De Grand, "Mussolini's Follies," 138.
87	Ibid., 145.
88	Alexander De Grand, "Cracks in the Facade: The Failure of Fascist Totalitarianism in Italy, 1935–9," *European History Quarterly* 21 (October 1991): 526.
89	Ibid., 520.
90	Ibid., 521.
91	Giuseppe Bottai, *Diario*, a cura di Giordano Bruno Guerri (Milan: BUR, 2006), 38.
92	Ibid., 53.
93	Ibid., 65.
94	Ibid., 77.
95	Ibid., 113
96	Ibid., 129.
97	Ibid., 131.
98	Ibid., 132.
99	De Grand, "Cracks in the Facade," 524.
100	Ibid., 522.
101	Alexander De Grand, *Italian Fascism: Its Origins and Development*, 3rd ed. (Lincoln: University of Nebraska Press, 2000), 113.
102	Bottai, *Diario*, 247.
103	Ibid., 285. "Visita a un campo di lavoratori italiani, verso la triste Dachau dei campi di concentramento. E' triste anche questo, di campo. Una serie di baracche in legno, che sanno di caserma e d'ospizio, ospitano questi poveri italiani spaesati, nostalgici, i quali, quando rimonto in macchina per andarmene, mi si serrano d'attorno invocando "pastasciutta! pastasciutta!" E anche questo loro grido fa pena."
104	Ibid., 301.
105	Ibid., 378.

106 Ibid., 471. "[A]nche la bugia di propaganda rivela il genio nazionale. Gl'italiani le dicono e le ascoltano facendo finta di crederci: e arrivano a tanto, nel loro piccolo machiavellismo quotidiano, da non credere neppure più alla verità."

107 Ibid., 349.

108 Ibid., 473.

109 Piero Gobetti, "Elogio della ghigliottina," *La Rivoluzione Liberale* (23 November 1922).

110 Piero Gobetti, "Questioni di tattica," *La Rivoluzione Liberale* (23 November 1922).

111 Benedetto Croce, "Perché non possiamo non dirci cristiani," *La Critica* (20 November 1942).

112 Bottai, *Diario*, 375.

113 Gaetano Salvemini, "Il mito dell'uomo-dio," *Quaderni di Giustizia e Libertà* (March 1932).The publication intended to focus on anti-fascism not as "negativo e indistinto" but "costruttivo." Cf: "Attraverso le riviste fasciste," *Quaderni di Giustizia e Libertà* (January 1932): 55.

114 Renzo De Felice maintains that the Ethiopian campaign marked the height of the *Duce*'s fame. But how many Mussolini's were there? Bottai would write in his diary in 1940: "That the personality of a man is manifold, everyone undertands this, and says that a man's personality is multiple and contradictory, often dramatic, shocking and always lost due to neglect. And that a man of command, rather than give in to this, rules over these aspects of his character and uses them as weapons for governance and rule – this too is also quite clear. The policy of the politician begins from him, from inside and recognizes and guides the conflicting parties as they struggle and fight within him. But in an exceptional man without scruples the liberal use of these characterisctics leads to paradox and cynicism. How many Mussolinis do people talk about? An infinite number. We ought to limit him to the essential: two. And forget about the minor Mussolinis; these are but calculated appearances, a demonstration of his versatility and what he can offer to the public. You have the Mussolini as farmer, soldier; Mussolini as athlete, miner, worker, cosmopolitan man, etc. – these are other reincarnations of an actor and, within limits, useful and necessary for a leader. And we have the Mussolini who's gloomy, happy, tragic, fun, deep, frowning, humorous, curious, sententious, paradoxical, who lives in *Palazzo Venezia* and surprises his visitors each time – even the ones that stop by often … The first Mussolini: a beast that senses everything – as he likes to say, very sensitive to

historical connections and to the secret meaning of events. The Mussolini
endowed with a remarkable power of miraculous intuition, especially
the history of dowsing, a true genius of history, and in Him whose
knowledge is translated into action … Can't imitate him, this Mussolini,
but he is exemplary: a star leading the way even if it is not at the end of
your journey, as a lantern might be. But this unreachable example – a few
pick up on it: it is hard to bear and doesn't give immediate satisfaction.
And so the rest turn to that imitation of Mussolini which is possible. In
other words, that is, Mussolini number two: a man who lives a normal
everyday life, immersed in his 'everyday' existence; a smart man, small,
petty, a jealous man with that jealosy that common men have. And ready
to lie, to deceive, fraud, and not keep his promises, promises not kept,
disloyal, treacherous, a coward, without a word, without love, incapable
of loyalty and love and quite capable of getting rid of his most faithful
followers. And it is this Mussolini – the 'versatile' and 'manifold' one
– just like you would see at the theatre, which I wrote of above. This
Mussolini is one that conceals under his clothes and by mask that nature
which is that of a betrayer and is low – just like the ringleader of a gang.
This is an imitation that is suitable for easy imitation by most. This is the
one on which leaders are made and remade, like coinage. Those same
that go from office to office or province and imitate him by echoing his
oratory, aping his poses, his frown, his abrupt rudeness, his cold arro-
gance, his closed-minded pride.We're forced to live between these two
Mussolinis. With a fidelity that is much too aware not to suffer until we
reach a level of disgust and rebellion. And with the consciousness that
must serve him by defending ourselves from him, love him by negating
him from us, offer him life by saving it. It's a bitter fate: sort of like an
unspeakable love." Bottai, *Diario*, ff. 952, in De Felice, *Mussolini il duce*,
257–8.

115 Bottai, *Diario*, 485. Bottai actually does not quote this passage. He recalls
the Psalm and writes down a few verses liberally inspired by Psalm 56.
Bottai eventually spent a few years in the French Foreign Legion and
returned to Italy thanks to the amnesty of 1947.

116 Wanrooij, "The Rise and Fall of Italian Fascism," 401–18.

117 Strauss, *The City and Man*, 147–8.

Selected Bibliography

1925–1995: la Treccani compie 70 anni: mostra storico-documentaria. Presentazione di Rita Levi-Montalcini. Rome: Treccani, Istituto della enciclopedia italiana, 1995.

Albanese, Giulia. *La marcia su Roma: violenza e politica nella crisi dello stato liberale*. Rome-Bari: Laterza, 2006.

Alfieri, Dino and Luigi Freddi, eds. *Mostra della Rivoluzione Fascista. Guida storica. 1. Decennale della marcia su Roma*. Rome: Partito nazionale fascista, 1933.

Angelini, Maria Clotilde, ed. *Il Baretti (1924–1928)*. Rome: Edizioni dell'Ateneo & Bizzari, 1978.

Bacigalupi, Marcella and Piero Fossati. *Da plebe a popolo. L'educazione popolare nei libri di scuola dall'Unità d'Italia alla Repubblica*. Florence: La Nuova Italia, 1986.

Benadusi, Lorenzo. *Il nemico dell'uomo nuovo: l'omosessualità nell'esperimento totalitario fascista*. Milan: Feltrinelli, 2005.

Ben-Ghiat, Ruth. *La cultura fascista*. Bologna: Il Mulino, 2000.

– *Fascist Modernities: Italy, 1922–1945*. Berkley: University of California Press, 2001.

Benjamin, Walter. *The Work of Art in the Age of Its Technological Reproducibility, and Other Writings on Media*. Edited by Michael W. Jennings, Brigid Doherty, and Thomas Y. Levin. Translated by Edmund Jephcott, Rodney Livingstone, Howard Eiland, et al. Cambridge, MA: Belknap Press, 2008.

Berezin, Mabel. *Making the Fascist Self: The Political War of Interwar Italy*. Ithaca and London: Cornell University Press, 1997.

Bolognesi, Cesare. *Quattro libelli inediti di Arnaldo Fusinato. Saggio sulla vita giovanile del poeta e quattro appendici*. Vicenza: Officine Grafiche STA, 1967.

Bonsaver, Guido. *Elio Vittorini: The Writer and the Written*. Leeds, UK: Northern University Press, 2000.

Bosworth, R.J.B. *Mussolini*. London: Bloomsbury, 2010.
– *Whispering City: Modern Rome and Its Histories*. New Haven, CT: Yale University Press, 2011.
Bowen, James. *A History of Western Education*. Vol. 3. New York: St. Martin's Press, 1981.
Brezzi, Camillo, and Luigi Ganapini, eds. *Cultura e società negli anni del fascismo*. Milan: Cordani Editore, 1987.
Bruno, Giuliana. *Public Intimacy: Architecture and the Visual Arts*. Cambridge, MA: MIT Press, 2007.
Burke, Frank, and Marguerite R. Waller, eds. *Federico Fellini: Contemporary Perspectives*. Toronto: University of Toronto Press, 2002.
Cannistraro, Philip. *La fabbrica del consenso: fascismo e mass media*. Prefazione di Renzo De Felice. Rome-Bari: Laterza, 1975.
Cannistraro, Philip V., and Brian R. Sullivan. *Il Duce's Other Woman: The Untold Story of Margherita Sarfatti, Benito Mussolini's Jewish Mistress, and How She Helped Him Come to Power*. New York: William Morrow, 1993.
Carli, Mario. *Con D'Annunzio a Fiume*. 1920. Foggia: Felice-Miranda Editore, 1992.
– *L'Italiano di Mussolini: romanzo dell'era fascista*. 2nd ed. Milan: Mondadori, 1936.
Cione, Edmondo. *Bibliografia crociana*. Milan: Fratelli Bocca Editori, 1956.
Coverdale, John. *Italian Intervention in the Spanish Civil War*. Princeton, NJ: Princeton University Press, 1975.
Croce, Benedetto. *Storia d'Europa*. Bari: Laterza, 1931.
Croce, Benedetto. *Storia d'Europa*. Milan: Adelphi, 1991.
Crovi, Raffaele. *Vittorini cavalcava la tigre*. Rome: Avagliano Editore, 2006.
D'Annunzio, Gabriele. *Prose di ricerca*. Milan: Mondadori, 2005.
De Ambris, Alceste. *La Carta del Carnaro. Nei testi di Alceste De Ambris e di Gabriele D'Annunzio*. Edited by Renzo De Felice. Bologna: Il Mulino, 1974.
Degl'Innocenti, Maurizio. *L'epoca giovane. Generazioni, fascismo e antifascismo*. Manduria: Piero Lacaita Editore, 2002.
De Felice, Renzo. *Antologia sul fascismo. Il giudizio storico*. Roma-Bari: Laterza, 1977.
– *D'Annunzio politico. 1918–1938*. Rome-Bari: Laterza, 1978.
– *Mussolini il duce: Gli anni del consenso 1929–1936*. Turin: Einaudi, 1974.
De Grand, Alexander. *Italian Fascism: Its Origins and Development*. 3rd ed. Lincoln: University of Nebraska Press, 2000.
– *The Italian Nationalist Association and the Rise of Fascism in Italy*. Lincoln: University of Nebraska Press, 1978.

Dombroski, Robert. "The Rise and Fall of Fascism, 1910–45." In *The Cambridge History of Italian Literature*, edited by Peter Brand and Lino Pertile, 491–530. Cambridge: Cambridge University Press, 1996.

Durkheim, Emile. *The Elementary Forms of the Religious Life*. London: Allen and Unwin, 1976.

Encyclopedia of Aesthetics. 4 vols. New York and Oxford: Oxford University Press, 1998.

Falasca-Zamponi, Simonetta. *Fascist Spectacle: The Aesthetics of Power in Mussolini's Italy*. Berkley: University of California Press, 2000.

Finney, Patrick. *Remembering the Road to World War Two: International History, National Identity, Collective Memory*. New York: Routledge, 2010.

Fogu, Claudio. "Actualism and the Fascist Historic Imaginary." *History and Theory* 42, no. 2 (2003): 196–221.

– "Fascism and Historical Representations: The 1932 Garibaldian Celebrations." In "The Aesthetics of Fascism." Special issue, *Journal of Contemporary History* 31, no. 2 (April 1996): 317–45.

Folin, Alberto and Mario Quaranta, eds. *Le riviste giovanili del periodo fascista*. Treviso: Canova, 1977.

Forgacs, David. *Rethinking Italian Fascism*. London: Lawrence & Wishart, 1986.

Foss, Clive. "Teaching Fascism: Schoolbooks of Mussolini's Italy." *Harvard Library Bulletin* 8 (1997): 5–30.

Frattarolo, Renzo. *Problemi di critica e correnti letteraria tra primo e secondo Novecento. Le riviste*. Rome: Editrice Elia, 1972.

Galfré, Monica. *Il regime degli editori. Libri, scuola e fascismo*. Rome-Bari: Laterza, 2005.

Garin, Eugenio. *Intellettuali italiani del XX secolo*. Rome: Editori Riuniti, 1975.

Gentile, Emilio. *Il culto dell littorio. La sacralizzazione della politica nell'Italia fascista*. Roma-Bari: Laterza, 1993.

– *La Grande Italia: The Myth of the Nation in the 20th Century*. Madison: University of Wisconsin Press, 2009.

– *Politics as Religion*. Princeton, NJ: Princeton University Press, 2006.

– *The Sacralization of Politics in Fascist Italy*. Cambridge, MA: Harvard University Press, 1996.

– *La Voce e l'età giolittiana*. Milan: Pan, 1972.

Gervasoni, Marco. *L'intellettuale come eroe. Piero Gobetti e le culture del Novecento*. Florence: La Nuova Italia, 2000.

Gillis, John R., "Memory and Identity: The History of a Relationship." In *Commemorations: The Politics of National Identity*, edited by John R. Gillis, 3–24. Princeton, NJ: Princeton University Press, 1994.

Giovannetti, Eugenio. *Il cinema e le arti mecchaniche*. Palermo: Casa Editrice Remo Sandron, 1930.

Gobetti, Piero. *La Rivoluzione liberale*. Prefazione di Umberto Morra. Turin: Einaudi, 1948.

Gravelli, Asvero. *I canti della Rivoluzione, Nuova Europa*. Rome: Nuova Europa, 1926.

Griffin, Roger. *Modernism and Fascism*. Basingstoke, UK: Palgrave Macmillian, 2007.

– *The Nature of Fascism*. London and New York: Routledge, 1993.

Griffiths, C.E.J., *The Theatrical Works of Giovacchino Forzano: Drama for Mussolini's Italy*. Lewiston, NY: Edwin Mellen Press, 2000.

Gumbrecht, Hans Ulrich. "I redentori della vittoria: On Fiume's Place in the Genealogy of Fascism." In "The Aesthetics of Fascism." Special issue, *Journal of Contemporary History* 31, no. 2 (April 1996): 253–72.

Guzzetta, Lia Fava. *Solaria e la narrative italiana intorno al 1930*. Ravenna: Longo Editore, 1973.

Harrison, Thomas. *1910: The Emancipation of Dissonance*. Berkeley: University of California Press, 1996.

Iannaccone, Giuseppe. *Il fascismo sintetico*. Milan: Greco & Greco, 1999.

Isnenghi, Mario. *L'educazione dell'italiano. Il fascismo e l'organizzazione della cultura*. Bologna: Cappelli, 1979.

Koon, Tracy. *Believe, Obey, Fight: Political Socialization of Youth in Fascist Italy*. Chapel Hill: University of North Carolina Press, 1985.

Langella, Giuseppe. *Il secolo delle riviste*. Milan: Vita e Pensiero, 1982.

La Rovere, Luca. *Storia dei GUF*. Turin: Bollati Boringhieri, 2003.

Ledeen, Michael. *D'Annunzio a Fiume*. Rome-Bari: Laterza, 1975.

Luti, Giorgio. *La letteratura nel ventennio fascista*. Florence: La Nuova Italia, 1972.

Lyttelton, Adrian. *The Seizure of Power: Fascism in Italy, 1919–1929*. London: Scribner, 1973.

Mack Smith, Denis. *Mussolini*. New York: Alfred A. Knopf, 1982.

Malaparte, Curzio. *Fughe in prigione*. Florence: Vallecchi, 1943.

Manacorda, Giuliano. *Letteratura e cultura del periodo fascista*. Milan: Principato Editore, 1974.

– ed. *Lettere a Solaria*. Rome: Riuniti, 1979.

Mancini, Elaine. *Struggles of the Italian Film Industry during Fascism, 1930–1935*. Ann Arbor, MI: UMI Research Press, 1985.

Mangoni, Luisa. *L'interventismo della cultura*. Rome: Laterza, 1974.

Mastrangelo, Emanuele. *I Canti del Littorio*. Bologna: Lo Scarabeo, 2006.

Mazzocchi, Luigi and Domenico Rubinacci. *L'istruzione popolare in Italia dal XVIII secolo ai nostri giorni*. Milan: Giuffrè, 1975.

Meneghello, Luigi. *Fiori Italiani*. Milan: Rizzoli, 1976.

Minoia, Carlo, ed. *I Libri, la città, il mondo: Lettere 1933–1943*. Turin: Einaudi, 1985.

Moretti, Franco. "Conjectures on World Literature," *New Left Review* 1, (January–February, 2000): 54–68.

Mosse, George L. *L'uomo e le masse nelle ideologie nazionaliste*. Rome-Bari: Laterza, 1982.

Mussolini, Benito. *Opera omnia*. Edited by Edoardo and Duilio Susmel. 44 vols. Florence: La Fenice, 1951–1980.

– *Talks with Mussolini*. Interviews by Emil Ludwig. New York: AMS Press, 1982.

Nacci, Michela. *Tecnica e cultura della crisi, 1914–1939*. Turin: Loescher, 1982.

Panicali, Anna. *Elio Vittorini*. Milan: Mursia, 1994.

– *Il primo Vittorini*. Milan: Celuc libri, 1974.

Parlato, Giuseppe. *La sinistra fascista. Storia di un progetto mancato*. Bologna: Il Mulino, 2000.

Passerini, Luisa. *Fascism in Popular Memory: The Cultural Experience of the Turin Working Class*. Translated by Robert Lumley and Jude Bloomfield. Cambridge: Cambridge University Press, 1987.

Paxton, Robert O. *The Anatomy of Fascism*. New York: Alfred A. Knopf, 2004.

Pugliese, Stanislao, ed. *Italian Fascism and Antifascism: A Critical Anthology*. With introduction, notes, and vocabulary by Stanislao Pugliese. Manchester, UK: Manchester University Press, 2001.

Roberts, David D. "How Not to Think about Fascist Ideology, Intellectual Antecedents, and Historical Meaning," *Journal of Contemporary History* 35, no. 2 (April 2000): 185–211.

Santoro, Vito. *Letteratura e tempi moderni, Il lungo dibattito negli anni Trenta*. Bari: Palomar, 2005.

Schnapp, Jeffrey T. *Anno X. La Mostra della Rivoluzione Fascista del 1932*. Pisa-Rome: Istituti Editoriali e Poligrafici Internazionali, 2003.

Scritti politici editi ed inediti di Giuseppe Mazzini. Vol. 2. Imola: Cooperativa Tipografia Editore Paolo Galeati, 1907.

Siciliana, Enzo, ed. *Antologia di Solaria*. Milan: Lerici, 1958.

Silone, Ignazio. *La scuola dei dittatori*. Milan: Mondadori, 1974.

Spackman, Barbara. *Fascist Virilities: Rhetoric, Ideology, and Social Fantasy in Italy*. Minneapolis: University of Minnesota Press, 1996.

Spirito, Ugo. *Memoirs of the Twentieth Century*. Translated from Italian and edited by Anthony G. Costantini. Amsterdam: Rodopi, 2000.

Sternhell, Zeev. *The Birth of Fascist Ideology: From Cultural Rebellion to Political Revolution*. With Mario Sznajder and Maia Asheri. Translated by David Maisel. Princeton, NJ: Princeton University Press, 1994.

– "Modernity and Its Enemies: From the Revolt against the Enlightenment to the Undermining of Democracy." In *The Intellectual Revolt against Liberal Democracy, 1870–1945*, edited by Zeev Sternhell, 11–29. Jerusalem: Israel Academy of Sciences and Humanities, 1996.

Stone, Marla. *The Patron State*. Princeton, NJ: Princeton University Press, 1998.

Strauss, Leo. *The City and Man*. Chicago: University of Chicago Press, 1978.

Sturzo, Luigi. *Miscellanea londinese*. Bologna: Zanichelli, 1967.

Tarchi, Marco. *Fascismo. Teorie, interpretazioni e modelli*. Rome-Bari: Laterza, 2003.

Turi, Gabriele. *Il fascismo e il consenso degli intellettuali*. Bologna: Il Mulino, 1980.

– *Il mecenate, il filosofo e il gesuita: l'"Enciclopedia Italiana," specchio dellanazione*. Bologna: Il Mulino, 2002.

Venè, Gian Franco. *Letteratura e capitalism in Italia dal '700 ad oggi*. Milan: Mondadori, 1992.

Vittorini, Elio. *Conversazione in Sicilia*. Milan: Rizzoli, 1986.

– *Diario in pubblico*. Milan: Bompiani, 1957.

– *Il garofano rosso*. Milan: Mondadori, 1997.

– *Le opere narrative*. Edited by Maria Corti. Milan: Mondadori, 1974.

Zagarrio, Vito. *Cinema e fascismo: film, modelli, immaginari*. Venice: Marsilio, 2004.

Zangrandi, Ruggero. *Il lungo viaggio attraverso il fascismo*. Milan: Feltrinelli, 1962.

Zucconi, Ernesto. *Liberazione!: dietro la maschera del mito*. Pinerolo: RA.RA, 1998.

Zunino, Pier Giorgio. *L'ideologia del fascismo: miti, credenze e valori*. Bologna: Il Mulino, 1985.

Index